The Many Passions of Michael Hardwick

ALSO BY MARTIN PADGETT

A Night at the Sweet Gum Head

The Many Passions of Michael Hardwick

SEX AND THE
SUPREME COURT IN
THE AGE OF AIDS

MARTIN PADGETT

W. W. NORTON & COMPANY
Independent Publishers Since 1923

Copyright © 2025 by Martin Padgett

All rights reserved
Printed in the United States of America
First Edition

For information about permission to reproduce selections from this book, write to Permissions, W. W. Norton & Company, Inc., 500 Fifth Avenue, New York, NY 10110

For information about special discounts for bulk purchases, please contact W. W. Norton Special Sales at specialsales@wwnorton.com or 800-233-4830

Manufacturing by Lakeside Book Company
Book design by Dana Sloan
Production manager: Louise Mattarelliano

Library of Congress Cataloging-in-Publication Data is available.

ISBN 978-1-32403-541-1

W. W. Norton & Company, Inc., 500 Fifth Avenue,
New York, NY 10110
www.wwnorton.com

W. W. Norton & Company Ltd., 15 Carlisle Street,
London W1D 3BS

10 9 8 7 6 5 4 3 2 1

*For Susan, who reminds me to
love deeply and without fear*

What will it cost me?
What will you make me pay?

—SYLVESTER, "DO YOU WANNA FUNK"

Contents

Preface — xi
Prologue — xvii

I: AWAKENING
Adrift — 3
Devils and Gods — 11
Atlanta — 27

II: CONVICTION
Crime of Passion — 49
Private Matters — 71
The Boys of Summer — 95

III: CRUCIFIXION
Justified — 105
Theater — 137
Reversal — 153

IV: RESURRECTION
Backlash — 171
At Liberty — 191
March — 211

V: METAMORPHOSIS
Bliss — 225
Silence — 251
Landslide — 275

Epilogue — 279
Acknowledgments — 291
Sources — 299
Notes — 303
Index — 331

Preface

When people hear my name, they think of a radical cocksucker. People don't know anything else about me.

—MICHAEL HARDWICK[1]

I came to Atlanta in 1997, full of the hope that many young queer people often bring with them when they move to cities with thriving queer communities. Atlanta promised so much—new people to meet, new worlds to explore—but in the throes of the HIV epidemic it also threatened death as well as criminal conviction. Until 1998, almost all consensual sex acts that took place between adults outside of marriage in the state of Georgia were against the law. I chased a lot of men anyway, with the dangers left unspoken but fully understood. Every time I had sex, I placed myself in peril. Every time I had sex, I became a felon.

In that time, queer people knew the legal risks their lives entailed, if for no other reason than the bravery of a man who led the gay-rights movement to the steps of the U.S. Supreme Court in 1986, as the tide of an epidemic washed over a community, nearly drowning it in grief. On August 3, 1982, Atlanta police officer Keith R. Torick climbed the steps to the bungalow at 811 Ponce de Leon Place, where he intended to serve a warrant for public drinking. Bartender and artist Michael Hardwick had been ticketed but had missed a court date. The officer found him in his bedroom, engaged in consensual sex with a male partner. The act violated Georgia's centuries-old sodomy law and carried a potential twenty-year prison sentence. Hardwick was arrested, along with his companion, and over the next four years he would lay bare the conflict between state law and the U.S. Constitution's implied rights of privacy.

Hardwick fought all the way to the Supreme Court, where, on June 30, 1986, in *Bowers v. Hardwick*, the court found that Georgia had the right to patrol its citizens' sex lives. In one of the most widely reviled rulings of its time, the court wrote that homosexual intercourse could be evil, that queer people had violated public morality, and that discrimination based on sexual identity could remain legal. Activists likened Hardwick's case to those of Dred Scott, who despite fleeing north out of slavery for several years was found to still be owned by his plantation master, and Homer Plessy, a Black Louisianan whose loss in a case to desegregate transportation gave the stamp of approval to "separate but equal" public accommodations. Each of them had been deemed inferior by virtue of their unalterable identity, a second-class status granted the imprimatur of the law, the state, and the courts.

The lives of Scott and Plessy would not be documented in their deserved depth for decades. That has also been the case with Michael Hardwick. The mostly bloodless procession of the history of *Bowers v. Hardwick* has been devoted to legal arcana. That has left behind a pale rendering of his truth. I want to change that.

He was a child of divorce, of psychedelia, of the spiritual awakening that led many away from Christianity. Michael Hardwick was a child of Stonewall. He was made a pawn of the courts, first by chance, then by his own choice. In turn he became a galvanizing force for the gay-rights movement. He became its John Brown when he bequeathed a version of himself to the public discourse around queer sex and queer lives. As his body weakened, he became part of the legacy of America's shameful treatment of queer people during a time of tragedy. Hardwick's life provides us with nothing less than stark, haunting lessons on the sexual politics of the United States from the dawn of the Pill to the dawn of the HIV/AIDS epidemic.

His outsized life forced America to come to grips with queer people and to acknowledge its moral failures toward some of its most marginalized citizens. Yet not long after his death in 1991, Hardwick had largely been forgotten, save for the moment when the Supreme Court overturned the decision bearing his name with another: 2003's *Lawrence v. Texas*, the text of which held that *Bowers v. Hardwick* had been "wrong the day it was decided." Today the memory of Hardwick has faded even more as queer life has made notable progress in the courts, in popular media, and in American culture.

That progress has not included all queer people, however. Through selective and even distorted readings of the principles of liberty enshrined in the Constitution, today's Supreme Court has dismantled privacy protections established over a half century of decisions, including the recently overturned 1973 ruling on abortion, *Roe v. Wade*. That judicial activism has authorized renewed surveillance of the most intimate aspects of our lives—and has been enjoined by a new wave of anti-queer hatred. From manufactured anti-transgender panics to the threat of renewed enforcement of still-extant sodomy laws—more than sixty years after those laws began to be dismantled—queer people remain at risk, and on watch.

Hardwick's life describes the toll exacted upon queer people in the contest for equality, as it becomes clear that the contest has been re-engaged. It demonstrates how tenuous the definition of liberty is, and how precious we should hold our privacy in an age where it faces a renewed and vigorous existential threat. It is invaluable in this moment to remind us of the power of resistance. His life maps out the terrain for queer people who must fight for their very existence and for their rights, knowing they may lose, only to establish a foundation for others to continue to fight after them.

I write this as someone who swam in the grief of the queer world of the 1980s and '90s, nurturing my emerging self while I navigated the ever-present danger of death. I write from behind other barriers to objectivity, too, but even more challenging have been the barriers to knowledge. Hardwick did not leave much in the way of a written record of his life. He didn't keep a journal. He rarely wrote letters or cards. He lived before the internet turned our lives into byte-sized confessionals. Forty years have passed. Timelines are incomplete, and months of his life go undocumented.

I have tried to resist the impulse to fashion a hero out of him, knowing he would resist the label. His heroic actions are to be lauded, for sure. But each of us has the right to behave privately in ways others might not condone; to fail; to react outrageously or incoherently; to abuse ourselves in ways that seem unconscionable while we seek a salve for untold psychic wounds.

Heroes are myths. Michael Hardwick was no myth. He was a human being worth knowing, loving, understanding—and reclaiming.

Queer people must continually claim and reclaim our rights as well as our history. To do so, we first must know that history. On June 13, 2021, thirty years to the day that Hardwick died of complications from AIDS, I made the first Zoom call with a close friend of his from Atlanta. It was only then, as I started to reassemble the mosaic of his life, that I realized how much his life had been buried by the *Bowers* decision. He was an accomplished artist, a thoughtful student, and a careful lover. He rooted his life in nature; it was the law that labeled his identity a "crime against nature" that was the artifice. Out of a sense of duty, he allowed himself to become the proxy for culture wars over privacy and sexuality as they raged. When he did, his arrest, his resistance, and his HIV status placed his body in contention at the highest levels of power for the rest of his short life. His arrest did not define his life, but it played a part in creating it as we now know it. It determined his trajectory. It wrote his epitaph.

What I have gathered here emerged in thousands of fragments, like the pieces of the mosaic he puzzled together during his 1989 interview with Robrt Pela of the *Advocate*. His life itself emerged in an overlapping, sometimes discontinuous narrative. Often, Hardwick was an unreliable narrator of his life. He adapted his story to focus on the cause of gay rights and to minimize the effects of trauma he had endured or was enduring. In some cases, he embellished the truth to make his life seem more worthy of the heroism that became attached to it—or to obscure relationships that he sought to keep private. In many instances I have presented conflicting memories of the events of his life, in the interest of transparency. For clarity, I have quoted him in a few ways. When a quote came from Hardwick directly, whether through home movies, published interviews, or written affidavits, I have placed those quotes inside the usual quotation marks, and cited them in the endnotes. When others have remembered how he spoke or reacted, I have put those sentiments in italics, knowing that they approximate distant memories relayed through someone else's recollection sometimes six decades later. The rest of the story comes from dozens of interviews with family, friends, and colleagues.

History is too fragile to remember him perfectly. The forces that shaped Hardwick's life are just as critical to identify and cross-examine. I confess that there are moments when I cannot tell you what he was doing—but even in those moments, I can tell you what was being done to him.

Prologue

Fireworks soared over Piedmont Park and beyond on July 4, 1982, chasing the final glints of day from the sky. They pock-pocked and sizzled, each tracing its own arc toward the infinite, falling shy, and then spinning and looping into dizzy orbits, their pink-orange fire snuffed and turned to ash before they fell to the ground. Each one crackled in an explosion of joy as Michael Hardwick worked on the Cove's lighting. While regulars cruised each other and newcomers gawked at the seamy side of Atlanta's gay nightlife, he stuffed insulation back into the ceiling of the room that would soon be the club's new dance floor.

"Finally," an ad in Atlanta's queer bar rag *Cruise* promised, "a place to boogie down after the others close!"[1]

Small and rectangular like an old ranch-style house, the Cove, opened in 1968 by Jim Nalley and Frank Powell, had been expanded time and time again ever since, a maze missing its minotaur. From the front door, the coat check on the left led into the main bar area, with its filthy carpet that never was cleaned. Off to the right, the bar sold hot dogs and cheeseburgers from a tiny, closet-like space, which made it a restaurant according to the letter of the law, and thus it could steer clear of Atlanta's stringent nightlife codes and closing times.

Next to the food, a small restroom offered one of the Cove's many safe harbors for furtive sex. Farther down the hall, past owner Lloyd Russell's office, an open room with open urinals offered no privacy, just approving nods in the direction of the back of the building. At the end of the line, another single restroom with a locking door formed the Cove's inner sanctum. Its users wouldn't hold up the line by having sex; they did their lines and pills and moved elsewhere for other transactions.

Hotly promoted as "the ultimate in disco light, sound and atmosphere," the new dance floor would double, even triple, the bar's size—but the Cove still was best known as the home of the one-night stand. Patrons drank and cruised as they eased their inhibitions with a cocktail or three, or fired up with speed or coke, loitering on the horny frontier between sexual desire and the ability to perform sex itself. They did it under a cloak of privacy: Bar memberships kept outsiders away from its dark confines; the front door took the names and addresses of anyone who wanted to step inside, vetting them against lists of people barred from other gay clubs in Atlanta, protecting them from unwanted attention from the police.

The new disco space would open to the left of the main entrance, where the buzz of construction noise distracted a few of the crowd that thickened at midnight and still pulsed at sunrise. The Cove's crew had tacked up curtains of slitted black vinyl to disguise the entrance to the new dance floor. Bartenders dubbed it the Car Wash and hoped to be stationed at the tiny bar that until then had been a dead end. Now the new room—with its "acoustically designed floor with built-in shock absorbers for hours of tireless dancing, five times the air conditioning to create a cool meat market, and three new T-rooms, as well as a Kudzu Court"—would make the small serving station a star attraction.[2]

The disco floor had not yet acquired the dank, cloying smell of cigarette smoke and sex that permeated every pore of the main bar. It had an industrial tone: a single small light casting erotic shadows on its ladders and scaffolding. It looked like a porn set, and even though no one was supposed to go in yet, people did anyway, including the staff. Bartenders were supposed to shoo cruisers out of the unfinished space, but on more than one occasion they'd be called out by their own patrons: *You're trying to keep us out, but you're in here getting yours!*[3]

The room had a door for easy access to the outside, where most of the sex happened. Men lined up across the length of the building in semidarkness, facing the homes on Dutch Valley Road, where most people slept unaware of or unwilling to acknowledge what could easily be seen from a kitchen window, especially at dawn, when the Cove finally emptied out some of its patrons, sending them home for rest before another round.

Unfinished and unready, the Cove had opened to members over that Fourth of July weekend in 1982. For most of a steamy Sunday afternoon, the Cove's patrons had chatted and writhed in the throes of a "tea dance"—a daytime gay dance party infused with the acrid odor of poppers and fueled by all kinds of substances. As the tea dance ended at nine o'clock, streaks of red, white, and blue fired into the still-warm sky. Hardwick's intermittent curses syncopated with heavy dance beats as he finished his work so he could go home.

The crackles grew more profuse over Atlanta as the humid evening air grew dark. Independence Day fireworks waited for their chance to burn at nearby Lenox Mall, while the sound of early celebrations ricocheted off the Cove's windows and across the sky as revelers lit Roman candles, fired off bottle rockets, and shone in the haunting glow of sparklers. At 8:52 p.m., Atlanta–Fulton County Stadium hurtled $12,000 worth of explosives over the home of the Braves and Hank Aaron's 715th home run. At Stone Mountain, where a laser-drawn General Robert E. Lee charged across the Civil War figures that were carved into the granite fifteen years before, above the very spot where the Ku Klux Klan had burned effigies of Black men at its base, a $15,000 fireworks extravaganza underwrote the notion that the South—*that* South—would rise again.[4]

A painful recession had dampened the national spirit, but pundits had offered signs that America might be turning the tide against a relentless battery of bad news on the 206th anniversary of the Declaration of Independence. No one had died in war so far in 1982. Interest rates had fallen, and so had tax rates. President Ronald Reagan had begun to talk to the Soviet Union about strategic cuts in nuclear weapons. Unemployment still was soaring, but on this July 4, America congratulated itself even while the national symbol of freedom, the Statue of Liberty, was falling to pieces. Broken-off bits floated in the water nearby, and the seams between the sheets of copper that formed the ninety-six-year-old statue's robe had begun to split. Rain poured into the cracks as wind buffeted the frail iron frame, while salt air and acid rain broke down its viridian patina. The mixture of metals, iron and copper, had turned her gown into a fragile network of barely-there lace. The torch and arm were deemed dangerous. A presidential commission led by Chrysler's Lee Iacocca had been charged with raising $200 million to renovate the gift from the French, but if its work wasn't completed with due haste, the monument to liberty would be in peril.

The Cove peaked in the early morning hours, long after other bars had closed, in the gloaming between four and seven o'clock, when DJ Aron Siegel spun the newest 12-inch dance remixes, pitting old disco standards against new hits that had emerged under the label of "dance" when disco wore out its welcome, as its essential queerness became toxic for casual straight fans. Soft Cell's "Tainted Love" and Yaz's "Situation" poked eerie tendrils of synthesizer into the club's darker corners, while the latest dance workout from Sylvester and Patrick Cowley went into heavy rotation. "Do You Wanna Funk" brought the electronic side of dance music into the foreground while it muted the rubbery thrust of funk bass that had shoved disco out of the closet in the first place.

Sylvester had launched his pop career into the stratosphere with the outré gender- and genre-bending 1978 disco hit "You Make Me Feel (Mighty Real)," a song originally written as a gospel-inflected midtempo ballad. With "Do You Wanna Funk" released on July 4, 1982, Cowley stripped the track down to an insistent beat driven by cowbell and lifted to the sky with synth whirls and Sylvester's predatory falsetto, a force of androgynous nature that shot through the track. High energy infused Sylvester's performance, but it betrayed the story behind the song. Early in the year, his writing partner Cowley had been hospitalized with symptoms like those of the mounting number of victims of "gay cancer." Cowley had lost eighty pounds and had begged to be allowed to die. Sylvester went to his hospital room, held his hand, begged in return for him to live, then commanded him: "Get your ass up out of bed so we can go to work." Cowley soon recovered enough to leave the hospital and to resume work on what would become "Do You Wanna Funk".[5]

Sylvester's persona and music already had gained widespread fame and had become shorthand for the gay experience—a pop-cultural fact and part of the new fiction of a postmodern America, the fiction of acceptance. Media had begun to depict a new and unrestrained sexuality, to inject a boundless sense of potential other worlds into the American psyche—but that psyche still understood homosexuality as a pathology.[6] Even as queer culture was becoming mainstream culture, it was met with age-old disgust for queer people.

Hardwick gave up his work long after he and the fireworks had exhausted themselves, after fending off the hands that offered him ecstasy as he moved through the Cove. The Cove's bartenders ranged from leather daddies to lithe, skinny men—a Village People palette that made Hardwick's thick brows, prominent cheekbones, and strong, jutting chin stand out in high-fashion contrast. He dressed in preppy clothes: a fedora-like hat, an unbuttoned collared shirt, a tie knotted loosely around his neck. He wedded his natural good looks, his ineffable charisma, and his ability to connect with strangers into a popular, profitable persona. He liked people and attended well to his customers, whether they were attracted to him or not. Most were. He made hundreds of dollars in tips every night he worked the bar.

He rarely talked about the darker times of his life, how he had been punished in a state-sanctioned drug-treatment program that was all but brainwashing. He kept quiet about the silent prophet who guided him toward a life that cherished the act of love, above all. He had studied landscape design and botany in college, and lived near his exuberantly Mohawked lesbian sister, Alice, who built fantastic sculptures and artwork that garnered buzz in their Florida hometown's queer community.[7] He learned from her and had begun to show the same bright promise. He habitually flirted with drugs, with straight women, and with partnered men, until, he claimed, one broke his spirit. He retreated to the Appalachian Mountains, where he practiced silence and strove for a peaceful existence, guided by Billie Holiday records through the heartache that came after a passionate but complicated affair broke apart.

He had rejoined the vibrant queer world in Atlanta, where owner Lloyd Russell installed him at the Car Wash bar so he could coach newer bartenders like his scrawny friend Jim, a 110-pound chicken posted to entice the hawks who strafed by on the hunt for the latest and newest arrivals. Jim would gladly take the leftovers, after Hardwick made his nightly choice from the field of contestants who followed him and hoped to be plucked from the crowd. Usually, that meant someone who could hang around until dawn's early light, when he finally got off.

Hardwick stepped down from the ladder for the final time sometime that morning, took a bottle of beer offered by another bartender, and walked out of the Cove, green-glass bottle of Molson in hand. A few moments more at the bar, a few more goodbyes to friends, and Hardwick might have missed the drive-by glare of Atlanta police officer Keith R. Torick, who cruised south down Monroe Drive to scour out the vandalism, prostitution, even murder on the rise in Midtown Atlanta and the fringes of surrounding Ansley Park and Virginia Highland. Torick, a muscular and compact black-haired Detroit native, had joined the Atlanta force in 1980. Despite Detroit's epic crime waves, Torick had to venture south to find work, far from the Polish family that had taught him that boys don't cry. At fourteen years old, Torick had been propositioned by a man who wanted to pay him $5 for sex in a gas-station bathroom. He turned it down and ran.[8]

Hardwick left the Cove at the precise moment, around six in the morning, when Torick's patrol car cruised by. A white, college-educated artist would normally be protected by the warm embrace of the law in many circumstances, especially in Atlanta. But the beer bottle Torick said he saw in Hardwick's hand violated Atlanta's open-container laws, even though Hardwick tossed it in the trash can just outside the bar when he saw the police cruiser troll by.

The two would dispute the events that followed, in court, in newspapers, and on television over the next half-decade. Hardwick would say that Torick stopped him and demanded to know *Where's the beer? I saw you throw it away when I drove by.* When he tried to explain, Torick ordered him into the backseat of his squad car, and for twenty minutes or so, the two squabbled. Exactly what was said would never be made clear. Hardwick wasn't free to leave, and since he'd come out of Atlanta's most notorious gay bar, he thought—he *knew*—that Torick was hassling him for being gay. He told Torick that he'd chucked the beer in the trash, but Torick told him he couldn't see the bottle from the car.[9]

Fine, Hardwick said, *just give me a ticket for drinking in public.* It could cost him $50 or more, as much as a new Sony Walkman, but he'd had enough. Maybe he'd ask his boss about it: Lloyd Russell had been studying at Georgia State to become an attorney. Or maybe he'd just go down to court and take care of it on Wednesday, the day he believed Torick had written at the top of the ticket. He had plenty of cash from a night tending bar and would have so much more in a few weeks after the Hotlanta Raft Race. He had to be back at work that afternoon and wasn't in the mood for all of this, not with another tea dance starting in eight hours.

Fuming, he headed wearily toward home and his air-conditioned room in the Craftsman bungalow at 811 Ponce de Leon Place, out of the stifling summer air. The humidity had made his shirt cling to him in wet patches. It was an unwelcome presence that invaded every square inch of his exposed skin.

AWAKENING

Adrift

Before the law branded Michael Hardwick a sodomite, before he wasted, before his life dissolved into quicksilver and whispers, he was Mike, a chubby, golden-haired boy bobbing in the gentle surf of the Atlantic Ocean, on a raft that floated in the glaring sun.

His father, Rick, had built the raft from old tires and scraps of wood lashed together with rope. Rick could build just about anything. On the off days when he could dismiss the squall of his fire station's siren, Rick installed air conditioners for extra money. He couldn't keep his hands still. He cobbled together a go-kart for his children, which his eldest, daredevil Alice, promptly ran into a building, sending her and her older brother Patrick into wails of despair, while Mike and his sister Susan steered clear of the ensuing maelstrom.

Rick had strapped the raft to the roof of their station wagon, then closed his children and his wife, Kitty, inside. They drove nearly an hour from southwest Miami to the beach, where they gathered with Rick's fellow firefighters and their families for big barbecues. The smell of burgers and beer wafted along the shore and drifted away as the scene repeated, family after family. It faded on the southernmost tip of the beach, where other men cavorted together, where Mike would bask one day.

Rick launched the raft into the ocean and climbed onto it, then dared his children to push him off and fight for the chance to be king. Kitty relaxed with her mother, Kathleen, whom the children called Nanny, and waded into the surf with her camera to take photos of her family adrift before she splashed back to her beach chair. When they grew tired of the water, Mike and Susan came to shore and continued with their own version of king of the mountain, jumping in turn over Nanny while she dozed. Their skin pinked, then turned red.

Rick repacked the wagon for the drive home when the sun had taken its toll. They took their places, their wet bathing suits and sweat sticking them to the car's vinyl seats, and cruised back to their newly minted suburb, to a home that had already begun to break.

Kitty was the granddaughter of Clemens J. Huelsenkamp and Catherine Zair Filer, who sat for a long-exposure family portrait at perhaps the height of their wealth, him dapper in a three-piece suit that smirked at the Florida heat and humidity. C.J.'s parted and receding hair capped plaintive eyes over a walrus mustache, while Catherine's lavish bonnet of hair married with her Gibson-girl white shirtwaist and dark skirt. C.J. had worked in the railroads and speculated on land in swampy, nearly uninhabited stretches of Florida, selling one parcel near Fort Myers to Thomas Alva Edison.[1] After a stint as a commissary officer in Cuba during the Spanish-American War, he moved his family there, to the town of Bacuranao, where his company built a pineapple-jam factory.

Huelsenkamp deduced how to clarify lime juice without chemicals, a major concern in an era of food safety, when foods were routinely and without acknowledgment cut and altered with additives. A small empire flourished. He invented a carbonated blend of pineapple, grapefruit, and papaya and called it Pin-a-Pola. When he moved the family back to Miami in 1915, he built a Pin-a-Pola factory, ready to consume all the fruit grown on 20,000 acres in the Miami area, with more imported from the Bahamas and Cuba.[2] During the 1920s, vicious hurricanes and a real-estate bust ate at the roots of the family business, and Huelsenkamp sold off real estate for a fraction of its presumed value.[3] When he died of heart disease in 1932, the entrepreneur left little behind, save for the old mansion on Northwest Thirty-First Street where his widow, Catherine, lived, close to her children—son William and daughters Bertha, Alice, and Kathleen. Kathleen, a kindergarten teacher, had married Harvey Blalock and given birth to a daughter in 1928. She named her Kathleen, but everyone called the girl Kitty.

Billy Dale Hardwick, called Rick as long as anyone could recall, did not know the generations before him. He had been orphaned in Kansas City, along with a brother who was adopted by Charles and Mary Alice Pitcock. When the boy died not long after they took him away, the Pitcocks returned to the orphanage for Rick.

Rick grew up in Kansas and Missouri and enlisted in the navy a little more than a month before his eighteenth birthday. The military shipped him to Pearl Harbor in 1942 and stationed him on a destroyer.[4] On leave in the summer of 1944, he met Kitty at a USO dance at Miami Beach. He left Miami for a stopover in Boston before he reported back for duty, and Kitty followed with her mother. The young couple married on August 13, 1944, at Trinity Episcopal Church, the bride draped in white crepe and wearing a white orchid corsage. Kitty returned to Florida while Rick went off to war.

Their family grew almost as soon as the navy discharged Rick on November 30, 1945. Kitty gave birth to Alice Dale on September 16, 1946; Patrick arrived on January 26, 1948. The family lived due west of Haulover Beach when Susan was born four years later. Kitty had her fourth and last child, Michael David Hardwick, on February 13, 1954.

Kitty leaned on her mother for help in raising the children. Nanny Kathleen had divorced Harvey Blalock back in 1951, after she discovered that he had started a second family in the Caribbean, where he worked for long stretches of time designing runways for airports. By the time she became a grandmother, Nanny lived alone in a home that she filled with the rustic art she created, where she wrote poetry and meditated in a garden she dedicated to Saint Francis. She painted the home's walkways to resemble cobblestones and grew flowers to festoon an entry arch.

As the clan's matriarch, Nanny watched her grandchildren on the weekends so Rick and Kitty could drink and dance without a curfew, then rustled the children into their Sunday clothes the next morning to take them to church. She painted Easter eggs with them, decorating the shells with a chorus of angels or a grouping of Hawaiian dancers. She studded them with fragments of her jewelry and fastened pictures of her family to them until she had made about a hundred of them.

She opened her home to her flock on high holidays, until it spilled over with Space Age children who orbited Depression-hardened aunts and uncles and war-veteran parents. One relative caught it all on film: his home movies captured the tropicalia of Nanny's yard in spring, when the house's jalousie windows opened to greet the scents of a yard in full Florida bloom, where the bromeliads arched high above the grass. Another film lingered over a white church with an elaborate four-story steeple, where Mike and Susan streamed out with baskets in hand, ready to pounce upon Easter eggs found in the yard among the palm trees. As the filmstrips jumped jaggedly to another year, Mike and Alice did a jitterbug on a New Year's Eve while Kitty fawned in a sateen dress and cat-eye glasses and Rick's spit-curl hung on his forehead in beatnik defiance. They looked like the kind of family that the postwar generation had been promised could stay intact.

Kitty planted palm trees at the new house she and Rick bought at 5741 SW Fourth Street and framed it with gardenias that scented the air around her bedroom. Solidly middle class by then, the Hardwicks had been lured by the promise of more space for their large family and for their hobbies. Kitty's lush plantings relieved the cookie-cutter staleness that had already set into the vast tracts of suburbia once the trees were felled, swamps drained, land cleared, and three or four styles of houses stamped over hundreds of acres to house the flood of people moving to Florida and having families.

Rick toyed with the idea of building a pool in the backyard. He toyed with the family version of democracy, even asked the kids and Kitty to vote on it: should they dig up the yard and have such a luxury, or should they build a fallout shelter instead? They held a vote: five were for the pool. The one who wasn't was Rick. During the Cuban Missile Crisis, he worked as a radiological monitoring instructor for Miami, the fear of war driven home on a daily basis. The kids could swim at the lake nearby, Rick half-joked, or Kitty could fish a dime from her purse to send them down to the public pool at the end of the road. She sent them there often, locking them out of the house and only letting them back in for a peanut-butter sandwich before she instructed the older kids to put Susan and Mike down for a nap.

Soon, the Hardwicks were the first on their block to have a safe house in case of a nuclear attack. When the backhoe arrived to dig the shelter, it dug a grave instead for a world that still existed. Roughly fifteen feet square, the fallout shelter sat under a heavy steel door. Rick drilled his family in its use. They practiced getting into it and stayed down there for a whole weekend, a dry run in case they ever had to be in it all together for even longer. For high schoolers Alice and Pat, the test run was hell, having to pump water to keep the floor dry, then sleep on narrow beds lined up against the walls along with the weeks' worth of canned foods. Rick taught them that if anyone were to come to the door of the shelter, they should shoot to kill. Mostly, the bomb shelter sat unused, a sort of novelty that neighbors both chuckled over and envied. When it rained, the rising water table soaked its floor.

Aboveground, Kitty and Rick gave their children free rein to be themselves. Teenage Alice Dale and younger Susan, who shared a bedroom, marked a line down the center of it. Alice's side was a hovel and Susan's, pin-neat. Alice and Kitty shared a passion for horses and bought one that they stabled nearby, but by the time Alice entered Southwest Miami Senior High, they argued often. Alice had reached her breaking point. She had raised her younger siblings, in a way, and rarely expressed joy. In high school she adopted the beatnik ethos and traded her formal skirts for dark pants, in a first stage of rebellion. In 1966 she married Gerald Hehr and soon after gave birth to a daughter of her own.

Pat and Mike shared another bedroom with bunk beds for as long as Pat stuck around. Pat had gone greaser, never far from the cigarettes he rolled into his sleeve, and a shock of hair tamed into the duck's-ass style that was in vogue. He was the first to get suspended from school, his dyslexia undetected. He was the first to learn how to drive and, when he stole a car, was the first to get arrested. Pat had nominated himself Susan's protector. When a teenage kid had told her that Santa wasn't real, he chased the child out of the Hardwick yard with a BB gun, spraying pellets into the boy's rear end. In March of 1965, when he was sixteen, Pat married the young woman he had gotten pregnant and started work as a tree climber and carpenter.

Often left home alone, Susan and Mike distracted themselves in nature. They filled a toy wagon with the mangoes that fell from the tree in their yard and tried to sell them for candy money, not realizing that most of their neighbors had mango trees too. They assembled a menagerie of animals: a rabbit, a dog named Tippy, even an alligator, George, whom they fed raw hamburger until he grew too large to keep as a pet. They watched TV—cartoons mostly, and soap operas, where they could see family dramas that showed people struggling inwardly while outwardly, they lived a life richer than dreams.

Rick remained involved with his older children even after they had moved on and created new lives for themselves. He and Pat worked on their cars together, sometimes with Alice turning a wrench. His younger children were more distant to him. Susan kept quiet and slipped through Rick's moments of anger, staying under the radar. Mike and his father never seemed to connect. They were too unalike, aside from their physical resemblance that grew sharper as Mike grew older. Mike had begun to wonder why his father would not hug him or say he loved him. He was gentle, while his father and brother had a hard edge.[5]

Kitty had taken a job with the city, in charge of the police department's motor pool. She had let her children mature with that distance. She didn't read to them, and she didn't like to cook and wasn't very good at it. They went out almost every night to the diners in the neighborhood, though Rick would occasionally make ambrosia salad, or ribs, or hamburgers spiked with hot sauce. Susan eventually took over the chore.

The distance between family members grew wider and less easy to bridge. Susan and Mike had become latchkey kids who let themselves back into their home after school while their parents worked or, increasingly, went their separate ways. Rick bicycled around town with a six-pack of beer. Kitty drove her turquoise Thunderbird around the neighborhood and flirted with policemen. She craved the attention of other men, just as Rick sought it from other women. Prosperity had given them cars, hobbies, a home, a shelter—and it had also given them permission to dream about different lives imbued with different freedoms.

They had met by chance and built something delicate. It grew more fragile as they neared twenty-five years together. By the time Mike reached middle school, his family as he had known it had begun to disintegrate. Kitty's mother, Kathleen, died in 1966. Rick drank, and that did not relent. Both Rick and Kitty strayed. After he lost his wedding ring in a bar, she filed for divorce. Dade County granted it in April of 1967, on grounds of "extreme cruelty."[6]

Devils and Gods

On mornings when the milkman delivered to the Hardwicks' southwest Miami neighborhood, the loose gang of boys—Mike, Gene, and two other teenagers, all still awake at five o'clock in the morning—would lie in wait, ready to pounce. When the driver disappeared to hand off heavy cream and butter, they circled the truck and raided it for chocolate milk. Then they waited for the bread truck that made its rounds before dawn too. They had cleaned out the bomb shelter behind Mike's house and turned it into a hangout where they caroused all night long. It was hungry work.

Mike saw his father, Rick, sometimes. Gene's dad had left when he was two. Fathers weren't really part of the equation. Gene never knew Mike even had a father.[1]

The group would ride their ten-speed bikes to Miami International Airport just to the north, sneak inside the fence, and park under the lights to watch jets take off and land. Sometimes, the gang went inside the terminal to wander around. Or they'd ride all night to a quarry lake, climb a fringe of trees, and jump in for a swim, never mind what dwelled in the lake's depths. The boys were becoming young men, on their own.

Sometimes they would hang out at the home of another high

school buddy, David. David's sister Patty had a crush on Mike. He smiled a lot, and she thought he was handsome and cool. Patty's single mother had taken in her brother, a Vietnam veteran who liked to party. When the beer and drugs began to flow, her mother sent Patty to stay with an aunt. A lot of kids, including Mike, stayed.[2]

After they discovered drugs, Mike and his friends could easily score what they wanted. Sometimes they rode down to Coconut Grove and hung out at the parks, which had become hippie havens, with the usual pot and Quaaludes. Miami was a pill capital, an acid capital, a town where any of the three grades of pot—Mexican, Jamaican, Colombian—was easily available at anywhere from $20 to $25 a lid. They could buy cocaine, but it was more expensive. They should have gotten into more trouble than they did.[3]

Mike had shed his baby fat, and his sophomore yearbook revealed a leaner young man with a prominent jaw, straight hair gone a shade darker than blond, with a choker around his neck. He never had a girlfriend, as far as his friend Gene knew, but he had a way of talking to women. Mike would call up girls for his shy friend and convince them that they should be interested in Gene. There was never any thought that Mike might be gay. It wasn't discussed, it wasn't part of the vocabulary, at least in their group.[4]

But it was not unknown. The boys had been indoctrinated against the very idea at school and on television. On April 19, 1966, Miami TV station WTVJ aired a documentary special under its "FYI" banner. *The Homosexual* looked at the topic, starting with footage from one of Miami's junior high schools, where students were taught the evils of the aberrant sex practice.

"It can happen to anybody," Detective Sergeant John Sorensen of the Dade County Sheriff's Department of Morals said to the audience of eighth graders.

Officers had been speaking at PTA meetings and schools for

months to alert parents and students about the dangers of being queer. For some, it would be the first time they heard about homosexuality. Sex education belonged in the home, but many parents were too embarrassed to broach the subject. Lacking information, the report suggested, boys could be cruised by a homosexual and convinced to have sex. They might become male prostitutes or, worse, become homosexuals themselves. Queer people were made, not born, according to the ideology of the time. Queerness was absorbed or induced. It was unnatural.

A homosexual could be a man who looked or acted like a woman, though some appeared outwardly unremarkable, with unaffected speech and dress. They could lead a public life, without public knowledge of their identity. Even if it were discovered, none could be prosecuted for being gay or lesbian alone. Florida law since 1917 made "unnatural and lascivious" acts between people of the same sex a misdemeanor.[5] Such a "crime against nature" could damage a person's standing in the community, according to Detective Sorensen. Those who could afford to pay others for silence could return to the community, he said, but even after an acquittal on such charges, they were damaged. The stigma would remain with them for the rest of their lives.

As in many towns across the country, Miami police surveilled gay hot spots in the hopes of catching queer people in the act. The news special aired film that had been shot from a high vantage point at Twenty-First Street down onto Miami Beach. The footage was broadcast as an invert—as a film negative, to prevent public knowledge of identities, or possibly to remove the risk of libel. A straight person on that beach could be slandered if they were called gay. The news show said it had hidden telescopic lenses nearby to capture people in the act of perversion. What they caught were scenes of men cavorting in the water, some on each other's shoulders, some lying next to each other on the sand, close enough to leave no space between them. Some sat on a berm and spoke with others. Some openly flirted with each other. They weren't breaking the law.

After a segment in which a male sex worker was rendered a spectacle—the report offered him as an example of what would happen once a young man was exposed to queer sex—the documentary turned to Richard Inman, the president of the Mattachine Society of Florida. Inman had been afraid that his interview would be edited to make his case unsympathetic, so the documentary disclaimed that.

Mattachine existed to bridge the gulf between queer people and the law, he said, and to increase the understanding of queer lives. It had the side goal of reducing friction with the law as it stood. The present legal schema was untenable, Inman said in carefully measured words. The nation needed to replace its unenforceable laws against queer sexuality. It needed a whole new approach.

Inman attempted to neuter the concern that queer people might one day want the right to marry and to adopt children. "Homosexuals do not want that," he said emphatically, though "you might find some fringe character someplace who says that that's what he wants for himself." What Mattachine wanted, he said, were laws such as those in Europe that condoned any private act of sex between consenting adults. "Present laws give the adult homosexual only the choice of being, to simplify the matter, heterosexual and legal or homosexual and illegal. This to a homosexual is no choice at all."

Inman would go on to say that homosexuality was "not a desirable way of life," but since they could not find happiness with the opposite sex, "they should indeed not be denied the right to find . . . a measure of happiness and love in their life." Inman said he had given up queer sex in any case, since he had been robbed, been subjected to a blackmail attempt, and been picked up in gay-bar raids in 1954 and 1960. If the community would just counsel queer youth about the "miserable life" that would be theirs unless they reformed, he said, they might be able to prevent some family tragedy. Without the stigma of law enforcement, he said, there would be no deterrent—and if there were no laws against crimes of nature, queer people could live and act in private while straight adults might be prosecuted for adultery or fornication.

"This is not equality," he said.

In January of 1969 Kitty married her second husband, Joseph Melville Alamillo, a veteran of World War II and of two wartime marriages that had long since soured. Joe and Kitty were an affectionate couple together. He was a recovering alcoholic and Kitty had helped him get sober.

Mike lived with Kitty and Joe in a single-wide mobile home that permitted him to continue to attend Southwest Miami High. He had what he considered to be a normal life, like any teenager in any high school, anywhere.[6] He said he ran the streets with his friends, did gymnastics, flirted and cracked jokes in class, and had a girlfriend whom he persuaded to get an abortion.

Unafraid to experiment, Mike had easy access to just about any drug he wanted. To the palette of drugs he had tried, he added heroin. He could always ride the bus to the southernmost point of Miami Beach, where along its fishing pier and in the nearby park, teenagers played loud music from their cars parked in the public lots, drinking beer, smoking weed, occasionally throwing Frisbees.[7] The area near the pier had long been known as a major drug destination, where teenagers and adults could obtain "alcohol, Quaaludes, diazepam, marijuana, cocaine, amphetamines, and chalice vine and LSD."

President Nixon had proclaimed a national drug epidemic during the summer of 1971. Drug use was "public enemy number one," and had rooted itself in America's schools. A federal commission cited studies that purported to show levels of drug addiction at 559,000 people nationwide in 1971, much of it in schools. Some 6 percent of the country's high schoolers had tried heroin, equaling some 1.5 million students; 2 million had tried LSD, mescaline, or peyote; 5 percent cocaine; 8 percent speed; 7 percent barbiturates; and 5 percent painkillers like morphine.[8] During the ensuing panic dubbed the "War on Drugs," the park on Miami Beach became a visible point of civic shame.

That shame descended on Mike's home in 1971, when police called Kitty late one night to tell her that her son had been arrested with a carload of friends who were speeding on the highway. When he was arrested, he faced a judge who gave his mother the option of putting him in jail or in a reform program started locally in Miami the year before. Given the choice, Kitty chose reform, and Mike was ordered into the Seed.[9]

The Seed had been founded by Arthur Robert Barker on September 23, 1970, in Fort Lauderdale. With a deep widow's peak combed into his graying blond hair and a pointed face framed by long sideburns, the five-foot-seven Barker was a persistent smoker with "a hair-trigger temper."[10] The New Yorker had come to Miami, where, according to his self-authored legend, he sold peanuts at the Flagler Kennel Club for 5 cents a bag. The son of an alcoholic who died when Barker was fourteen, Barker claimed a military career as an air force pilot and an eighth-grade education. He married briefly and experienced homelessness during a period in New York.[11]

Barker began a low-key movie career and then became a comedian, where he used his drinking problem to a Dean Martin effect. He claimed it netted him enough cash to purchase a forty-six-foot yacht.[12] When he found sobriety, he credited it in part to his second wife, Shelly. He would later say he had been an AA sponsor to Art Carney and Jackie Gleason.[13]

The Seed had been an informal extension of his own sobriety since the late 1960s and early '70s, when he hosted meetings on a boat. The Seed's first fixed address was in a stucco house in Fort Lauderdale. He named the group for what he misunderstood from a Bible passage, that "a little mustard seed can move a mountain." When he was told the quote was incorrect, Barker chuckled and shucked it off as proof of a plucky lack of sophistication.[14]

Part encounter group, part harassment, the Seed combined deprivation of family with peer pressure to harangue teenagers into sobriety. First, Seedlings were removed from their homes and placed with the families of others in the program who had been judged capable of moving to the next phase. Parents were allowed to visit twice a week during open houses, where community members were also allowed. Barker deployed former Seedlings as security guards who checked the IDs of anyone who wanted access. Seedlings were subjected to routine searches of clothing from head to toe, down to the bras of female Seedlings. All personal papers, including driver's licenses, were taken.

Silence was the first mandate: for three days, new Seedlings remained quiet while others spoke about what had brought them there and the program's effect on them. The convocations took place under a circuslike tent in a parking lot, where dozens of Seedlings sat in often brutal heat from ten in the morning until ten at night. When they were permitted to join these "rap sessions," newer Seedlings were subjected to the verbal abuse of others. Those close to matriculation or those who had remained as volunteers were essentially the staff, since Barker and his wife were among the very few employees of the group. No therapists, doctors, or other addiction specialists were among them. Food consisted of what volunteers and parents could provide: Kool-Aid to drink, and peanut butter or baloney sandwiches made in big batches and brought from home. The Seed exercised group power over those subjected to it by confining them, their habits, their relationships, even their thoughts. It gave "love, understanding, openness, honesty, and a kick in the pants" when Seedlings needed it, Shelly Barker said.[15]

Most meetings ended with a final homily, the almost-compulsory "I love you, Mom and Dad. I love you, group."[16]

Barker drew on celebrity and notoriety to feed the Seed's public image and colluded with the powerful to fuel its growth. The federal government supported it despite thin record-keeping and almost nonexistent medical supervision. Judges steered children into the program. Parents handed over their children to the Seed without any proof of drug use; behavioral conflicts were enough for some.

The Seed drew the attention of politicians and celebrities eager to attach themselves to a program that seemed to ease the tension of a drug-fueled conflict between generations. Sammy Davis Jr. sang for the Seedlings in the grim ninety-degree heat of reflective pavement and bare shade of the canvas tent in April of 1972. He had visited soldiers in Vietnam undergoing drug treatment and served on Nixon's Committee on Drug Abuse. "I'm here because I wanted to say I've been here," Davis said before he broke into song, "I've gotta be me, I've gotta be free."[17]

The Seedlings had a song of their own. Sung to the traditional "Greensleeves," it rewrote the carol with propaganda as it instructed Seedlings that "The Seed, indeed, is all you need, to stay off the junk and the pills and the weed."[18]

Seedlings spent hours chanting songs and ridiculing one another, hurling epithets such as "loser." The inquisition would continue when they were asked who had tried amphetamines, who had experimented with heroin, who had smoked pot. On one occasion, nine of the Seedlings raised their hands when asked if they were there simply because of behavioral issues. One claimed to have had ten friends who had died of overdoses and of having put a syringe in a friend's coffin as a fitting tribute.[19] Seed meetings were produced as theater, with Barker the master of ceremonies.

On the day Sammy Davis Jr. sang, one forty-two-day veteran Seedling sat in the back row. The longer Seedlings behaved, the further they moved from the glare of Barker's front-row antics. A Seedling—named Mike—had grown distracted, and Barker called him out.[20]

"What were you fantasizing about?" Barker rasped at Mike. "You thinking of sticking something in your arm or being on some island with a chick and you as Tarzan?" Ushers promptly moved Mike back to a seat up front.

"I wasn't really fantasizing," the teenager later told the reporter. "I just wasn't listening."[21]

Once a Seedling completed the intake stage of the program—anywhere from two weeks to the four weeks demanded when a Seedling had been admitted by court order—they attended meetings three times a week at the Fort Lauderdale compound at 1311 South Andrews Street, as well as one day of meetings over the weekend. During this phase, their parents could open their homes to new Seedlings, as Kitty did when Mike returned home. She drove him and her new foundlings from Miami to Fort Lauderdale, an hour away and back, while she worked, bringing sandwiches she'd made as part of the group's social pact. She felt motherly toward these boys, and she believed the program to be the best of all the possible outcomes. She believed the drugs would have killed Mike.

The program bred dependence by confining Seedlings and then keeping them in its orbit for at least three months before they could return to their former lives—to school, or for many, to whatever place they could find where they would not be ostracized. Before they could graduate from the program, Seedlings had to abstain not only from drugs or alcohol but also from former friends who doubted the program. They were not allowed to take telephone calls from anyone outside the circle of trust. Enforcement came from the network of those who had graduated and survived it. Once out, former Seedlings were only supposed to be in contact with other Seed members. Any other contact would be reported back to Barker through his growing surveillance network. Barker boasted that he had "the greatest CIA in the world" working for him.[22]

The Seed used children to treat children, and that led to inevitable cruelty and abuse.[23] Some parents claimed the program turned their children into zombies. Some equated it with a concentration camp.

Some of Barker's former advisors and supporters became concerned about the program. Dr. Ben Sheppard, who had consulted with Barker and had been considered at the forefront of the drug-rehabilitation field in the state, said that half the Seedlings would not have been accepted by other treatment programs. A survey had found some 17 percent of those admitted had never experimented with drugs and there only to resolve "attitudinal" problems.[24] He said the Seed was "brainwashing" and called for its closure. A guidance counselor at one Dade County high school complained that the Seedlings who returned "straight" from the program behaved like robots, segregating themselves from other students and using the school's payphone to report other Seedlings for behavioral infractions.[25]

Evidence mounted that the Seed's success rate might be far less than the 90 percent claimed by Barker.[26] Nevertheless, in 1972, had been given $177,200 by the National Institute of Mental Health, money to be used for the rehabilitation of roughly 600 Seedlings.[27] Barker bore the cost of the facility, and some of the cost to feed the Seedlings, but little money was apportioned to employees, since there were so few of them. Barker himself drew an annual salary of $14,500 and paid his wife, Shelly, $6,500.[28]

New demands for oversight zeroed in on Barker's lack of records for Seedlings. A check of files found that only 41 percent of those taken in had finished the program and that 90 percent were never followed up with after they left. Barker would not provide treatment records for 72 percent of the Seedlings whose cases were checked, a red flag for state overseers who fretted that the program "could have disastrous effects on the youth with an unrecorded history of psychological disorder."[29] Barker's "psychological reconditioning" program had grown quickly in just eighteen months, and that drew the attention of media and then, the unwanted attention of regulators.

"I have nothing to hide," Barker said as he sloughed off charges of corruption. "I don't have any great political empire. I don't have any millions of dollars. All I have is kids."[30]

The reformed and tattooed alcoholic wheeled around in a blue Oldsmobile convertible with the defiance of the well-connected. Some thought he was a "fly-by-night mystic" and a "showbiz prophet," while some of the Seedlings saw him as "divinely inspired."

"They call you devil," he dismissed his critics, "or call you god."

Hardwick would later say that he moved out of his mother's house when he was seventeen, which would have been in 1971. The length of his involvement at the Seed would remain private, even to some within his family. His siblings had moved out and away, and had children of their own to raise. Gradually Mike rejoined the outside world. He had straightened out, his family believed, and he had changed physically to mirror the change they presumed had taken root within him. He had grown into a young adult. The golden-blond straight hair was gone. His hair had become beautifully kinky. He had entered the Seed an adolescent and emerged an adult Adonis, one with a new distaste for unfounded authority.

For a while, Mike worked as a pool cleaner, sanitizing them with harsh chemicals that clung in the humid air. At one job, the woman who hired him spoke to him about his life, about metaphysics, and about becoming his own master.

"And I looked around me," she read aloud to him, "and saw so many people who were totally controlled by their minds."[31] He seemed to absorb the message as a call to find a new structure for his life, and he found that structure in part through the teachings of a self-anointed god who had inspired his sister Alice.

Meher Baba, born in Poona, India, of Persian descent in February 1894, claimed to be one of five earthly incarnations of the universe itself, inseparable from God—a "perfect master."[32] He was the Rama, the Buddha, Krishna and Jesus and Muhammad; all were him too. His very existence, it was said, freed love from all its physical limitations. He did not claim to be a yogi or a guru like Maharishi Mahesh, who had enticed the Beatles to India on a sojourn that ended in the *White Album*. Instead, Baba dubbed himself the Ancient One, or the Avatar of the Age—another in a long line of prophets who were merely the expression of the true god of the universe.[33]

Those who believed in the aphorisms and asceticism of Baba often had another motivation. Many were recent refugees from programs like the Seed, where they had been excoriated and abused, only to leave, still faced with their addictions. Many sought a loving spiritualism as a medium between harsh drug-treatment programs and the freewheeling society they had shut out of their view. Baba disavowed all drugs, particularly hallucinogens and marijuana. His very claim—"I am the highest of the high."—spoke for itself.[34]

A new terrain of mysticism and spiritual beliefs attracted those who had experimented with psychedelics. The spiritual observance gave cover to what actually was happening: they were learning how to live without drugs. Baba love had not been a very widespread belief system until the mid-1960s.³⁵ But the jump in drug rehabilitation and the War on Drugs meant there were people ripe for conversion to Baba and other similar beliefs. Denigrated often as "cults," groups like Baba lovers nonetheless functioned as a sort of spiritual halfway house, where people could reintegrate into society while still holding on to some of the tenets that had driven them away from conventional societal constraints.³⁶

These groups also gave free space for queer identity to emerge, since core among Baba's beliefs was that sexuality was fluid, so long as it was practiced within monogamous relationships. Baba legend held that he had even created a rainbow flag a half century before queer people adopted it as a symbol of community. Long before a belief system formed around him, Baba had brokered a peace between Muslim and Hindu factions in his hometown of Meherabad. The groups had debated over the color of a flag that would be flown to steer goats and cattle from trampling on jasmine. The Muslims wanted a green flag, the Hindu, red. Baba is said to have proposed a rainbow flag that moved from its lowest red stripe—which stood for anger and lust—through the orange of love and yellow of sacrifice, on a spiritual ladder through renunciation's green band, knowledge's violet, and control's purple—with the top band in sky blue, symbolic of a surrender to the infinite and to union with the universe.

Baba's following grew as his teachings spread through the written word, but the prophet himself retreated from celebrity into silence. From July 10, 1925, until his death some forty-four years later, Meher Baba did not speak other than to himself. "You have had enough of my words," he told his flock. "Now is the time to live by them."³⁷ He communicated as needed through a lettered board that he touched to create messages. He had said that his silence would end before he passed out of the physical realm and that his last word would renew the spiritual energy of man, but he did not speak again. He retired to a cave a hundred miles from Bombay in 1965.[38]

When he died on January 31, 1969, thousands came in pilgrimage to get a final glimpse of the body, which was placed in a tomb he had ordered built and covered in roses. Baba lovers gathered at Kennedy Airport to fly to his memorial. When they returned, they said they had experienced heaven. They felt vibrations that emanated from what they perceived as his love. They experienced visions and manifestations of him, though he had died. Some were stricken with physical illness, so intense were their emotions. But they would forget all that as they came together and formed a family of believers and renewed their pledge to follow their prophet's mantra: *Don't worry, be happy,* Baba had taught.

Alice was the first in her family to plunge into the world of Baba. She had always been first to do something extravagantly different, to unleash herself from normality. Though she knew she was queer, she had married Gerald Hehr in New York in 1966, and inside of two years, they had a daughter, who grew into her angelic white hair. In the early 1970s, Alice decided she had to do something for Baba. She packed her sister Susan, Susan's son Robert, and her own daughter into an old VW Beetle and drove to Manhattan, where they sold crepe-paper flowers on the sidewalks. Alice's deft hands made beautiful buds that attracted the attention of soul belter Janis Joplin, who stopped to buy some from her and played with the children.[39]

The family left New York days later, with less than $20 on hand and only a loaf of bread and some peanut butter and jelly to eat. When a stranger who had run them off the road gave them money for their troubles, they adjusted their path and stopped in Myrtle Beach, at the center where Baba lovers had built a home for their devotion. Alice had dreamed of going there, but it was an unhappy visit. Baba was dead, and the followers at the center did not give the group the reception they expected.

This did not deter their belief in Baba. The Baptist and Episcopalian religions that Alice and Susan had been born into had failed them, cast them as outsiders because of their status as women and single mothers. Christianity, Islam, Judaism—all had been responsible for limiting the lives of their adherents as they proscribed evil and prescribed what was good. The wave of alternative belief systems that washed over the Western world during the 1960s and '70s promised a completely different vision: the innate purity of humanity and its innate perfection, love and forgiveness given freely, not subject to being earned. Whether it was EST or the Maharishi or Meher Baba, the lure of New Age philosophies came on strongly while the fusty old religions warred over contraceptives and recoiled in horror at the idea of female equality or even the existence of gays and lesbians.

Alice's influence on Mike bled into his spiritual life. Perhaps at her urging, he began to attend meetings held by Baba follower Ann Forbes, who had come to Miami from Germany in 1958. Forbes had met Baba in New York in 1956, in a transcendent moment that she preached to others. "As it was, I felt Baba's hand touching my wrist gently and drawing me up," she would later recall. "Before I knew it, I was face to face with the Compassionate Father and in His all-embracing arms. Baba held me so wholeheartedly for what seemed to me such a long time that I was in wonderment at what had happened to me. I found myself in utter amazement as the thought came—'Is it possible, me in the arms of God?'"[40] She had met the Avatar.

At one meeting where Forbes spoke of her Baba love and experiences, she walked through the crowd of believers, each anxious for a deeply held spiritual moment. Among them all, she approached Mike directly. She leaned toward him and whispered in his ear.

"You will stray many times," she said, "but you will return."[41]

Atlanta

From trails cut decades before through the vast Austin Cary Forest, Michael Hardwick could watch gopher tortoises skitter across dusty paths, listen for redheaded woodpeckers tapping the trees for grub, and slither along with frosted flatwoods salamanders and diamondback rattlesnakes through the bluestem and sedge grass. All forests are teachers, but this forest became his sage.[1] It instilled in him the belief that he was one with nature, both a voyeur and an intimate.

He had emerged from the Seed with a desire to find his truth. For the moment, that desire had led him north. He had moved far from his childhood home in Miami to Gainesville, where he lived near his sister Susan and studied Sanskrit and landscape design at Santa Fe Community College. He had matured into a slim-hipped, confident young man, one possessed of the striking good looks of a model, with piercing, wide-set eyes and a pronounced chin set under heart-shaped lips, all girded by an earthy voice.

The rest of the Hardwick family had spread out as parents remarried and as children became parents. By the mid-1970s, Rick had retired from the fire department and moved back to Missouri with his second wife, Mary Lou, and bought a huge house outside of Webb City. The home—his children called it a mansion—had a third-floor ballroom and a basement that had been an underground passage on the Prohibition circuit, where people played cards and drank in the contorted morality of the era. Rick filled the house with furniture from the Sears Roebuck catalog and let animals roam and defecate all over the house. He and Mary Lou decorated their home like the haunted house it resembled, hosted Halloween costume parties, and hired help to pop out of coffins in a theatrical display so impressive, the local television crew covered it.

Mike's brother Pat had divorced his high-school bride and had been arrested for barbiturate possession in 1971. His schools and parents hadn't been able to address his dyslexia, but in time he taught himself how to play chess and to how to read. After his charges were dismissed, he remarried and found steady work.

Alice Dale had moved to Missouri and lived down the road from Rick for a long time. She waited tables, tended to her daughter, and told her family she was a lesbian. Her father accepted it, and bought her tools for Christmas, as he had for Pat. He knew his older children better than he knew Susan and Mike, who got cash.

Susan had stayed in Gainesville after some college. There she met her second husband and had a second child, Jasmine. Susan immersed herself in learning how to raise her daughter, who had cerebral palsy. She wanted to ensure Jasmine had a vibrant life, although none of the Hardwick family knew what that life might look like.

Mike Hardwick lived an hour away in Waldo, where he spent three years living in relative isolation, as he seriously considered becoming a practicing Buddhist. His Episcopalian mother and his atheist father were wary.[2] Rick's whole orthodoxy of how men were defined had been defied by Mike's groomed appearance and work as a model, and in some part, by the extravagantly different beliefs he now espoused.

Hardwick's family saw him infrequently and knew little about the inner turmoil he had begun to smooth over and resolve. But when

Susan gave birth to Jasmine, he had driven the fifty miles to be there for the birth. He cradled Jasmine with a wide-eyed look of amazement. She offered him living proof that life could be created anew.

In 1976, Hardwick broke from the solace of the pine flatwoods and cypress wetlands to visit a female friend in Atlanta. When she introduced him to her gay male friend, Hardwick fell for him, without hesitation, without regret. They kissed, and it didn't scare him. If anything, it seemed perfectly normal to him.[3] Alice had come out years earlier to the family, and that had made it easier for Hardwick to see himself as gay. He had wanted to experience affection and closeness for so long. When it happened, he fell in love.

He wanted to be honest with his family. He told his mother that he was attracted to men, while he prepared to move to Atlanta. She peppered him with questions about how gay relationships worked, but he was a novice. Kitty asked him if men in relationships took on traditional roles. He confessed he didn't know but was eager to find out. But when he arrived in Atlanta, he discovered his would-be lover already had a partner. It devastated him. He felt as if he had given up his manhood.[4]

His female friend and her lover tried to help him heal as they packed for a planned move to eastern Tennessee. They offered him a place to crash—*you've got to do something, you're a mess*—and he accepted. Hardwick said he spent six months in emotional recovery. Billie Holiday became his spiritual guide.[5] Billie knew the taste of soured love. She knew the sting of a heroin needle. She knew that she had at times been powerless to both.

By 1977 Hardwick returned to a south Florida that bristled with a newly vocal and political queer community. Long before the 1970s the city had become both a hub of queer life and a flashpoint for fury. In

1937, almost 200 Klansmen raided the queer club La Paloma in northwest Miami and set fire to a cross in front of the bar. In 1954 Miami police raided public bathrooms, as they had in other cities then and earlier. In the early 1970s, Miami police converged on gay bathhouses to make mass arrests. Even so, a thriving queer scene flourished in Miami Beach, Coral Gables, and Coconut Grove, with an emerging outpost to the north to Fort Lauderdale.

Miami had its gay clubs and gay bathhouses, but "Fort Liquordale" had college-age drinking—and it had the Marlin Beach Hotel. The Marlin Beach had been built in 1952 as a kitschy hotel with more than a hundred rooms and balconies adorned with ironwork renditions of coral and seahorses. Its main bar wrapped around a ceiling-high tank where performers swam in mermaid costumes to entertain those seated at its bar. The Marlin hosted stars like Joan Blondell in suites like the Jules Verne Room, which had windows that looked out on the fishbowl-shaped pool where the mermaids would swim in a school of fancy.

The Marlin had been the setting for the 1960 film *Where the Boys Are*, with Dolores Hart, Paula Prentiss, Yvette Mimieux, and George Hamilton. The town had become a popular haven for college students as early as the 1930s. It surged in popularity in the 1960s, with the release of the movie, but began a decline by mid-decade as newer hotels rose and dotted the shore. Real-estate developer Bill Hovan bought the Marlin in 1966 when it was past its heterosexual prime. His gay employees had begun to bring in their gay friends long before he began marketing specifically to the queer community in 1972. At that point, Hovan alerted guests to the transition. Families that had visited the Marlin when the heart-shaped pool was filled with women would be greeted by a sign that read "This is a gay bar. If homosexuals or homosexuality offend you . . . STAY OUT!"[6] One man who had checked in with his young son promptly checked out when the son went for a swim and came back to the room, telling his father, "Two men are kissing at the pool."[7]

Gay men nicknamed it the "Marlena," and in the early 1970s the hotel became known worldwide for the scene at its pool, for the gay beach across the street, and for the action in its rooms and in its twin discos, the Lower Deck and the Poop Deck. It attracted a global audience of queers who soaked up the sun, then took in the latest disco during its afternoon tea dance while being served drinks by hot shooter boys in tight shorts known as the "Poopettes." To close each night, the disco would play the Connie Francis plaintive ballad from the movie that had made the Marlin famous. Some guests would show up dressed as the singer.[8] By 1977, the Marlin became one of the beach's best-known hotels, grossing more than $2 million in a year.[9] It became part of a distinct queer geography, one that stretched from Key West and Provincetown to Bondi Beach in Sydney to the Marais in Paris to a gritty back alley or two in Tokyo's Shinjuku district—a newly drawn queer map of the world, woven together in an imagined community and in a real one, linked by telephones, magazines, television, airplanes, and by word of mouth.

The Marlin's status as a queer destination aroused the ire of civic groups, who blamed it for rising problems with drifters and hustlers. Mayor E. Clay Shaw Jr. wanted Midwestern families to think of the town as their own retreat. If they came and saw men having sex on the beach, he complained, "What will they think? They'll never come back." Shaw vowed to stamp out the hotel's status as a queer mecca, even to stamp out homosexuality itself.[10] When police arrested some gay sex workers near the Marlin, Shaw tried to form a grand jury to hear complaints about them and their association with the hotel. A city attorney told Shaw there was nothing to investigate.[11] Legally, Shaw could do nothing to prevent gays and lesbians from flocking to Fort Lauderdale's flat, pale-yellow sand and its see-forever beaches, where sunsets would cast the water and sky the colors of a tourmaline, from deep aqua to rosy pink.

Shaw gave up in frustration. The Marlin Beach partied on. The queer community had won the latest round. It would be a rare victory, and a fleeting one.

By the 1970s, queer people had begun to resist the hundred-year project to detect them, define them, and deny them the basic privileges and protections of society. Before the turn of the twentieth century, queer people had more loosely been deemed degenerates and deviants because they broke free of the orthodoxy of God, marriage, and traditional family. More nebulous forms of discrimination were codified after World War II, as the compulsory heterosexuality of the postwar decade gave license to the state and its actors—doctors, police, the courts, relatives, and even strangers—to freely surveil and disrupt queer lives.[12] The oppression had a perverse effect from what had been intended. The tightening constraints of the law fueled the first of America's queer political movements, among them the Mattachine Society and the Daughters of Bilitis. Faced with increased scrutiny, persecution, and prosecution, a politically silent community began to pierce the anti-queer hysteria as it found its political voice.

The oppressive conservative morality of the era had begun to dissolve during the prior decade along all sorts of lines, from cultural flashpoints of literature, film, and music (Nabokov's *Lolita* to *The Asphalt Jungle* to Elvis "The Pelvis" Presley) to the legal code that underwrote it all. In 1958 the Supreme Court reversed an appellate court ruling in *One Inc. v. Oleson*, in which lower courts had deemed queer-oriented magazines obscene.[13] The decision found that even material that depicted queer-friendly content carried the protection of the First Amendment with it through the U.S. Postal Service. Magazines that showed bodybuilders posing nude had the same legal standing as the latest issue of *Life*. Once queer people could see their desires in print, they could see themselves.

The laws that governed sex itself were next on the docket. Sodomy statutes and codes against "crimes of nature" had been toughened in the prewar era, but during the 1960s states began to reconsider the sexual surveillance of their citizens. It had become obvious that extramarital, oral, and anal sex were widely practiced, and could not easily be patrolled. In 1961, Illinois became the first state to repeal its sodomy laws while other states maintained theirs and used them to prosecute people selectively based on their gender and sex. America's sexual landscape had been forever altered by the growth of cities, the greater political independence of women, the technologies of sex from the zipper to the Pill and penicillin. The law struggled to keep up, whether the sex in question took place in the home, in parked cars, or in public restrooms.

Sodomy inside of marriage had become a norm; outside of marriage it still inspired disgust and became a highly selective tool for the prosecution of queer sexuality. Even as police began to target them for the sex they enjoyed, queer people advanced the cause of sexual liberty. In 1963 the first gay bar opened in San Francisco's Castro district. In 1965, queer people in Los Angeles fought back against police power at a cafeteria they had claimed as a gathering space. In the same year in Atlanta, they rose up after a Halloween costume party ended with a hundred cross-dressing revelers in paddy wagons. Then, explosively, at the Stonewall bar in New York, in June of 1969, a four-day queer uprising left the bar scorched, the police battered, and the queers united in the belief that their time had come.

The skirmishes in the battle for sexual liberty proceeded apace in the Supreme Court, where justices had decided cases such as 1965's *Griswold v. Connecticut*, 1972's *Eisenstadt v. Baird*, and 1973's *Roe v. Wade*, which expanded the idea of privacy to include contraception and abortion and associated rights of reproductive privacy. The same court denied that it had any power to rule on an early same-sex marriage case, 1972's *Baker v. Carr*. Yet, it decided in 1976's *Doe v. Commonwealth's Attorney of Richmond* that the states had the right to write and enforce anti-queer sodomy laws. Queer sex, the court found, was still a "crime against nature."

By 1977, the progressive sexual politics of the women's- and gay-rights movements were met by the rise of the darker and decidedly anti-feminist, anti-queer conservatism of Anita Bryant. The former beauty queen and television star had emerged as the latest in a long chain of prophets, politicians, and attention-seekers who used queer people to platform themselves on a national stage. Bryant had discovered she could use the media to marshal a band of morality warriors against the gay-rights movement.

In 1977, Bryant lured money from groups against school desegregation to form her "Save Our Children" movement, which forced a recall vote on a gay-rights ordinance that had been enacted earlier that year in Miami. The ordinance had stated that discrimination against gays and lesbians was banned in private education, housing, unions, and employment in Dade County. Miami had passed it on January 18, 1977, and the blowback ensued immediately. By the end of February, Save Our Children had amassed enough signatures to trigger a referendum on June 7.

Bryant would be taken to task on a new CBS program that aired in the spring of 1977. On *Who's Who*, which was conceived of as a companion to *60 Minutes* but was more in the tone of *People* magazine, Bryant exchanged some heated words with journalist Barbara Howar, who visited the pop singer cum politician at her twenty-seven-room Miami mansion, where she lived with husband Bob Green and their four children.[14]

Bryant, Howar reported, "says she feels that God has singled her out to spearhead a crusade to prevent admitted homosexuals from teaching her children."[15] Awash in the imagery of Protestant family virtue, Bryant baked cookies with her children for a video clip before verbally jousting with Howar, who asked her bluntly: "Why are you taking this stand now and perhaps jeopardizing that?"

"According to the word of God, it's an abomination, uh, to practice homosexuality," Bryant answered, prickly.

"Anita, suppose one of your children came to you, suppose you found out in some way that one of your children was a homosexual," Howar asked. "What would you do?"

The singer's expression fell flat. She said she would love them and not disown them but would try to deal with "that problem" and love the sinners as God instructed. "God made mothers so that we could reproduce," she said. "Homosexuals cannot reproduce biologically, but they have to reproduce by recruiting our children."[16]

Bryant's movement had broken a taboo. It had forced TV and newspapers to discuss queer sex in frank ways. It also mobilized a wave of gay-rights activists, both queer people and allies alike. But it could not rally the rest of the Miami–Dade community in sufficient numbers. When Bryant's referendum to repeal the human-rights ordinance went before the voters, the anti-gay forces won 69 percent to 31 percent carrying every section of Miami except for Coconut Grove. Even the traditionally liberal voting blocs voted against the ordinance. A planned victory party at the Marlin Beach Hotel fizzled. The Miami gay-rights community staged a Pride protest where hundreds sang, shouted, and spoke about the defeat, before and after they marched down Grand Avenue in Coconut Grove.[17]

Hardwick was one of the thousands of queer people whose civil rights had been put to a popular vote. He lived in Coconut Grove while he worked in businesses that catered to gays and lesbians. Tucked away south of Miami past the seventy-two-room Vizcaya mansion built by John Deering, the hamlet had been named for the huge groves of coconut trees planted in 1870. It occupied a bank of coral ridges on the blue water of Biscayne Bay. It was almost hidden in a forest of poinciana and banyans, its tree-covered roads shaded by massive oaks and pines, its homes tucked behind coral-stone walls where hibiscus and palm trees and orchids flourished. Some of the town's pioneers were Bahamians who had built homes and the massive Peacock Inn in the town.[18]

The Grove had fashioned itself a hippie haven in the 1960s along the lines of Sausalito or Greenwich Village, but by the late 1970s it had begun to gentrify. The queer hideaway's mix of "super-rich matrons, freaked-out kids, artists and Audubonists" had made the Grove "a place of refuge from the plastic world all about," but now they were joined by the Collins Avenue nouveau riche that came with them.[19] Its leather and ceramics shops were joined by galleries that sold metal sculptures and jewelry in chic boutiques. The bohemian feel extended to its diet: the Oak Feed Store now stocked caviar and pheasant along with its wheat germ.[20]

The Grove read the temperature of the new Miami that had formed in the shadow of celebrity and notoriety. It was the home of the Mutiny Hotel, a hot spot that hosted celebrities from Fleetwood Mac to the Cars to Neil Young. Described as Miami's Studio 54, it included a tiki bar, restaurant, and a private disco. Cuban exiles and Miamians nearby had begun peddling marijuana there, aware of the ways to avoid detection in the isolated stretches of coastline found even around metro Miami. Cocaine was the step up from there and dominated the drug and crime scene so pervasively by the end of the 1970s, it had turned Miami into a sort of failed state.[21] As the ecosystem of stars, sex, and money attracted the Miami drug trade, the Mutiny became a hub for the cocaine industry.

While Hardwick became a familiar, popular face at the restaurants and bars in the Grove, he juggled connections with several men. He and an early lover, Jorge Vazquez, remained friends, though their romantic relationship had ended after a year and a half. By then, Hardwick had begun another relationship, with the Marlin Beach Hotel's manager, Cliff Hovan.

Cliff was the adopted son of Marlin owner Bill Hovan. Tall and muscular, with dark hair and a brushy clone mustache, Cliff had been born Cliff Pomeroy in Panama City, Florida, in 1954. He had met Bill Hovan, who was twenty-seven years older than him, and the two became a couple. With no legal recognition of their relationship possible, Bill adopted Cliff and hired him to run the front office of the hotel. Together, they lived in a well-off part of Fort Lauderdale, close to Birch Park and the central area where gay bars were clustered, not far from the condo building that Bill had developed before he purchased the Marlin Beach.

The unorthodox relationship between Bill and Cliff expanded to include Michael. Whether it was by mutual agreement, whether they all enjoyed a romantic triad, or whether Cliff and Michael kept their romance a secret, even Hardwick's family would not know. Queer relationships could have extraordinary fluidity. Without the blessing of the state or the church, those involved in such relationships had to negotiate status and standing, truth and secrecy. Their very identity was deemed by some an offense against God. They were damned anyway, no matter what kind of relationships they chose.

Every sex act they performed fit the legal definition of sodomy, an ancient and vague term still defined in the era's dictionaries as "unnatural" sex acts (either with persons or animals). Typically, it meant both oral sex and anal sex, which were also practiced by heterosexuals.[22] It was sinful, but thanks to Anita Bryant, it was fodder for casual conversation, even for newspaper advice columns. In the January 31, 1978

"Marriage Doctor" advice column in the *Miami Herald*, a reader asked Dr. Joseph Trainer the basics: "What is 'oral sex' and is what homosexuals do to each other the same as sodomy?" Trainer defined oral sex, and answered that it was a fundamentally natural act, estimating that about three-quarters of Americans, straight and queer alike, indulged in it. Its very prevalence gave states a legitimate reason to repeal their sodomy laws, even as the Supreme Court's *Doe v. Commonwealth* decision of 1976 had ratified the states' right to enact anti-sodomy laws. How could something so popular be illegal? Supreme Court or no, queer people had scientific proof that their sex lives were very much like those of their straight neighbors. Unwittingly, Anita Bryant had become their mouthpiece.

Still, Bryant would not relent as she pressured followers to press her agenda. In a letter to supporters of her newly renamed "Protect America's Children" campaign, she wrote a warning to the faithful in the summer of 1978. "Militant homosexuals across America are planning a national celebration—'Gay Pride Day,' June 25th—a day when militant homosexuals will strut down the main streets of every major city in our country flaunting their sexual perversions. From what I have heard and read, this celebration is just the beginning of a major operation to try to legally enforce homosexuality as a 'civil right!'" Bryant instructed believers to take the letter to their minister to organize a day of prayer on that same date, in the hopes that "you and I may be able to turn hundreds of them away from joining in these perverted activities." Her political power had overturned gay-rights ordinances in Miami, St. Paul, and Wichita, and she sought more money to mount more attacks.

Bryant's success in Miami–Dade had wounded the gay-rights movement but had not killed it. Many were aghast at the idea that America was in retrograde. The crusade triggered those allies to stand and be counted. The vigorous public debate about gay civil rights that followed had convinced some gay people that their political power had begun its ascendancy. All they had to do was drown out the growing backlash to queer power. Victories in court might accomplish that—victories against sodomy laws, first and foremost.

Hardwick would later recall protesting Anita Bryant, but mostly, he worked. By 1978, he bartended in queer-friendly restaurants and clubs, while he started his own landscaping business. Growth Concept Environmental Design attracted a clientele from contacts he had built up serving the elite in Coconut Grove.[23] He planted a lavish array of tropicalia on the patio at a new restaurant, Serendipity, that opened in Coconut Grove in late 1979, briefly living in a spare room at the owner's home on Miami Avenue with his friend Jorge.[24]

In one restaurant, he worked alongside a Black woman named Blanche, who he felt had been "blessed with second sight." One day as they talked about civil rights, Blanche made a prediction that would stick with him for the rest of his life.

"One day," she told him, "you will stand before thousands of people and speak on the issue of human rights."[25]

Bryant had sparked defiance in the queer community and urged it to organize better. It did so through the usual queer conduits. The bars and baths remained hubs of queer culture. South Florida queers could cruise to Keith's Cruise Bar in Hallandale Beach, where drag performers curated a satire of the straight world for the late-late-late crowd while they collected money for anti-Bryant efforts. Gay men could disrobe at the Club Baths in Miami, where they could commune in an oval pool or wander among a jungle of palms and orchids to find more secluded niches for private acts, under the protection of an owner who had sued the city's police to stop the legal persecution and won. Queer people had established a footprint from the south end of Miami Beach, where they mingled when the sun was at its apogee, blazing their skin red, all the way north to Fort Lauderdale, where they could spend the evening under a starry curtain of lights scattered by the Marlin Beach Hotel's mirror ball, with Bill and Cliff Hovan at the helm, Hardwick somewhere in their orbit.

Hardwick was spending time with Cliff during these months. After about a year and a half of landscaping and catering and waiting tables, he said, he decided that he had issues he still wanted to resolve. He planned another departure from Miami to find the answers to questions that he still had about his life and his homosexuality. He sold his half of the landscaping operation to his business partner, packed his things, and headed north once more to Tennessee—to Gatlinburg, where Hovan would join him.[26]

The beige Jeep Wrangler bounded over the dirt, through the hills of eastern Tennessee, where Michael said he had gone to heal. He clambered up the hill with family visiting from Gainesville: Susan; her children, Robert and Jasmine; and Susan's boyfriend, Mike Chriss, all crammed into the sport-ute, followed by another car filled with Cliff and other friends that they had brought to Tennessee or made there. Hardwick and Hovan had made Gatlinburg their place. They lived together, adopted a pet ferret together, and purchased a lot in Smoke Rise Mountain Community on April 2, 1979, paying $6,450 for the land that one day might be a home.

In the 8-track deck in the Jeep's dash, Fleetwood Mac's *Rumours* cycled through its eleven paeans to love and heartbreak, from the ballad "Dreams" to the fiery "Go Your Own Way," recorded in Hardwick's Coconut Grove neighborhood just two years before. The two-car crew drove on rutted dirt roads up to Smoke Rise, where they reached the side of a mountain, on a hill that faced the sunrise. One day, Hardwick said, he and Hovan would live there, where they could watch summer storms clatter tree trunks together or see distant mountain ridges through spindly birches in winter.

While they planned the future, they shared an apartment near Emerts Cove Road, on the steep side of a mountain near an old cemetery, next to a river that rushed in white froth around the rocks, where the sun set fire to the ridge every evening. They hiked about forty miles each week, at Laurel Falls and Clingman's Dome and Cades Cove, the collection of oases where Hardwick found peace.

Gatlinburg attracted nature lovers from all walks of life, but at its core, it was steeped in devout Christian beliefs—so devout, it was home to a tiny church on the main strip where services were recorded on VHS tapes and made available for anyone to play in a TV/VCR provided for worship. A neighboring burg hosted its own passion play: Fashioned after the day-long dramatization of the crucifixion of Christ, the Gatlinburg area's version competed with rivals in South Dakota, Arkansas, and Strasburg, Virginia.[27]

Hardwick relied on a different cast of teachers from those offered by the Christianity in which he had been raised, in which he now was steeped. He had learned from Meher Baba. Now he studied Carlos Castaneda, a Peruvian émigré to the United States who had written a series of books about his journeys and apprenticeship to a Yaqui Indian sorcerer. Castaneda absorbed hallucinogens to observe their effects, and in his first Don Yaqui volume, *The Teachings of Don Juan: A Yaqui Way of Knowledge*, the author wrote about the spirit that lived in nature, the mescaline, and about the use of yerba del diablo, or jimsonweed, to induce divinely inspired visions of lizards and of flight.[28]

The New Age philosophies filled a void in those who sought out his books as spiritual guides, as a generation parted with traditional Western religion and the dogma that challenged the tenets of their daily lives.[29] Castaneda's universal themes of self-improvement and of the magic in everyday life resonated strongly and subtly throughout popular culture. George Lucas had read the author's tales of Don Yaqui and patterned the relationship between Luke Skywalker and Obi-Wan Kenobi in *Star Wars* on the Castaneda series.[30]

The books held Hardwick in a thrall. The mythic creation Don Juan Yaqui spoke of the need to detach oneself from the external world and from the idea of death, in the pursuit of the life of a "warrior." In his dreams Hardwick became that warrior. He had experienced the passions of youth, of nature, of substances, of realizing he was queer. He now understood what that meant to him, both physically and spiritually. He knew that the chance to pursue passion could be infinitesimally brief, that he must seize it, embracing it headlong. Castaneda had taught him to accept that his life would take him to places unknown only if he discarded the fear of death.

"The dying sun will glow on you without burning, as it has done today," Castaneda had written. "The wind will be soft and mellow and your hilltop will tremble. As you reach the end of your dance you will look at the sun, for you will never see it again in waking or in dreaming, and then your death will point to the south. To the vastness."[31]

Hardwick spent much time and much money opening a health-food store called Pegasus in Windmill Towne, a shopping center with some eighteen stores on the main road heading northeast from Gatlinburg. A windmill stood outside of the shop, nearly the size of those in the Netherlands. Hardwick, now with short hair and often warmed by a plaid shirt, enlisted the family to help get the store up and running; they came for about two weeks, making tofu scrambles they stuffed into pockets of pita bread and blending the smoothies that Hardwick and his friends sold from the small store that always smelled of smoke from Hardwick's and his business partners' cigarettes.

One night during the family visit, nine of them sat for dinner at the expensive French restaurant on the top of a nearby mountain. Mike Chriss laughed louder and harder as the men around him cracked jokes and showed their campy gay side, Hardwick included.[32] "She's a mess in a dirty dress and she needs to be healed," Cliff would say cuttingly, to cackles. When the bill came, Hovan paid for all of them. As far as Susan and Mike knew, Michael's new boyfriend was rich.

Hardwick clicked with Susan's new love. Hardwick had a natural gift for connecting with people, which he had honed working in bars and restaurants. When he felt it necessary, he toned down the voice he used with queer friends, changing it to sound deeper and more stereotypically masculine. He could swing a hammer. He rarely dressed in anything more than overalls or jeans and a T-shirt. He code-switched constantly, whether it was among his friends, his customers, or his family. When his sister's flock got to Gatlinburg, Hardwick made a deal with Susan's boyfriend: he would trade his Jeep for the week for Mike's old '66 Ford pickup. The deal sealed their mutual respect.

So did Hardwick's eagerness for the outdoors. During their stay, the family took to the favorite trails that had given Michael solace. They climbed and hiked around Cades Cove, where native Cherokee had hunted for hundreds of years but was now a one-way road where tourists could stop at preserved homesteads, churches, and barns to see how families had lived in the not-too-distant past. They plodded the mucky trail that led to Rainbow Falls, where the almost three-mile hike rose 1,500 feet to reach an 80-foot-tall waterfall that grabbed afternoon light and splashed a namesake sign of hope overhead.

Charlie's Bunion was the most treacherous and rewarding hike of them all. It rose to more than 5,500 feet on the state line between Tennessee and North Carolina. Once it had been covered with heavy old-growth forest, but in the 1920s a massive fire had scoured what had been left behind by loggers who had stripped the mountainside clear of vegetation—before massive rains washed away the sterile soil in a landslide to uncover the rocky outcrops that give it its name, a bunion-like growth on the northern face of the mountain, one of the few like it in the Smoky Mountains.

It would be challenging for experienced hikers, to say nothing for a child with different abilities. Five-year-old Jasmine could not yet walk but was too heavy to carry the whole way. Hardwick and his friends conveyed her down the trails, hoisting Jasmine on their shoulders, carrying her in the backpack harness, trading off with one another as they grew tired. Hardwick stopped to carve her a bear knife, whittling it out of wood—for protection, he told her, from whatever might lurk nearby. When Jasmine dropped it as they stepped over a stream, Hardwick picked it up and put it back in her hand. He had become a protector, a warrior, the patriarch of this family despite his youth, one who would have a deep influence on them all. Days after her family had returned home, Susan would listen and smile as Robert picked out Fleetwood Mac tunes on their piano.

Hardwick's health-food store died a quick death. Both he and Pegasus show up in the Gatlinburg phone book—all nine pages of it—in October of 1979, but by September of 1980 only he was listed. By late 1980, he disappeared entirely from phone books and city directories. "I lost my ass in the health food store," he would later recall, "but at the same time I gained a lot of knowledge of myself and became a friend to myself, which is what I was really seeking to do."[33]

After Gatlinburg, Hardwick wandered. He spent time in New York. He told friends and family that he had dated the Marlboro Man—likely Christian Haren, the ex-army Californian who had some success as a television and Broadway actor, with a bit part in Vincente Minnelli's *Bells Are Ringing* before he became the sixth and perhaps the only queer Marlboro Man during the cigarette brand's long ad campaign run.

Hardwick's female friends from Atlanta urged him to come for another visit after they had returned from Tennessee and offered him a place to stay if he decided to make the city his next home. He took them up on the offer. By November of 1980, he had taken a job tending bar at one of the city's best-known gay clubs, Backstreet.

Hardwick was in Atlanta, nearly twenty-seven years old, when he received word that his father was dying in Missouri. Rick had taken a container of hot grease to the back steps and then had fallen on them. The grease left third-degree burns all over his body. When the doctors performed X-rays, they found cancer in his lung. It had progressed rapidly. His children were with him at Webb City's Oak Hill Hospital when Rick Hardwick died on February 15, 1981.[34]

Hardwick's father had never been able to come to terms with his son's identity. Being queer was a fad the boy would outgrow.[35] They would never bridge that difference, but Hardwick had flown to Missouri to be by his side anyway. He had done all he could. After the funeral, he went home and resumed his arc through the dizzy orbit of Atlanta nightlife. He reveled in the attention of men, the joys he had chosen and earned, the peace he had found, all his awakening had granted him.

CONVICTION

Crime of Passion

Backstreet's dance floor pulsed with New Year's Eve revelers under a canopy of white and black streamers and balloons, as Michael Hardwick rang in 1982 behind the bar. The new year promised so much: new friends, new worlds to explore, a rediscovered freedom. He lived in an apartment across the street from the Cove nightclub on Monroe Drive, in the Monroe Manor complex that gay men knew by its nickname: Vaseline Valley. While most people slept, he could be found behind the bar at the famed Atlanta disco.

Carmine Vara and his children, Vicki and Henry, opened Backstreet as Peaches Back Door in 1975, flush with money from their other gay bars, Boston's Punch Bowl and Provincetown's Crown & Anchor.[1] They turned a former furniture store into a disco temple that held worship until four in the morning. The club rose to national renown as an essential must-do, round-the-clock party. Resident DJ Angelo flew to New York to advise record executives on dance tracks about to be released. Backstreet hosted a White Party, where everyone wore white, with thousands of white balloons at the top of the room over the dance floor, long white ribbons and a white feather tied to the end of each of them.

Backstreet bouncers ushered those who were young or white or attractive into the club, while others were charged more, held in line outside, or denied entry. Shirtless, wired, slicked with sweat and dancing as closely as humanly possible, they hustled and bumped to the latest of a new breed of dance hits, from Devo's "Whip It" to Diana Ross's unintentional gay anthem, "I'm Coming Out." Backstreet would relax its door policy, but the club would stay predominantly gay, white, male, and pretty.

The chosen queer elite who walked into the club faced a huge mirror on a wooden wall, then emerged into a sunken space where the owners had plunked white furniture down on forest-green carpet. Mirrors on the ceiling reflected a dance floor that lit up to cast an infinite number of reflections from the cluster of mirror balls of different sizes that hung overhead like a solar system. Above the dance floor on the mezzanine, clubgoers could look down into an aviary filled with exotic birds of red, gold, and green.

One upstairs alcove had been lined with mirrors and a neon-lit glass-block bar capped by what looked like a huge contact lens that was filled with Chinese goldfish—huge animals with tails at least eight inches long.[2] Hardwick tended bar there often, with the help of his barback Jim Bass, and entertained guest performers—Grace Jones, Evelyn "Champagne" King, France Jolie—who lingered in the quieter space. He had a view of the dance floor and would gesture to people he knew, communicating with his hands like he did with his niece Jasmine. He staked his claim to the space, signing the wall behind the bar with a marker, as if to leave his mark for posterity.

Hardwick raked in tips. Some older bartenders donned leather apparel while others cashed in on their reed-thin, bright-eyed youth. Hardwick dressed and groomed himself to a preppy veneer, his hazel and green eyes set off against dirty-blond hair. His ingratiating smile beamed his charisma at friends and clients. He could be gregarious and polite and flirty, all at once.

Backstreet put its stamp on Atlanta nightlife. It served as a proxy for the Atlanta the city had come to be or at least wanted to be—"fabulous," according to a lesbian interviewed for the *Atlanta Constitution*. Atlanta was "the gay capital of the Southeast," according to reporter Barbara Gervais Street, a "Mecca and a haven for homosexuals from the rural outback and middle-sized towns, a magnet drawing them to a subculture that may number as many as 250,000 men and women."[3] No reliable way existed to count queer people, but a casual census could count thousands where they gathered.[4] Those queer places included three bowling leagues, gay TV and radio shows, gay-affirming churches, seven or eight gay and lesbian softball teams, and some thirty-odd bars and bathhouses across the city—discos, leather bars, drag bars like the Sweet Gum Head, and the most popular queer hangout of all, Backstreet.

As queer Atlanta grew more confident in its public spaces, political organization followed. First Tuesday and its two hundred members politicked to vault queer candidates into contention for local elected office. A Lesbian/Gay Rights chapter of the American Civil Liberties Union taught the community how to deal with the city's police force. Though Atlanta's Chief of Police George Napper engaged in regular conversation with gay and lesbian leaders, harassment still happened too often, even after Napper and the ACLU put in place a mechanism to register complaints against the force.[5] The Atlanta Gay Center offered an introduction to it all. The center took more than 20,000 calls each year from gay and lesbian newcomers, could-be Atlantans, and citizens on a range of topics, from where to find treatment for sexually transmitted infections to how to avoid confrontation with the law.

The political evolution had to happen because Atlanta, like most cities, denied basic equality to its many queer citizens, even as scions of the civil-rights era ascended to its leadership. Andrew Young had been elected mayor in 1981, and during his tenure, he talked about how he was happy to serve as mayor in a city that had once jailed him for nonviolent protest.[6] President Jimmy Carter's ambassador to the United Nations, and Georgia's first Black member of Congress since Reconstruction, Young had already aroused the ire of queer Atlanta. In his first year in office, he had met with the community only once and had refused to sign a Gay Pride Week proclamation. Relations with the police department under his command were, "at best, a truce."[7]

The mayor complained that he had little control over Fulton County's legal authority or over codes that singled out queer people, such as sodomy laws. Hinson McAuliffe, the county's solicitor, arrested more than two hundred men in adult bookstores for sodomy in 1980 alone, and Young said he could do little about it. While he denied that he had any authority to certify any sexual behavior, he hinted that he would be inclined to support anyone faced with any kind of discrimination. The government, after all, had tried to blackmail civil-rights leaders with charges of homosexuality.[8]

Young acknowledged the unfinished business at hand in a city that thought of itself as "too busy to hate"—a convenient bit of sloganeering that had been coined during the Ivan Allen administration from 1969 to 1973. As the Black civil-rights struggle had demonstrated, the slogan could broadcast a simple and effective message of justice and equality, at least until it ran headlong into the reality experienced by those outside of the usual orbits of power. The gay-rights movement faced bitter resistance in its pleas for social change. In that respect, the two movements were kin.[9]

"The problem of the gay movement is not the gay community," Young said, "it's everybody else."[10]

Among those "else" were Young's own police. While the mayor brushed off complaints of entrapment, former police chief Reginald Eaves agreed with the queers who lobbed those charges. Decoy officers under his watch would put on "very, very tight pants," he said, and cruise men in Piedmont Park after dusk, then arrest anyone who approached or touched them.[11]

While they struggled to organize into useful political organizations, queer Atlantans had begun to worry about a new threat to their lives. Scientists had first sounded alarms during the summer of 1981 over a new illness among gay men. A constellation of infections signaled a breakdown of their immune systems. Chief among the infections were pneumocystis carinii and a rare kind of cancer known as Kaposi's sarcoma, which usually affected older people of Mediterranean ancestry and took years to develop. Patients had weight loss or developed lupus, anemia, cancers of the anus, or a fungal infection found on mucous membranes called thrush.

No one knew yet how the diseases were related, but they knew already that gay men were affected in much higher numbers than other groups. Still, at a congressional hearing in the spring of 1982, the National Cancer Institute's Dr. Bruce A. Chabner said the emerging condition was a problem "of concern to all Americans."[12] Researchers had begun to refer to it as gay-related immune deficiency (GRID) or, as it would come to be known, acquired immunodeficiency syndrome (AIDS).

The world faced an "immunological time bomb" with no clear way to disarm it. Researchers estimated that affected gay men had roughly a thousand sexual partners each—twice the number of the men studied who were not affected. It had already reached epidemic proportions, and as the NCI and Centers for Disease Control said, those cases that had been observed to date were likely "just the tip of the iceberg."[13] By the summer of 1982, the CDC revealed that at least 335 people had been diagnosed with the condition. It already had killed 136 of them.

The gurus who had guided Hardwick's spirit to Atlanta were joined by a cadre of earthbound gods that fed his other senses. They comprised an amazing variety, from conventional-looking men to fellow preppies to leather men. Hardwick shot to the top of many to-do lists: who wouldn't want to sleep with Michael Hardwick, they would ask?

As he cruised at Backstreet during his off hours, Hardwick met gorgeous, hairy-chested Ernie Mule, who lived and breathed the "clone" look, from his dark, thick mustache to his habit of wearing as little as possible when he danced. Almost three years younger than Hardwick, from a stretch of the New Jersey shore near Point Pleasant, Ernie worked at Bulldogs on Peachtree. They met, and then he all but disappeared for the first two weeks they were intimate. Hardwick tended to keep to himself anyway. He was gregarious and outgoing in public places, but his private business was his own. From what his friends and Ernie's friends could tell, they loved each other and spent days at a time affirming that affection behind closed doors.

When they came up for air, jealousy took root. Ernie saw Hardwick flirting with John Foutz in a corner at Backstreet's tea dance one afternoon. He recognized Foutz as someone Hardwick had tried to bed a few times, but Foutz had never acquiesced. At tea dance one Sunday, Foutz had been dancing in a corner when Ernie lurched at him from across the floor and slapped him: *you fucking whore, you're dating my boyfriend.* Foutz didn't know what he meant until Hardwick appeared and pulled Ernie off him. Months later, Ernie went to Bulldogs and sat down for an interview with the bar's manager and co-owner—Foutz.

Foutz hired Ernie anyway, and hired Ernie's roommate too. Queer men could let many things slide. Romeos, Lotharios, even those mythic sexual conquistadors were no match for nor any template for queer people, many of whom coupled with abandon and mostly retained their status in the community even when they did so. Hardwick spent his sexual currency freely—and he and Ernie were on and off together anyway, just as Hardwick had been on and off with other men he dated.

Hardwick flirted with just about everyone, including a beautiful woman from South Asia who hung around with some of his other friends. Hardwick propositioned her and her male friend, frequently and insistently. Everyone was sleeping with everyone; it didn't matter.[14]

Backstreet brought Hardwick a sort of fame within the demimonde of night people. Soon, his popularity and the standard turmoil of bar life—who got better shifts, or a better station—led him to leave for a job at the Cove, where he worked for "Papa" Lloyd Russell, whose graying, receding hair and rounded glasses gave him an avuncular look. Russell assigned him to the spot at the edge of the new disco floor under construction. The Cove peaked when other bars closed, from four in the morning to seven, every corner and crevice filled with high-energy music and a high-energy crowd revved up by whatever means it could obtain. Once the dance floor opened, Russell knew, business would boom, simply because the Cove was one of the only places in town that would be open at those hours.

Hardwick sought attention on the other side of the bar. When he left work, usually around dawn, he would cue his friends to the next party at 811 Ponce de Leon Place, the spartan bachelor pad he'd moved to and shared with a roommate. Hardwick wasn't someone who did well on his own. When friends promised to come see him at the bar or at home and didn't show on time, he would get anxious and would phone them: *Where are you? When are you coming in?* He liked to be the center of attention. At Ponce Place, he had an open-door policy and welcomed anyone to play Uno at the dining-room table while he poured drinks from the butler's pantry. Some guests would crash on the couch; some would rest in Hardwick's bed in the first bedroom on the left, down the hallway in the Craftsman bungalow. They may have partied a lot, but Hardwick never lost control. He was one of the most grounded people in his crowd. Even when he smoked and snorted, he never seemed to show the ill effects.

The cast of characters was as fluid as the relationships between them. Hardwick had a brief fling with Woody, whom he had served at Backstreet, then turned into a friend. He partied with his fellow Backstreet alum Robert Davis at work and at home. They all hung out with Miss Puss, the lesbian glue that held their band of brothers together. Puss had discovered Atlanta's queer bars in the late 1970s, dancing at Backstreet and watching drag shows at the Sweet Gum Head, where she couldn't believe the beauty of performers like Rachel Wells. Puss had introduced Hardwick to Ernie, by then his ex-lover. Hardwick let Puss use his room and his bed for the torrid affair she had begun with a woman whose parents would have found the liaison beyond the pale.

The all-hours agenda didn't start until dawn, and usually went on through the day, and sometimes the next day, even as they hit the bars where they worked. They drank at Backstreet with disco doyenne France Jolie. They caroused with Colin Hay and the Aussie band Men at Work just as their first single, "Who Can It Be Now?" clawed its way onto the Billboard chart. They played cards and got high at

Hardwick's house. His roommate worked days and rarely was there when they descended on the house. They had the run of the place. When Hardwick left for work, he asked only that they lock up when they left. He was the center of attention, the party-maker and the caretaker, even when he wasn't there.

One Saturday night during the summer of 1982, Puss, Hardwick, Robert, and another pal, Chris Moore, zoomed past Midtown and Backstreet, to head for the Limelight to see its spectacular show before heading back to their home turf. Peter Gatien had opened the new Buckhead disco two years before, at a cost of millions of dollars. He had spent his way into notoriety, down to the glass floor that capped a tank of roaming sharks. Puss went in her car, while the men piled into another, and when it was time to head to Backstreet they got in their separate cars. When the men didn't show up, Puss worried and waited, then ultimately went home.

The next day she found out they had been jumped by gay bashers. Robert had been hurt the worst and had to have his jaw wired shut, which he laughed off by saying he needed to lose weight. The owners of Backstreet put together a fundraiser during their Sunday tea dance to raise money for his medical bills, opening on a Sunday afternoon just for the occasion. It was the first time Puss had seen Hardwick upset. He had been her protector—*Hey Puss, I'm getting ready to leave, are you OK?*—when they were at the bar. Now he was angry and confused. He always wanted to see the good in people. Why would anyone have done that to him and his friends?

In his ease at life in the queer parts of town, Hardwick had forgotten a basic truth. Queer people had to worry about their safety, always. They observed a cardinal rule: never walk home drunk or alone. No wall kept angry straight men out of the gay neighborhood.

Queer people could be more comfortable in Atlanta than anywhere else in the South, but the threat of violence remained.[15]

They could not rely on the police, who did little to protect them. In mid-June of 1982, Atlanta police arrested five teenagers who had roamed into Piedmont Park after dark. Suspected of attacking queer men in the park on the two weekends prior, the three white and two Black men had chased a man up the hill, screaming, "We're going to kill all the faggots in the park!" before they beat the broken pieces of the man's glasses into his face.[16]

Queer people could not depend on the city to accept them. While the Atlanta City Council passed a resolution that declared Lesbian/Gay Male/Transperson Pride Day on June 26, Mayor Young refused to sign it. "I am withholding my signature," Young wrote in a statement, "because I believe that it is inappropriate for governments to proclaim or comment on the sexuality of private individuals."[17] He ignored it for eight days, which allowed it to take effect without his assent.

Neither could queer people rely on the law to protect them. On June 25, the evening prior to the 1982 Pride protest march, police arrested four men at the private Club Exile. Undercover officers had gone to the club, located on the third floor of the Peachtree Manor Hotel, and had given the desk clerk fake membership cards. They arrived on the third floor to find men engaged in sodomy—defined under Georgia law as contact between the mouth or anus of one person and the sex organs of another, whether they identified as straight, bisexual, gay, lesbian, transgender, or even if they were married. Police charged two hotel employees with maintaining a disorderly house and two other men with sodomy.

An arrest for sodomy could ruin a life. "Typically a sodomy defendant has no criminal record," said Winston Morris, attorney for one of the men engaged in consensual sex, "and is not emotionally prepared to deal with this like a hardened criminal would be."[18]

While police cuffed men for consensual sex in relative privacy, not a few miles away, Anita Bryant was in a rapture, one propelled by deep bass beats and the sizzle of a high hat. On a visit to Atlanta, Bryant had decided to visit her first disco—the Limelight in Buckhead, where Hardwick and his friends had been assaulted only days before. She hustled with Russ McCraw, a reverend from Montgomery, Alabama, who dubbed himself an evangelist to gay people who wanted to show them that "there is wholeness in Christ."

"I've been in that lifestyle," he said, "and I don't find it a wholesome lifestyle."[19]

Prayer partners Bryant and McCraw boogied for half an hour on the invitation of a parking valet, a relative of McCraw. Though it wasn't exclusively or predominantly queer, the club had a huge queer following, which was stunned to see the homophobe shaking her booty in enemy territory.

"This is my first trip to a nightclub in a long time," the forty-two-year-old Bryant said, before photographers realized who she was and began to snap away.[20] McCraw tried to turn her back toward them, but club photographer Guy D'Alema captured Bryant in mid-disco, her tongue grazing across her teeth, in a rapture of a different kind. McCraw tried to wave the lens off, but when he couldn't, the pair left the club.

When she found out she had been photographed, Bryant became upset and let it be known that she felt exploited. McCraw would not reveal where she was staying with friends in Atlanta and begged off on further comment: "She'd like to have her privacy, like anyone."[21]

Without the mayor's moral blessing, Pride went ahead in 1982. With a theme of "Stonewall Then, Atlanta Now," some 4,000 people protested at the foot of the Georgia State Capitol and its gold-leafed dome. Floats and marchers paraded from Tenth Street to Peachtree Street, then to the grassy field on the east of the Capitol Building, where speakers drove the rally's point home: queer people in Atlanta could gather in public, but they were still governed by laws that they did not help create and were patrolled by a political system of surveillance that sought to keep their criminal status intact.

Two, four, six, eight! Gay is just as good as straight![22] As they chanted in the strong afternoon sun, gawkers watched politely, except for the street preachers, who intervened and debated with marchers. The Gay Men's Chorus led the group that spooled out for more than a mile and spanned six people across, in marked contrast with the first official Pride protest march ten years earlier, when only a couple hundred people had marched. Police kept the parade moving along while plainclothes officers, some from the Georgia Bureau of Investigation and the FBI, watched and took photos for purposes unknown. When the parade reached the Capitol, organizers released a mass of lavender balloons that floated up and away past the gold-domed rotunda.

Some complained that the march was too long, too quiet at times, or that the carnival that had kicked off Pride Week had been too celebratory. But the crowd was larger than the year before, and more intent on making itself known. A handful of the core organizers were planning a new March on Washington like the one held in 1979—a protest that would underscore the need for equality and civil protections for queer people. Atlanta representatives would head to New York soon to begin the long process of organizing something that they hoped would number 100,000 people when it swarmed the U.S. Capitol.

Hardwick pushed the door at the Cove open early in the morning on July 5, long after Pride had subsided, after he had put some finishing touches on the club's new disco. He had taken a swig or three of the Molson Ale he had grabbed on the way out, but when he saw a police car roll by through the stifling summer heat, he chucked the green glass bottle in the trash a few feet outside the door. He had begun training as a beverage manager for the Peachtree Plaza Hotel, and as a bartender he was well versed on the city's public-drinking laws. Cautious and aware of how it might appear, Hardwick walked a few yards to Monroe Drive, turned right, and headed home. He saw the police car turn around near Orme Circle, where it wheeled around and drove toward him, then pulled to a stop.

Officer Keith R. Torick got out of his car and demanded to know where Hardwick had thrown the beer bottle while he frisked him. Torick had joined the Atlanta police force on April 14, 1980. That December he reported for duty at the city's airport. Since July 28, 1981, he had been assigned to Zone 2, the area surrounding the Cove, and he had gained a reputation for vigorously policing the area. Queer people claimed he often harassed them near the Cove and other gay bars.[23]

Hardwick had a temper, and it didn't take a lot to piss him off, but he usually let things blow over quickly too.[24] He believed the cop had stopped him because he knew Hardwick was gay.[25] When the officer asked him what happened to the beer, Hardwick pointed to the trash can about fifty yards back at the bar.

You're lying, Torick said. The officer said he saw him drinking the Molson, and that he had thrown away the bottle when he saw him.

Torick put Hardwick in the back of the squad car and peppered him with questions. The two bickered about the particulars until Torick drove him back to the Cove, where Hardwick said he could find the beer bottle in the trash. Torick told him he couldn't see it from the police car and would not allow Hardwick out to find it.

Hardwick could tell the officer would not budge. He thought the best thing to do would be to keep the situation under control. He thought it might grow more hostile if he didn't cooperate.[26] He gave up and told Torick to write him the ticket.[27]

The ticket had an appearance date in municipal court at 9:00 a.m. on July 13. The top left corner read "Wed Thurs." Hardwick assumed the thirteenth was Wednesday, based on the writing at top of the ticket. July 13, 1982, was a Tuesday.

A week later, Hardwick returned to his apartment after work and found his houseguest Kirk Slusser in a state of high agitation. Slusser and Hardwick had met at Backstreet months before, and for a time Slusser partied wherever Hardwick happened to be. They had intimate moments but hadn't had sex. Instead, they cruised together. They went to the Club Baths on Spring Street, where Kirk felt standoffish about people he didn't know while Michael paddled around in the swimming pool, sweated in the sauna, and disappeared with companions in the twin-bed-sized cubicles that lined the upstairs floor.

When Kirk had ended a prior relationship, Michael let him sleep on his chocolate-brown sofa in the living room. They kept few secrets from each other but talked little about Michael's past. Kirk sensed that Michael carried a fair amount of pain within him. He didn't talk about it, but it sat near the surface.

Kirk had been alone on the morning of July 13 when Officer Torick showed up at the door to serve Hardwick a warrant for his failure to appear in court. Torick had been at the courthouse when Hardwick missed the hearing, then filed for the warrant immediately afterward. Two hours after the scheduled hearing, Torick was on the doorstep at Ponce Place, where he entered the house and demanded Kirk's identification. Slusser told him Hardwick would be back by five in the afternoon. Torick checked the back of the house for Hardwick and ran instead into Bob Cheek, a friend of Hardwick's roommate. Satisfied that Hardwick wasn't home, Torick headed to the front door.

"Tell him I will be back," Torick told Slusser.[28]

Hardwick returned home that afternoon just before four. Still out of sorts, Kirk told him that a police officer with a warrant had been by but did not show him the warrant.

That's impossible, Hardwick thought. *My court date isn't until tomorrow.*

Only when he got the ticket out and looked at it again did he realize the confusing writing at the top of the ticket. He called the municipal court to find out what he could do to fix the situation. Told to be there the first thing in the morning, Hardwick arrived at the courthouse at 8:30 a.m. on July 14, 1982, and explained to Clerk of the Court Jerry G. Coots how he had misunderstood the conflicting days and dates written on the ticket.[29] Coots consulted with a judge, who decided that since Hardwick had tried to make amends for the missed court date, he could resolve the matter by paying a $50 fine, typical for a first offense.

The cop's already been at my house with a warrant, he told the clerk. Coots told him that was impossible, that it normally took forty-eight hours to process a warrant. Hardwick wondered how Torick had the legal right to enter his home. Coots wrote a receipt which stated that the fine had been paid. On the receipt Coots also wrote a message directly to Officer Torick: "if you are not going to enforce the warrant please come by and cancel it."

Hardwick had been arrested before and had dealt with the consequences. He had now made amends as instructed. He believed he had taken care of the ticket for good.[30]

He may have all but forgotten about it as he worked long hours at the Cove, as Atlanta hummed with queer activity all summer long. The Ramblin' Raft Race turned the city's mucky, undrinkable Chattahoochee River into a Thomas Eakins painting. Barely clothed men splashed on inner tubes and floated six-packs of beer while the "Vacation" by the Go-Go's blasted from portable radios. The original Raft Race had taken place on the Hooch during the 1970s and had grown to earn the *Guinness Book of World Records* title as the world's biggest participant sporting event. Drugs, drinking, and nudity generated a backlash, and a crackdown. After the 1980 race, organizers shut it down.

Queer people reclaimed it as their own. Mark McCutchan and others had started a gay version of Raft Race in 1979, with about five hundred queer people floating down the Chattahoochee, usually during the first weekend in August. By 1982 it drew a thousand people and spun off a half dozen weekend parties at gay venues. On the same weekend, the Hotlanta Softball League pitted fourteen teams from ten cities against each other in a tournament that ended on Sunday, August 1, followed by a beer bust at the Sports Page lesbian bar.

Kitty Hardwick had chosen that weekend to visit her son in Atlanta, on a stopover as she drove from Gainesville to Pennsylvania to visit a friend. When she went to sleep, Michael had borrowed her car to go to work. She found him unconscious the next morning in his roommate's bedroom. He had parked in front of the house at 6:30 a.m., he said, when one of three well-dressed men that he did not know called out his name. Before he could do anything else, the men grabbed and pummeled him, kicking him in the face and in his sides, knocking him senseless. He passed out on the sidewalk for a time. When he woke up, he struggled up the concrete steps to the house, hoping that his mother would not see him in such bad shape. His nose dripped blood the whole way down the hall to the back bedroom. Kitty found the trail when she woke, then found her passed-out son.[31]

When he woke, Hardwick couldn't tell his panicked mother what had happened. The men who had beaten him knew who he was, but he did not know them. His mother wanted to stay and tend to her son, but he brushed it off. He convinced Kitty that it had been a random attack by a pack of drunks. He pleaded with her until she relented, got back into her car, and drove on to Pennsylvania.[32]

A few decks of Uno cards lay on the dining-room table, their hands played out. The skunky smell of weed clung to the air, even when the door swung open to welcome someone new or release them back into the night. It was a typical night at Hardwick's house, now that the Hotlanta weekend had ended. His roommate had not been seen or heard from, but a crew of regulars hung out, including Puss, Woody, and Kirk.

A new face from Mobile joined them that night. Dwight Sawyer had come to look for a place to live for himself and his partner, Joey, who had stayed behind to pack up their house on Springhill Street. A burly, mustached, and balding man of twenty-seven, Dwight had squared eyebrows that framed a kind face. Joey, lean and brightly blue-eyed, had met Dwight in 1979 at the University of South Alabama, where Dwight studied for a double major in music and math. Joey found him warm and unaffected, and naturally handsome. Both had ex-lovers and a poor track record at monogamy. They decided to have an open relationship. While they had a torrid sex life together, they enjoyed the novelty and sometimes the convenience of strangers and new friends.

They didn't want to leave their life and friends in Mobile. They needed to leave. On March 21, 1981, two Klansmen kidnapped nineteen-year-old Michael Donald as he walked to a store. Henry Hays and James Knowles were enraged that a Black man on trial for killing a white police officer in Birmingham had been freed.[33] The men cut Donald's throat and hanged him from a tree on Herndon Avenue, not far from where Joey and Dwight lived. They had picked Donald at random and lynched him as a threat to other Black citizens of Alabama. Other Klansmen burned a cross on the city courthouse's lawn that evening.

Joey worked for the City of Mobile, while Dwight tutored, but those jobs were not worth their safety. The Klan had begun to encourage violence against gays and lesbians in its propaganda. The couple checked out other cities, but only Atlanta seemed like a good fit. After a raucous New Year's Eve at Backstreet, they decided it would be home. In the spring, Dwight took off for Atlanta to find work and an apartment. He met and bonded with Hardwick over pinball games at the Cove.[34] They grew as close as any two men who knew each other for that long could.

On the night of August 2, 1982, Hardwick took Slusser's car keys, put him in a cab, and told the driver to take him to 811 Ponce de Leon Place.[35] Slusser was there when Hardwick came home from work that morning, along with a few others who drifted out as dawn approached. By morning, everyone but Slusser and Dwight Sawyer had left. Sawyer had planned to go back to Mobile that afternoon to get his partner and to bring him back to Atlanta.[36] He and Hardwick had retired to the bedroom, where they smoked some weed and undressed.

Sometime before noon, Officer Torick parked his police cruiser in front of Hardwick's house and walked up the concrete steps to the front door, with what he believed to be a valid warrant.[37] He approached the front door. Sawyer would recall that it had been left open. Slusser would recall that he did not let the officer in, that he came in on his own. Startled by the encounter, Slusser did not know he had the right to turn the officer away. He grew paranoid that the officer might find the marijuana drying in the kitchen. He told Torick that he didn't know if Hardwick was in, but that he might be in his bedroom. While the officer walked to the back of the house, Slusser staggered to the kitchen and tried to hide the weed.[38]

During the night, the bedroom door had been closed. Hardwick's room had the only air conditioner in the house, and when Sawyer had gone down the hall to the bathroom, Hardwick asked him to shut the door.[39] Torick briefly paused outside what he stated was a door slightly ajar. Hardwick heard a noise and looked up—and, seeing no one, resumed having oral sex with Sawyer. Torick, on the other side of the door, said he saw two men, for a moment, engaged in mutual oral sex.

After thirty-five seconds, Hardwick later said, he heard another noise, and in the dim light of a candle saw a police officer standing in his room.

"My name is Officer Torick," he announced. "Michael Hardwick, you are under arrest."[40]

"For what?" Hardwick demanded, while he and his companion, naked, fumbled for composure, struggling through the haze of marijuana. "What are you doing in my bedroom?"[41]

Torick had a warrant for arrest, and though Hardwick told him the warrant wasn't valid because the ticket had been paid, Torick persisted.

"It doesn't matter," he said, because he had acted in good faith.[42]

Hardwick asked Torick to leave while he and Sawyer dressed. The men were still naked and erect. As they slipped on clothes, Hardwick a light gray sweatshirt, Torick did not break his stare. Hardwick asked him to at least turn around.

"I've already caught you," Torick told Hardwick. "Why should I bother?"[43]

Torick scanned the room and saw the small brown bowl of what he presumed was pot beside the bed, not more than a quarter ounce. He told them both that they were now also under arrest for possession, and since he did not ask any questions, he did not have to legally read them their rights. Hardwick pleaded with him, and said he had proof of the fine he had paid. If Torick would just call to verify the receipt was at the Cove, or even drive by the Cove, he could prove he had been compliant in the charge and the warrant.

No, he would not, nor did he have to call, Torick told Hardwick. As far as driving two blocks to the Cove for evidence, Torick said he did not "run a goddamn taxi service."[44]

Slusser watched as the men were taken away in the squad car, then scrambled to call others to find out what to do next.[45]

Torick drove to the police station on Ponce de Leon Boulevard. He had handcuffed the men to the floor in the backseat of the squad car. They sat for more than a half an hour while Torick went inside and spoke with his superior officers. The police debated whether Hardwick would be charged with solicitation and Sawyer with sodomy, and how they would be charged for the small amount of marijuana. When he returned, Torick told the two men they were headed downtown.

"You're under arrest," he said as they headed to the Atlanta jail.[46]

A dank, decrepit pile right out of a noir movie, the jail had been built in 1933 to hold 136 inmates, but its population swelled often to three times that.[47] In November, a few months after the men were brought there, it was considered "unfit for human habitation."[48] Guards broadcast the arrival of fresh meat: "Hey, these guys are in for sodomy!" "Oh, it's going to be a good time in the bullpen tonight!"[49]

Hardwick and Sawyer were moved from floor to floor of the jail, while they overheard officers denigrate them. "Fags shouldn't mind," an officer said. "That's why they're here."[50]

Hardwick felt like he was being treated like an animal, in shock over what had happened. The police kept moving them around, announcing that they were in for "cocksucking."[51] Sawyer was freaking out.[52] Hardwick was scared to death, worried that they would be sexually assaulted in prison.[53] All he wanted to do was to survive.[54]

At one point, an officer put them in a holding cell next to a pay phone. Sawyer's pocket jangled with quarters from a night of playing pinball. First, he called his partner, then he gave Hardwick a coin to call the Cove. He reached Lloyd Russell, who had Hardwick's receipt for his initial ticket, and within the hour, someone came to jail with bail money. But the police delayed processing them, and Hardwick and Sawyer were kept in a holding cell for about four hours before being moved again. The two weren't fingerprinted and processed until early evening, sometime between 6 and 8 p.m.[55] Hardwick finally bonded out at about 10 p.m. for $325.

Sawyer didn't have a similar connection to get bail money. After Hardwick got out, the guards changed their shifts. A Black officer was instructed to put Sawyer in a communal cell but put him somewhere safer. "I don't think you're going to have a very good time here tonight," he said. "I'm taking you and putting you in a cell by yourself."[56] Sawyer appreciated that small act of mercy.

Hardwick was able to go to where Sawyer was staying and get the cash that he had brought with him to Atlanta. Hardwick then took the cash to A&B Bonding, across the street from the city jail, and worked his charm on its bondswoman. Hardwick didn't own property, and he himself was on a bond, but after appealing to the agent he was able, with help from Lloyd Russell, to bond out Dwight for $275.[57]

In Mobile, Sawyer's partner, Joey Potter, had already gone down the street to some of the gay bars to take up a collection for bail money. Bartenders and next-door neighbors gave him money.[58] They could deal with the stray sex later. In the moment, Potter grew angrier as he rustled the money to pay back the kindness. He had been an activist in Mobile, and now he was furious.

"We're going to fight this!" Lloyd Russell told the Cove crew, without hesitation. He was on his way to finishing his law degree—even before, Russell would go to the mat for his employees, paying for their medical bills if they got out of hand. Anything they needed to do to fight this arrest, Russell said he would do.

The marijuana would be simple to handle. It was a $55 fine and ten days in jail, at most. The sodomy charge would be far more serious. Georgia's law and sentencing guidelines could lead to twenty years in prison if Hardwick were convicted.

"This is gonna stop," he told his bartenders and barbacks.[59]

Hardwick's first court date for the sodomy charge would be the next morning, at 9 a.m. The last seventy-two hours had been traumatic: his assault, his mother's panic, his sex life turned inside out, his arrest. Frustrated and angry, shot through with new and unfamiliar fear, Hardwick had his doubts about a fight. It would be his life upended, and no one else's.

It was that fear that the state used to keep queer people in submission. The jail was only the most visible symbol of the carceral archipelago. Everywhere they turned, queer people faced the judges of normality who watched them, reported them, and had them punished. The state had built an apparatus that it used to constrain them. Once that apparatus had been built, it took only one operator to throw its full weight into action.

Private Matters

Hardwick and Sawyer stood before the judge in Atlanta Municipal Court the next morning during a preliminary hearing and pled not guilty, then began to look for help. They needed someone to get them out of trouble.[1]

Before the next hearing, scheduled for September 14, they made trip after trip to the courthouse to request that the cases be dismissed, with no luck. A connection with a judge who might have been able to help went nowhere.[2] On one court visit a clerk realized Hardwick's case had been recorded incorrectly with a court date of August, not September 14. He could have been served with another warrant and arrested once again at any time on or after August 17.[3]

Sawyer didn't know that Hardwick had already been approached by Clint Sumrall of the American Civil Liberties Union of Georgia. Sumrall had been looking for a suitable case to test Georgia's sodomy law. The ACLU had its roots in the defense of birth control education, which had been imperiled by the Comstock Act of 1873, which forbade the distribution of obscenity via the mail. Gradually those free-speech cases extended into birth control itself. As early as 1932, ACLU founders felt birth control might be a constitutionally protected right.[4] In its more than half century of existence, the ACLU had become an important check to the power of the state and its intrusion into private lives, particularly into sex lives. It had built its own apparatus of power, one that sought out cases it could argue to challenge the existing order. Legal mills on all sides needed human examples as they defined and refined what the law said, and what it did not say.

ACLU attorney H. Judd Herndon met with both men and told them they could plead guilty as first offenders and likely face no further problems. If they pled not guilty, they risked conviction and the remote chance of a twenty-year prison sentence—but they could also alter the trajectory of the gay-rights movement. Herndon explained that the ACLU had been looking for five years for the test case that could invalidate Georgia's sodomy law, which made it a crime for any person "to perform or submit to any sexual act involving the sex organs of one person and the mouth or anus of another."[5] The challenge was finding a case without sullied circumstances—those in which a minor was involved or in which the act of sex had taken place in public—and one in which the defendant was not too frightened to take a public stand.[6] In the 1976 *Doe* sodomy case decided by the Supreme Court, the plaintiffs had chosen to remain anonymous. If someone were to go public with their case, it might encourage both straight and queer people to see sex and privacy as intimately connected and, in doing so, defuse the idea of any consensual sex as unnatural.

Sawyer retained Herndon as his lawyer, and believed that Hardwick had too. But after Sawyer had returned to Mobile, Hardwick met with a larger group of attorneys associated with Herndon who saw the potential to overturn the Georgia sodomy law. John Sweet led the group. Raised in Cincinnati, where his family once hosted activist musician Pete Seeger, Sweet became an avid musician who performed civil-rights protest songs, "the more radical the song the better."[7] He served on the Atlanta city council and worked alongside John Lewis, whom he would help to get elected to the council in 1981. When he met Hardwick for the first time that September, Sweet convinced him that freedom and the gay-rights movement were a struggle with an epic quality. If Hardwick pursued his right to privacy, he could change history.[8]

Hardwick sat next to Kitty, who had stopped in Atlanta on her way back from Pennsylvania once she heard her son had been arrested. They were surrounded by ten attorneys, including Herndon, Sweet, and Louis Levenson, who laid out the possible case and its gravity.

Levenson found Hardwick quiet, circumspect, and quite sanguine about what he was doing—about what had been done to him. *You're going to be quite notorious*, he told Hardwick. Rather than try to have the charges thrown out due to the questionable status of the warrant, the ACLU attorneys wanted Hardwick tried at the superior court level. They needed a conviction to challenge the sodomy law.

What's the worst that could happen? Hardwick wanted to know. *What's the best?*

The attorneys explained that the judge could sentence him to up to twenty years if he were convicted.

"Twenty years!" his mother exclaimed. "Do you realize I'll be dead before I see you again?"[9] Kitty didn't want her son to take the risk and urged him to drop the case.[10]

The lawyers in turn urged Hardwick to think about it. They asked him to write down what had happened that day. As he weighed the consequences, he wrote about his arrest in neat block letters that leaned left. As his story unfolded on paper, his handwriting grew larger and angled more sharply, his anger visible as it marched off the page. The arrest had traumatized him, and he hadn't begun to process it until he put it down in words. When he was done, he realized he had been horribly mistreated.[11]

It would have been easy to walk away, but Hardwick knew he would have to live with himself. He worked in gay clubs, wasn't a prominent person, and could afford to give up his privacy. Not every queer person could do so. He didn't think he would go to prison, not really.

Against his mother's wishes, Hardwick agreed to press his case.[12] He called John Sweet back.

"Let's go for it," he told Sweet.[13]

Attorneys and gay-rights advocates filled the small Courtroom No. 1 on September 14, 1982, in Atlanta Municipal Court. A few in the room laughed when a bailiff called out Hardwick's name before Judge Howard R. Johnson sat to hear the case.

Sawyer had returned only two days before from Mobile. As far as he knew, Hardwick had not yet decided how he would plead. He had not decided either. Only then did Sawyer meet Hardwick's attorneys: Sweet would represent Hardwick on his sodomy charge and Levenson on the marijuana charge. Sawyer had not been offered their services, and Herndon remained his lawyer.[14] Judge Johnson chuckled when he asked how they would plead. To the charges of possession and sodomy, both men pleaded not guilty.[15]

Officer Torick took the stand. He had gone to serve the warrant he had taken out two weeks earlier, he said, and knocked on the front door. He testified that Hardwick's roommate Kirk Slusser answered, and that because he had been there before, Slusser knew who he was.[16] Torick said when he asked if Hardwick was home, Slusser said he "didn't know" but opened the door and "told me I was welcome to come in and look for Mr. Hardwick." Slusser had not been asked to testify so could not refute this testimony.

Torick said he went down the hallway in the house, to the second door on the left, which was open approximately three inches. In the slip of light, Torick said that he observed the men in "an act of sodomy . . . that being oral sex. Each of the other had each of the others' penis in their mouths." After he identified himself, Torick said he saw a small brown ceramic bowl with what he thought to be marijuana.[17] Both men denied it was theirs, he said.

When he had ticketed Hardwick weeks earlier, he said he told Hardwick that he could have arrested him. He had a few people skip on warrants already. When asked, Torick said he hadn't tried to serve the warrant to Hardwick at the Cove because he usually got busy with calls when he started his shift at 6:30 in the morning. He had not checked to see if Hardwick had dealt with the warrant before going to arrest him, Torick said.

Once inside the house, was there "any reason why you did not announce or otherwise let your presence be known?" Herndon asked.

"I was at the door approximately one to two seconds before I announced my presence," Torick said.

Torick said Hardwick told him that he had a receipt for the fine, though the court advised people in his situation to keep all paperwork with them at all times.

"Did anything prevent you from making a call," Herndon asked, "to ascertain whether the man's allegations were true or not that he had appeared and paid a fine and disposed of the case?" His squad car had a radio, after all.

"Other than a busy court and a busy radio dispatcher," Torick responded, adding that he believed the warrant was valid and that he didn't need to check.

The judge checked in crisply: "Counsel, it doesn't matter whether the warrant was valid or not. No charges were brought as a result of that. The charge was brought as a result of what he observed after he got there. The validity of the warrant is not in question." The judge accepted Torick's insistence that he had been granted access to the house by Slusser.

John Sweet rose and made a motion to dismiss Hardwick's case as a violation of his First Amendment, Fifth Amendment, and Fourteenth Amendment rights, including his right to privacy. The judge denied the motion.

Herndon was able to get Dwight's marijuana charge dismissed, since it was not his home and since the marijuana had not been in his hands. But Judge Johnson would not relent on the sodomy charges. Both cases would be sent up to the Superior Court of Fulton County.

As the parties left the courtroom a man approached Officer Torick and shook his hand. The man, in his fifties and a plumbing inspector for the city, had come to the hearing because he was Hardwick's neighbor and the father of two teenage boys.

"I appreciate you cracking down," the neighbor told Torick. The parties, the nude sunbathing, it had all become too much.[18] Whatever privacy Hardwick had been entitled to was an afterthought.

As the ACLU-associated attorneys discussed in the coming days how to proceed, most of the coalition wanted the ACLU of Georgia to take up Hardwick's case. The timing seemed right. Two in the group did not agree. Attorney Buren Batson, who had been arrested by Atlanta undercover police in 1980 for solicitation of sodomy, believed the case would fail. The other person who wanted to make the case go away was Sawyer's attorney, Judd Herndon.

Fulton County Superior Court set a grand jury date of October 7, 1982, for Hardwick's case, but before it could be presented, District Attorney Lewis Slaton had it pulled from the docket.[19] Hardwick's attorneys surmised that the DA's office sensed the constitutional challenge in the works. The case in limbo, Hardwick faced the potential of prosecution for up to four years after his arrest—until August 3, 1986.

Slaton had deployed Georgia's sodomy law against sex workers and those engaged in public sex. He sometimes used it as a tool to induce a plea bargain in cases of sexual violence. He said he never had used the law to prosecute a queer person for having sex, if they were having sex in private. Though he expressed distaste for "that type of conduct among homosexuals or lesbians," he didn't think a jury would convict Hardwick, because of the implicit right to privacy.[20] He felt consensual sodomy should be a misdemeanor, not a felony.[21]

The ACLU grew impatient with Slaton's stance. Hardwick had met with them for a few hours each week as they practiced for his eventual testimony. At one meeting, the attorneys advised Hardwick that they needed to take a calculated risk. They needed to compel prosecution, on the grounds that Hardwick did not want the case hanging over his head.[22] But on January 7, 1983, Louis Levenson received a letter from the DA's office that said, "unless further evidence develops, the cases will remain as not presented to the Grand Jury."[23]

When Slaton would not budge, Hardwick's attorneys chose the radical course of filing a case in U.S. district court, one that charged the state's sodomy law and Hardwick's arrest were unconstitutional based on the Fourteenth Amendment's due process clause and its implicit right to privacy. Because John Sweet didn't practice in federal court, he gave the case to another ACLU attorney, Kathleen "Kathy" Wilde.

The case named Atlanta's chief of police and the district attorney as respondents, as well as Georgia attorney general Michael Bowers. Bowers, a West Point graduate in 1963, had joined the Georgia Office of the Attorney General in the 1970s and replaced decorated World War II serviceman Arthur Bolton as AG in 1981. He carried over Bolton's formalities of punctuality and of staying out of the press, but when it came to keeping work and private lives separate, Bowers faltered. Hardwick's case put Bowers into direct conflict with the law. Since January of that year, the attorney general had been involved in an extramarital affair with his secretary, Anne Davis. As far as the law was concerned, Bowers was a hypocrite.[24]

Hardwick had retreated from his usual circles in the weeks after the arrest, more so as weeks became months. When he saw Sawyer out in public, they did not discuss the case. Dwight and his partner Joey had found a small apartment near Piedmont Park, and they were relieved to hear that the DA's office did not intend to prosecute either of the men. As of January 1983, Sawyer did not know Hardwick had decided to pursue the case in district court. They saw each other a few times more, early that year. Then Sawyer never saw Hardwick again.[25]

Kirk Slusser had also seen Hardwick a few times after the initial flurry of court proceedings and watched him grow more angry than afraid. One day they met outside of a bar, not far from the house where Hardwick had been arrested. Slusser found him much more subdued than his usual self. They disagreed over some details about what had happened but parted, Slusser thought, on good terms. Hardwick had even said to Slusser, *Let's get together soon.* It never happened. Worried over his role in the unfolding passion play, Slusser left Atlanta to return to the Midwest. He had never wanted attention. It could threaten his job. It could threaten his life.

Hardwick began to withdraw from his close circle of friends. Puss never saw the inside of the Ponce house again. She had been there with her lover in the nights before the arrest. What if it had been them, instead of her friend? The consequences would have been grave for both women, but far more so for her lover.

Hardwick began to speak out more about what was right, and how he had been wronged. When word spread that he would take on Georgia's odious law in court, he became a symbol of hope that the queer world's second-class status would change. He came out as a plaintiff and when he did, he became more than a cautionary tale. In Atlanta's queer demimonde, he became a star.

Legal rights exist only in theory until they are claimed, exercised, and preserved. The conflict between Georgia law and the U.S. Constitution had to be challenged so that one would prevail, but unknowable questions vexed activists. Was the straight world ready to think of queer people as equals, or was Hardwick's challenge premature? Should the community wait until the culture and the courts had aligned in their favor? Should it now, when the facts were clear and perfect, offer the needed body?

Kathy Wilde believed that given the circumstances of Hardwick's arrest, the law could be undone. She had traveled in liberal legal circles but hadn't handled a Supreme Court–level case yet. Her ACLU colleague Sweet had a habit of taking on cases based on the community need and not on the available expertise. When he handed her the case, she had to learn quickly about sodomy law to draft the complaint. Sweet advised her to study a recent decision out of Texas in *Baker v. Wade*. Same-sex intercourse had been illegal in Texas since 1974, and in 1979 Dallas Gay Alliance president Donald Baker had been fired from his schoolteacher job for stating his queer identity on television. Baker filed suit later that year—and on August 17, 1982, U.S. District Judge Jerry Buchmeyer ruled that Texas had violated his right to privacy and equal protection. Wilde digested those arguments as she built the distinct case for Hardwick, which would rely on arguments for privacy rather than equal protection.

On February 14, 1983, Wilde filed suit in U.S. district court, and requested a declaratory judgment that Georgia's law was unconstitutional, a violation of the due process clause of the Fourteenth Amendment and its right to privacy. In the filing, Michael Hardwick, a twenty-nine-year-old U.S. citizen, asserted that he was "a practicing homosexual, who regularly engages in private homosexual acts and will do so in the future."

The case included the anonymous plaintiffs "John and Mary Doe," a lawfully married couple who "seek to engage in sexual activity now proscribed by Official Code of Georgia Annotated S/S16-6-2 (Ga. Code Ann. 26-2002) in the privacy of their home." The co-plaintiffs "have been chilled and deterred from engaging in personal, private sexual activity by the existence of the Georgia sodomy statute and the recent arrest of Plaintiff HARDWICK."

"The Georgia statute," the filing noted, "makes it a crime for all persons including married people, unmarried people, and homosexuals to engage in private, consensual sodomy." It also put Hardwick "in imminent danger of arrest, prosecution, and imprisonment," while it imposed upon the Doe couple "a burden upon and significantly interferes with the decisions of Plaintiffs Joe and Mary Doe in their personal, private sex life."

"Sexual conduct in private between consenting adults is protected by a fundamental right of privacy," Wilde wrote, "guaranteed by the First, Third, Fourth, Fifth, Ninth, and Fourteenth Amendments to the United States Constitution." The state law violated the Constitution because the state of Georgia had no compelling interest that could justify such a law; because the broadly written law did not distinguish between acts in public and acts in private; and because the sodomy statute deprived Georgians of a freedom to expression and association.

The case did not mention the gender of the person with whom Hardwick was having consensual sex. It bypassed the Georgia Constitution and courts' rulings, as far back as 1905, that a right to privacy existed in the state, in the haste to take the case directly to federal court, rather than state courts. That would prove a controversial choice, since gay-rights groups such as the National Gay Task Force had embarked on a strategy to repeal sodomy laws through legislatures and courts, state by state, avoiding any case that might wend its way to the Supreme Court. The case included no equal-protection claim, in part because its privacy claims seemed to hold such strength, but also because Georgia had prosecuted straight couples for the same acts.[26]

From the moment she began writing, Wilde steered the case toward the mainstream. She underscored the broad nature of the Georgia statute, which technically made oral and anal sex taboo even for married couples, though they were protected by prior Supreme Court decisions that had squared marital rights of privacy. To bolster the case, she had enlisted the Doe couple, acquaintances who were not thrilled with the prospect of participation but were willing because they believed in the principle. The brief muted any focus on gay rights, which had already amplified tension among the attorneys on the case. Some of the legal team—including Sawyer's lawyer, Herndon, who was himself gay—resented the fact that Wilde, who was straight, would be the one to defend a queer man.

Wilde had not met Hardwick when she was handed the assignment to take on his case. They saw each other for the first time the day the case was filed in federal court in downtown Atlanta. Hardwick felt they clicked: They both liked the outdoors, they were close to the same age, they saw eye to eye on the issues. He believed she was perfect for the case. She did not hesitate when he told her that he wished to remain out of the spotlight as much as possible: *I'm going to have my privacy,* he told her, *and keep it quiet.*

Wilde organized a press conference for the filing and had tried to get local coverage of the case, but producers at Atlanta TV channel WXIA told Wilde that the word "sodomy" had never been uttered on the air, and that it never would be. They sent reporter Paul Crawley anyway, and when Crawley filed his report, the station refused to run it. The word "sodomy" meant something different from oral sex, they demurred. While many people could picture themselves in the act of oral sex, sodomy also meant anal sex, and that might horrify them.[27] Was the public ready for someone so forthright about being gay, talking about their right to have sex and being arrested naked with an erection? Even though massage parlors and drag clubs had formed a queer strip in the close-in suburbs, Atlanta also gave quarter to a large religious population, Southern Baptists in particular. A sea change would make many people uncomfortable.

The TV station finally decided to air the segment. Wilde and Hardwick went their separate ways and would connect again in person only when something required it. Court cases could be like that: they exploded into view, lit brightly by flashes of public attention, then settled into long, dim pauses when nothing happened, except behind closed doors.

"Sodomy" carries specific religious and historical meanings that demonize sex—most often the sex lives of queer people. Across a patchwork of state codes, sodomy in 1982 could mean sexual assault, but could also mean consensual sex between married people, between unmarried people of the same sex, between unmarried people of different sexes, or even sexual relations between species. Invariably, the word carried the stain of moral condemnation.

Sodomy law in the United States derived from that found in English common law—it was a "detestable and abominable crime against nature," one with "a still deeper malignity," as described by William Blackstone in his *Commentaries on the Laws of England*. Published in America in 1772, the treatise emerged in an era when sodomy most often described anal sex between two men—and sometimes was punished by the death penalty.[28] Sodomy became fused to a concept of sex that happened outside of marriage. As America adapted English common law for its own purposes, legislators enshrined heterosexual, monogamous, marital, penile-vaginal sex as the only acceptable form of intercourse.[29] Othered into political reality, homosexuals became a legally distinct class by the late nineteenth century. Sodomy laws were honed to patrol them during the twentieth century.

The state's distaste for queer sex was laid bare as many laws were whittled down to punish only homosexual sodomy. Before 1961, sodomy was a crime in every state. In that year, Illinois became the first state to repeal its laws making certain acts of consensual sex in private between adults a crime. Other states, such as Georgia in 1968, reinforced their sodomy law by adding sex between women to the statutes. At the same time, the Supreme Court had begun to delve into the nuances of privacy law. Inadvertently they chipped away at the logic behind sodomy laws with some rulings, while they drew a bright line around homosexual sodomy with others. In *Stanley v. Georgia* (1969), the court acknowledged that it was constitutional to view obscene materials in the privacy of one's home, but in *Doe v. Commonwealth* (1976), the Supreme Court upheld the decision by a lower court that affirmed Virginia's sodomy law. However, in *Doe*, preceding lower court decisions included a dissent by Judge Robert Merhige that outlined the future thinking behind privacy and its linkage to queer sex. Individuals had the right to be free from government in private, intimate matters, Merhige wrote, and the choice of an intimate partner was "of the utmost private and intimate concern." Sodomy was not about morality, Merhige wrote, but about the constitutional right to privacy.[30]

These rulings did nothing to slow the actual practice of sodomy, but still were used as a crude cudgel with which to patrol and punish queer people as well as unmarried people. By the 1970s, queer groups had begun to organize and to recognize and challenge sodomy law, though the challenges were met with unease, even in legal circles. Arrests numbered in the thousands each year, not the tens or hundreds of thousands. The evolving laws raised uncomfortable new discussions in a public sphere still grappling with the existence of queer people, much less with what they did in their own homes. For most people, queer people included, sodomy law was a theoretical possibility that lingered like the scent of a joint toked the night before. Since it was unlikely a police officer would ever be present during such an act, so long as it was kept out of the park or any public place, it was not much worth worrying about, and prickly to discuss, in any case.

By then, the sexual revolution had collided with the evolving idea of privacy to greatly expand the idea of personal liberty. During the 1960s, the Supreme Court decided that the concept of substantive due process had always been intended to guarantee some rights that were not specifically mentioned in the Constitution—and though they were unenumerated, they were nonetheless real because of their interaction with other articles, amendments, and innate American ideals. The state was, and states were, prohibited from inhibiting or eroding those rights without a distinct purpose—one deemed important enough to supersede the constitutional right. As they were decided, a passel of privacy rulings laid a uniquely complicated minefield in the terrain of constitutional law, one that whipsawed back and forth in interpretation as justices retired or were replaced.

Privacy had been an almost foreign concept in the days of the early twentieth century, but in 1928, a dissent by Justice Louis Brandeis in a wiretapping case, *Olmstead v. United States*, seeded the notion of "the right to be let alone."[31] In *Poe v. Ullman* (1961), the Supreme Court rejected a case about contraception access in Connecticut, deciding that the plaintiffs had not yet been injured by the law that prohibited the distribution of information about contraceptives, and thus had no standing. But in a dissent, Justice John Marshall Harlan II wrote that due process did not only describe the judicial proceedings once a law had been broken. He concluded that it also described the actions of the state as they infringed upon understood liberties. Each time a justice wrote an opinion such as Harlan's, they created fertile intellectual ground for future decisions as well as dissents.

Under Chief Justice Earl Warren, the Supreme Court embarked on a series of decisions that more clearly delineated the right to privacy.[32] It ruled in a 7–2 decision in *Griswold v. Connecticut* (1965) that married couples had the right to use contraception under the "penumbra" of the Bill of Rights, though the decision also asserted the right to preserve laws concerning morality. Privacy also underwrote *Loving v. Virginia* (1967), a unanimous decision that held that interracial couples had the right to marry, since decisions about whom to love and with whom to procreate were personal and private. Virginia laws against miscegenation had no rational purpose but to draw an "odious" racial distinction, the court ruled, while the state had argued that because the law applied equally to Black and white citizens, it should stand.[33] In a 6–1 decision in *Eisenstadt v. Baird* (1972), the Supreme Court found that the state of Massachusetts had no just basis to interfere with the distribution of contraceptives to unmarried people, after a lower court had ruled that a lecturer at Boston University illegally gave away spermicidal foam to an unmarried person.[34] Then, in *Roe v. Wade* (1973), a woman sued the state of Texas for the right to have an abortion, arguing that Texas laws prohibiting the procedure were violations of the First, Fourth, Fifth, Ninth, and Fourteenth Amendments. In a 7–2 ruling the Supreme Court found that the right to privacy conferred a right to have an abortion, with varying implications throughout the course of a pregnancy.[35] In its totality, *Roe* established that privacy rights extended to medical decisions, to the fundamental choice of whether to parent or not, and to the very core of sexual activity—which it held to be a private matter.[36]

The ACLU of Georgia held out hope for a favorable decision from its first hearing in federal court, as it had been docketed with Judge Robert H. Hall, a 1979 Carter appointee and a friend of the former president. Almost instantly, Hall received a challenge from Lewis Slaton, who on March 7 filed to dismiss the case based on the Constitution, citing Blackstone's concept of a crime "of so dark a nature . . . that the very mention (of it) is a disgrace to human nature."[37] He wrote that *Griswold* had not been decided to protect homosexuality, quoting instead Justice Harlan's *Poe* dissent, which cited only the "intimacy of husband and wife" as an "essential and accepted feature of the institution of marriage, an institution which the State not only must allow, but which always and in every age it has fostered and protected."[38] Slaton added that the state had the right to patrol sex in other ways too. It could regulate marriage and disallow fornication and adultery. It could regulate how and when pregnancy could be aborted. It could test the blood of those who applied for marriage licenses for sexually transmitted infections, in the interest of public health.

Slaton cited sodomy laws as a defense against the emerging threat of disease among homosexuals. "With Acquired Immune Deficiency Syndrome (A. I. D. S.), medical science knows neither cause nor cure. It does know that there is a high incidence among homosexual men. To the extent that the enforcement of laws proscribing consensual sodomy achieves the goal of preventing transmission of these diseases, a legitimate, and constitutional state purpose is established." Slaton wrote that he respectfully prayed that the motion to dismiss be granted. Religious precepts had been so deeply embedded in the practice of law as to go unnoticed.

On April 15, 1983, Hall ruled against Hardwick. He dismissed the Doe plaintiffs, saying they had no case. They were unable to show that they had sustained or were in immediate danger of sustaining some direct injury because of the statute's enforcement. "As to plaintiff Hardwick," he wrote, "the Virginia statute challenged in that case is quite similar to the Georgia legislation in question here, and all the constitutional arguments made by Hardwick here were rejected in *Doe*. For these reasons, the motions to dismiss are GRANTED."[39]

The law had the power to dismiss the very idea of civil rights in this way. Never benign, the law could permit an activity under one cultural guise while it disallowed it under another. It absolved and convicted in the same act. It could argue from behind a curtain of innate cultural bias written into law centuries before, avoiding studiously the clear intent of the very words penned in founding documents. Hall ignored the repeal of sodomy laws in half the states, and claimed the law as it was written in the other half as cover.

Neither Wilde nor Hardwick had even seen the inside of Hall's courtroom. It had all been done through written motions and decisions in Hall's private chambers.

"Welcome to the annual parade of perverts down Peachtree!" Maria Helena Dolan bellowed to the crowd of Pride protesters in June of 1983. Dolan's fierce disrespect for propriety had a new reason to well up. "We know why we're here today. Because we're all criminals. Yes, in Georgia, to share love in any but the breeder/missionary position is a crime. They call it a 'crime against nature.'" Dolan charged that politicians ignored the real crimes: environmental policy, unchecked

Klan hatred of Black and queer people, and the Reagan administration's blind eye toward the epidemic surging in the queer community.

On May 26, Mayor Young had proclaimed AIDS Awareness Day, and about 400 people lit candles and marched from the gay bar Crazy Ray'z to Piedmont Park as they marked the somber occasion. Young had signed his first resolution designating Gay/Lesbian Pride Day on June 25, albeit with a hedge. In a letter to city council president Marvin Arrington, Young wrote, "As I indicated in my letter of June 16th, 1982, on this same subject, I believe that sexual orientation is not a subject for government certification or intervention. It must, however, be the role of government to protect the rights of its citizens and to prevent discrimination. My administration is committed to that end."[40]

The official theme of "Out Front, Out Loud, Outstanding" would be overwritten by the fears that riddled the queer community with anxiety: the fear of death and of continued second-class citizenship. With an estimated 2,000 people in the protest march, the city closed down Peachtree Street between Tenth and Eleventh for a rally where Susan McGreivy of the National Lesbian & Gay Rights Project told the crowd that they needed to support the Hardwick legal challenge of the sodomy law: "Protection of your civil rights—housing, employment, you can't get anything until you get rid of that law."

She critiqued the queer community itself. "When we don't go to demonstrations, when we don't write the necessary letters, when we don't register to vote, when we don't donate time or money to Queer causes—these are all crimes against nature. This is doing the patriarch's work for him. It's a form of self-strangulation. But we can stop strangling ourselves by altering our self-images. We need to see ourselves not just as lovers, but as protectors and providers for our people."[41]

Gay civil rights still were the rallying cry, as speakers commanded the crowd to channel their anger into organization and persistence. The next day, the Atlanta paper wrote it large: "Gays becoming a key factor in city politics."[42]

The 1983 parade had also been the first in which a "Stop AIDS" banner had been carried. The hard work of activism on behalf of civil rights had already drained so many people working for the cause when the virus began to tighten its grip. Now groups like AID Atlanta struggled under the weight of an epidemic that had already claimed dozens of lives in Atlanta and had put thousands in a state of panic.

"We are being overwhelmed," a representative of the group said. "We are the only organization of our kind in the southeast. We get over 30 calls a day from North Carolina to Florida. We are all volunteers but we are working people, too. We need help."[43]

"That's a crock of shit," Hardwick said flatly. *Cruise*, a queer community magazine, had sent its editor to ask him about his ongoing case, and diving into the emotional abyss once more lit his anger anew.

He still was the soft-spoken young man who had been stunned nearly a year earlier when he had been arrested for having sex with another man. He never saw himself as an activist. He never expected that a beer bottle tossed in the trash would become a turning point in the gay-rights movement.[44]

Now he answered all manner of questions about his private life in the belief that readers would understand Georgia's incoherent and outdated sodomy laws. "They say they don't enforce the law unless it is an aggravated case like rape," he spat. "What about entrapment? What about my case?" (No official records suggest that Torick was ever charged with entrapment or harassment.)

Hardwick said he had worked with lawyers for the past ten months "designing the case" and amassing some ten to fifteen expert witnesses, using the Texas decision in *Baker v. Wade* as a template for action. The man initially interested in his case, Clint Sumrall, had teamed with local club manager Ted Binkley to set up a group, Georgians Opposed to Archaic Laws, or GOAL, to help finance the legal effort. The case had been dismissed by U.S. district court, he said, which meant it could take months or years before a higher court decided to hear it—or declined to hear it.

The law had stripped Hardwick of the power he felt in his community. It had humiliated him. Coming out in public and fighting his arrest had restored some of that power. He claimed he wasn't involved to enjoy the spotlight or to become a celebrity. Instead, Hardwick saw himself as the means for change. He believed his case could set a precedent that could lead to an end to employment and housing discrimination. The investment of his time and the impact on his life had been worth it so far, he thought. He was happy with his decision and hoped his sacrifice would lead to some good.

"I think about the 10 to 15 people who are arrested on sodomy charges in Georgia each month," he said. "I think about the teacher who has spent six years in college and has to throw it all away. I think about the guy whose family doesn't know he's gay until they read about it in the papers. I want to make people aware of the law and let them know that they can do something about it. My family is aware... I'm very lucky. I'm very pleased by my legal help. They believe just as much as I do that the law needs to be changed. Even if we don't win, this will lay the foundation for changing the law."[45]

It had taken a toll, and more trauma accrued as the stakes in the case grew. When the case became public, Hardwick had been fired from training that would have made him the beverage manager at the Peachtree Plaza Hotel. He had gone in to check to see when his next shift would be, after the TV news had aired its report on his day in federal court. When he looked, he didn't find himself on the work schedule, and was told he would not be hired. He found work instead in a gay bar and with a florist.

Anxiety still tied him in knots. He worried that someone else might be planning to assault him, since he had been beaten before his arrest and was now more visible. He changed his phone number, put his lease in someone else's name, and moved.[46] The mere sight of a police officer made him nervous, and he studied passing faces for any sign of a religious zealot out to make a point.

"I'm worried," he said, "about getting blown away by a fundamentalist psycho."[47]

Hardwick had reason to worry. The city's newspaper granted column inches to vile speech that made light of the predicament of the queer community and, arguably, encouraged hatred, if not violence. Columnist Dick Williams, who had become known for his antiqueer screeds, wrote in the *Atlanta Journal* on July 3, 1983, that he had watched coverage of the Atlanta Pride protests on television the weekend before, and still had questions.

"What are these civil rights the homosexuals want?" he asked. "How are they being discriminated against?"

Williams complained that he had been accused of "fagbaiting" and that he could not find conditions or situations in housing, employment, or civil discourse that would require anything special for queer people. "It seems what homosexuals want most is audible advocacy for their lifestyles," he said. "They are not talking civil rights, they are talking civil wrongs."

His list of those wrongs ranged from queer people occupying public space in city parks to transgender sex workers practicing on the same Atlanta streets as other sex workers to teachers being allowed to "parade an illegal standard of morality past children." Queer people wanted legitimacy for something that 79 percent of Americans were against, Williams concluded. "Gay liberation doesn't mean freedom in the bedroom. It means freedom to proselytize."[48]

Queer people should be able to live where they want, "provided they follow the norms of society," he wrote. "Were I a landlord, I would defend my right not to rent to the leather-and-chains crowd. Were I hiring an employee, I would defend my right to fire him/her if he/she began coming to work as a transperson."

Williams finished on an inhumane note: "Close to a million homosexuals marched last weekend. The disease called AIDS was foremost on their banners. Science, we hope, will cure it. But like syphilis and gonorrhea, the control of AIDS is within the reach of those affected. Has the disease violated their civil rights? It hasn't, but it sure does discriminate."[49]

Williams's bigoted tirades were learned from a well-worn playbook. That summer, Jerry Falwell's July 1983 *Moral Majority Report* was sent to his flock with a shocking cover. Under the headline "Homosexual Diseases Threaten American Families," it showed a family of four white people in surgical masks. The stigma of being gay had been enshrined. Queer people were deemed a contagion.[50]

On August 5, 1983, Hardwick's legal team began the long process of appeal on Judge Hall's April order. Wilde and others spent hours behind closed doors at work on their response. They argued that the district court had erred when it dismissed the motion, and that the fundamental right of privacy extended to all consenting adults, including homosexuals.[51]

The chorus of voices in the case filings now included an amicus brief from Lambda Legal, an advocacy group established in 1973 to take up legal challenges specific to queer people, especially on issues of equality. In its brief, Lambda Legal wrote that in 1977's *Carey v. Population Services* abortion-funding case, the court had explicitly said that it had not yet answered to what extent private consensual sex could be governed. An appeals court could do as it wished, Lambda's brief argued, because the law had shifted since 1976 and *Doe*. Hardwick's case should be heard, so that the core issue of privacy could be explored better than in an impervious echo chamber such as the one offered by Judge Hall.[52]

More important, the Lambda brief floated the concept of personal autonomy as a legal right—the "right of the individual to conduct his own life as he sees fit."[53] The right to privacy governed how people interacted with the state, and that implied a personal sphere into which the public good could not and should not intrude.

Finally, Lambda reasoned that the courts should apply heightened scrutiny to the case. That meant Georgia would have to justify why and how it should be able to interfere with the constitutional right to privacy. The brief did not expect the courts to take an even tougher look at the case under so-called strict scrutiny. That would be applied if a law had been crafted with the plain objective to discriminate against a class of people. No court had yet held queer people as a class that deserved protected status, though commenters such as Laurence Tribe of Harvard University Law School had begun to urge the courts toward that logical conclusion.

Neither test should even be necessary to decide the case, Lambda's brief concluded. "Since the governmental interest suggested below fails to pass muster under either standard," it read, "this statute cannot survive any form of serious review." The government needed the means to protect citizens involved in pederasty, prostitution, and sexual violence, but it had "no legitimate interest in regulating private, consensual sexual conduct between adults which would justify an invasion of Constitutionally protected rights."[54]

The Georgia Attorney General's Office responded in a filing that none of the plaintiffs in the case, especially the Doe couple, had standing to challenge the lawsuit because none were under genuine threat of prosecution. The Supreme Court had been correct in 1976, AG Bowers's office responded, in that the precedent from the *Doe* sodomy case still held. The jousting continued when Hardwick's team turned Bowers's response against him, noting that the very cases cited by the attorney general's office underscored that Hardwick could still be arrested and prosecuted. The aim of their suit was legitimate, they wrote. Hardwick "should not be required to wait and undergo criminal prosecution as the sole means of seeking relief."

The case would go to the U.S. Court of Appeals for the Eleventh Circuit, and by the end of 1983, it settled into quiet stasis until it was heard. As it did, some of those attached to it were dismissed from the proceedings, in court and out of it. Dwight Sawyer's case disappeared from the docket, and most of the original legal team assembled on Hardwick's behalf had completed their work, as Kathy Wilde and representatives from Lambda Legal pressed onward. Officer Keith R. Torick had left the Atlanta police that summer, to later join a suburban Roswell police squad miles away from Atlanta.[55]

Hardwick remained in Atlanta, for the time being. His life had been upended, and he had gone into hiding within the semi-cloistered confines of the queer scene. A summer before he had been the center of attention and in command of his life. Now much of what happened to him was out of his control.

The Boys of Summer

In the time it took for his appeal to be heard, Michael Hardwick could be found bartending and waiting tables at one of Atlanta's queerest places. The Gallus filled the white wedding-cake building at 49 Sixth Street. A private home when built in 1893, in the early 1970s it became the Esperanto, a gay bar in the rapidly queering neighborhood of Midtown. It turned into the Gallus in 1974, its name a double entendre for the French word for "cock."

In January of 1984, the Gallus opened "The Third Floor Bar," hosting a gala to kick off the new space. It gleamed from the light cast by its iridescent rainbow-tinted milk-glass windows with green tulips cut and mounted in their frames. On the main level, each Gallus room had its own theme and white-tablecloth seating. It was, as the *Atlanta Journal* dubbed it, "one of the dining bastions for Atlanta's gay community, a kitschy combination of turn-of-the-century bordello and art deco overindulgence. The restaurant's interior is a dizzying combination of frosted, gold-framed mirrors, curlicued wood frames, marble top tables, dark red velvet walls, paintings, and plaster cherubs. But if you can get by the surroundings, you will enjoy one of Atlanta's more interesting dining venues."[1]

Hardwick worked mostly on the main floor, but sometimes

upstairs. He tried to keep his work separate from his case. His lawyers had agreed with him that, were his private life to be aired for public consumption, it could affect whatever path the U.S. Court of Appeals might take. He could be seen on the rare occasion at the Cove or at Backstreet, but for the most part he lived quietly, and even his old friends would share only a hello with him when they saw him at work.[2] There would be no return to the carefree days before his arrest.

Hardwick would later say that he had a platonic relationship with a woman during this period, one in which he felt more than the nonsexual bond that they shared. He "couldn't let it happen," he said. "I didn't want her to resent me when I wanted to see my male friends. She moved out."[3]

Hardwick had learned to keep to himself. The more he revealed, the more he could be surveilled. The staggering ubiquity of personal information available to strangers—telephone numbers, street addresses, city directories, and in his case newspaper biographies and on-site TV interviews—had given the world details about where he slept, where he worked, who he had sex with, and how he preferred to have sex. The idea of the loss of privacy had saturated American culture already as camcorders and cell phones became more prevalent. Still, few people were subjected to the fearsomely efficient intersection of technologies as Hardwick had already been.

There still were places where one could hide in plain sight, though. The Gallus was one.

On April 23, 1984, U.S. Health and Human Services Secretary Margaret Heckler confirmed a scientific breakthrough. The root cause of AIDS had been discovered—as the "LAV" virus at the Institut Pasteur in Paris by a team led by Dr. Luc Montagnier and as HTLV-III in the United States by a team led by Dr. Anthony Gallo.[4] The discovery came too late for many thousands of people. Already, 880 new cases of AIDS had been reported in the first three months of the year.[5]

The disease could not be diagnosed until it flourished in the person's immune system. Even as it killed their helper cells, pocked their skin, and ravaged their brains, people were uncertain if they had it. Were they already sick? Who had given it to them, and to whom had they passed it as an unwitting carrier? A vaccine could take years, time many people did not have. Would they die before anyone cared?

AIDS had come, and it mattered critically to whom it came first: queer people and people of color. So long as it affected them, those underclasses of people could be held responsible for a contagion that could be ignored or muted until it threatened to feast on the powerful. Society privileged some forms of sex while it pathologized others, as Michel Foucault had written in his *History of Sexuality*. Society had taken a common act of sex and refashioned it as homosexuality, an idea it used to amass power and wield it against queer people. Homosexuality was no longer a natural act between members of the same gender. It became an identity. "The sodomite had been a temporary aberration," Foucault wrote. "The homosexual was now a species," one to be dominated.

The very idea of queerness mutated into a condition that the state used to prosecute and persecute lives through all kinds of modern institutions, from the courts to prisons to law enforcement.[6] But in his dissection of power's pervasive nature, Foucault detected its inevitable opposition. "Where there is power," he reasoned, "there is resistance." The two were inseparable.

Foucault's psychosocial dissections of sexuality seemed even more prescient in the year prophesied by George Orwell in *1984*. The novel evoked the post–World War II generation's queasiness at the speed of technological progress and the growing power of the state long before Foucault. An anti-romance novel floating in dystopian horror, *1984* cast sexuality as political peril in a tale of rebels and lovers tamed by cruel psychological and omnipotent political force.

In the year 1984, the paranoia personified by Orwell's Big Brother embedded itself into the American psyche. It became a most convenient metaphor for a fervent strain of conservatism on the rise. President Ronald Reagan sold the idea during that year's elections as "Morning in America," but many held it to be an encroaching darkness, an era in which, as Orwell declared, "private life came to an end."[7]

Both Orwell and Foucault foresaw the time when privacy and sexuality would become ever more entwined in a passionate contest between power and desire. Orwell died in 1950, before that embrace would be codified by an epidemic. Foucault would become one of the epidemic's casualties. The writer and philosopher, whose speaking tours of the United States turned into a visiting professorship at the University of California at Berkeley in 1980, was known to be an enthusiastic visitor to the bathhouses in nearby San Francisco—an enthusiasm he described in interviews even as the epidemic took its shape and name.

It was, he said at first, a "dreamed-up disease." In 1983 he became ill. Diagnosed with AIDS, Foucault went to the Pitié-Salpêtrière Hospital in Paris, where he died on June 25, 1984.

Hardwick already knew many who had died of AIDS. Don Stevenson had been the first.

Don was close to Hardwick's friend Puss and also Puss's mother, Winnie, who took care of gay men in her daughter's circle. She mothered them when no one else would. When Don became gravely ill in the fall of 1982, he went to Atlanta's Grady Hospital, the ominous Deco pile downtown, where Winnie found a plate of hospital food sitting outside Don's door.

What's that? Winnie asked.

The nurses explained it was Stevenson's food—and that they wouldn't enter the room. Winnie demanded a fresh tray for him.

I'll take it in, she said. They instructed her to put on a mask, gown, and gloves. Winnie stared at them. *Just give me a new plate of food.*

Even Puss was shocked by her mother's hardline stance. They got the food and took it into Don's room. Their friend sat at the end of his hospital bed, in his gown, tracing patterns in the air like he had been drawing in the sand. He had lost most of his attachment to the world. Puss and Winnie got on either side of him and helped him back into bed, and something clicked. He was alive again, if only for a moment, and was genuinely happy to see them. Winnie rubbed his arm, the reassuring gesture that the well give to the sick so that both can be comforted. It must have been the first time Don had been touched in a humane way since he entered Grady, Puss thought.

On October 17, 1982, Don became the first of Hardwick's circle to "tour." That was how Puss's Broadway-crazed family put it. When someone died, they didn't die. Of course not. They went on a "major tour." Somehow the idea that they could be trapped in a never-ending production—of *Mame*, for example—in theaters unknown to them, blunted the incredible pain of their loss.

After Don, the new reality of life and death came home to them all. Puss would tell her gay male friends—Hardwick included—that she worried for them. She knew gay men, and how they were.

We're careful. And still some of them didn't take precautions, at least before they were showing symptoms, or maybe they were and disguised them well.

Don't worry. It wouldn't affect them because they were careful. And even so, there would be a cure or something coming soon.

We're fine. But they weren't. Fatalism proved the easiest way to handle the trauma of the unknown. They had begun the watch. They knew that it was too late. Soon they would lose more people than most people lose in a lifetime.

Bars and baths closed. Apartments went empty. Funeral homes prospered. Hospitals converted wings, even entire buildings, to AIDS-only facilities. The Gallus thrived.

In the basement, the Gallus's owners had converted a narrow but long space into a sort of speakeasy, with a bar that took up more than half the dark-wood-paneled rumpus room. Disco music blared all the time. Cruisy and fun, the Gallus basement was a dive bar, with a few video games and barstools.

Hardwick worked the basement bar on occasion. It suited his need for privacy, since its customers paid and tipped in cash, and since its profile was kept low by its patrons. In the dimly lit room Hardwick could be surrounded by casual friends and former lovers—and hustlers and pimps and drunks, too; by the lawyer who would park his limousine outside and lure hustlers into it with cocaine; by the men who would meet and go outside to the bushes behind the basement bar.

The Gallus had, in an era long ago, been a funeral home. The basement had once been the building's crematorium. The hustlers plied their trade where the dead had been ushered into the fire. The dining rooms upstairs had been funeral parlors where mourners had come to remember the dead. As Hardwick poured drinks and served them with his usual wide smile, the dead were among them.

ABC Evening News reported on November 23, 1984, that AIDS cases were doubling every six months, and that a quarter million gay men could soon be infected, if they were not already. There were nearly 7,000 known cases.[8] Of those, 3,342 people had died. Anywhere from one-third to two-thirds of the men who sought care from venereal-disease clinics in New York and San Francisco showed antibodies to

AIDS in their blood. And while the CDC and FDA promised that a test to detect those antibodies would be widely available in just a few months, the Atlanta Gay Center and others were advising men to be wary of it.[9] The test was not a test for AIDS, they said, and it would not be 100 percent accurate. A positive test only meant that the person had developed antibodies: AIDS was a condition of progression and multiple pathways. A negative test could mean the person had not been exposed to the virus, or it could mean it had not been long enough for the body to have had a measurable reaction. The Gay Center recommended that people ask if their blood was being tested, and if so, to refuse the test until more information was known.[10]

Ironically the rapid spread of the epidemic reduced some fear among gay men, the report noted. While some people had changed their behavior—fewer men were going to bathhouses—others who had seen friends die had realized that life would always come to an end, sooner or later. Many decided to live as they had before AIDS, in defiance.

In the Gallus dining areas, the managers played quieter music, "The Way We Were" by Barbra Streisand, or Dusty Springfield. In the basement the disco pumped out harder, more insistent fare like "Relax," a thumping dance hit by British band Frankie Goes to Hollywood. The song leapt off the vinyl with an introductory blast of saxophone, a muezzin cry that sounded as if it blared from atop a minaret in Morocco—a call to a distant Mecca for a prayer of a different kind. The video would be banned from MTV; the band, with queer frontman Holly Johnson, had filmed some of the most risqué queer footage it could, setting the song in a den of iniquity populated by bare-chested leather men, an emperor being shaved by servants, circus animals, and a visual feast of ambiguously gendered stage performers—all backdrop for the lead singer, who strips off a jacket, removes his tie, and loops it around a man's neck to use as a harness.[11]

It was an underground orgy that would be damned as "disgusting" by the kind of rock-and-rollers who owned the music airwaves.

The song harnessed the frenetic energy of a community on the edge of collapse. They had marched across the dewy grass at Piedmont Park, held each other closely, plunked coins in the same jukebox, lit a cigarette for each other, splashed Chattahoochee River into each other's faces, called a cab for one another when the Cove crowd broke up. Now they were in it together to the end, in a silent exchange between friends and lovers who sealed their relationship one final way.

That winter, the Gallus had just put another song into its jukebox, Don Henley's latest single, "The Boys of Summer." Henley's song wistfully documented the fading glow of an era, coining an instant nostalgia for a time when life could have gone on, not when it was ending for so many. The boys of summer from just a year or two before now were dying.

Another song in the jukebox, another man in the hustler basement, another in the hospital. Life for queer people still went on, but it came with the sense that what was done, was done, and now what was left was to await the inevitable. Beautiful humans with good souls withered away to nothing. As they were dying, they knew themselves differently from how many others knew them: as worthy of life. So they ate, and they drank, and they coupled, and they danced. At the Gallus they feasted on what remained, consumed by a bacchanalia in the basement of a funeral home.

CRUCIFIXION

Justified

Hardwick had waited nearly two years for the U.S. Court of Appeals for the Eleventh Circuit to hear his plea when on January 7, 1985, it pulled his case free from a quagmire of motions and stays. The three-judge panel selected to hear it—Elbert P. Tuttle Sr., Phyllis Kravitch, and Frank Johnson—thrilled Kathy Wilde. Tuttle had ruled that James Meredith could be admitted to the University of Mississippi and that Martin Luther King Jr. and followers could demonstrate in Albany, Georgia.[1] Johnson had sat on the three-judge panel that struck down the Montgomery bus-segregation law that placed Rosa Parks at the forefront of the national civil-rights movement.[2]

The tone of their inquiry gave Wilde hope from the first volleys. Johnson fired off the most pointed questions for the state's attorney, Michael Hobbs, about the justification of the law. When Hobbs reiterated that public morality was the only justification for the law, Johnson stared and asked: "Do you understand that this is two consenting adults in the privacy of their bedroom?"

Wilde left the courtroom optimistic, though Judge Kravitch had parried with her over the 1976 *Doe* sodomy ruling in Virginia. Wilde told the court that recent developments in other cases had left open the question whether the *Doe* decision still applied. She cited some of

Kravitch's own recent rulings, which suggested that the state had no right to confine personal behavior to a moral code.

Having their sex lives controlled by the state was just one of the everyday oppressions that queer people endured, but Hardwick's case offered a glimmer of hope. A decision in his favor could send the case back to district court with the instructions for a criminal trial in which the state would have to justify how its sodomy laws were not in conflict with the Constitution.[3] It could also send it up to the Supreme Court if conflicting lower-court decisions were deemed worthy of its review.

The Supreme Court had little exposure to date on the issue of constitutional rights for queer people. In 1967 it upheld the deportation of Canadian citizen Clive Boutilier, because it deemed the plaintiff had been "afflicted with a psychopathic personality"—a diagnosis that would be applied to queer people until the American Medical Association depathologized homosexuality in 1973. The Immigration and Nationality Act of 1952 effectively barred queer people from U.S. entry because they were considered and labeled morally and medically defective.

In January 1984, British citizen Richard Longstaff petitioned the Supreme Court to decide whether homosexuality could preclude one from becoming a U.S. citizen. Longstaff had emigrated to the United States in 1965 and had not disclosed his homosexuality in his application for permanent residency. The application used the term "psychopathic personality," which Longstaff did not know was used to describe homosexuals. When he filed for citizenship, Longstaff was found to be ineligible because he had failed to establish "good moral character." The Supreme Court turned down Longstaff's plea for a hearing, and as the INS prepared to deport him, Longstaff returned to his clothing store and hair salon to epithets of "faggot" left on his answering machine.[4]

By October of 1984, the Supreme Court confronted its first queer free-speech case. A public-school teacher in Oklahoma had been warned to not speak about his identity since the state had written into a 1978 law its ability to fire any teacher who either engaged in "public homosexual activity" or "public homosexual conduct." The former was precisely defined as the sex act itself, but the latter was worded to include advocacy for any expression of queerness, whether private or public. An Oklahoma district court found for the board of education, but the Tenth Circuit of the U.S. Court of Appeals reversed that decision in part when it found that "conduct" was an overly broad assault on free speech. The board of ed petitioned the Supreme Court, which granted certiorari—an official review of lower court proceedings—in *Board of Education of Oklahoma City v. National Gay Task Force* in the fall of 1984. The National Gay Task Force brought on Laurence Tribe to argue on behalf of the teacher's right to free speech. That March, with Justice Lewis F. Powell out on medical leave, the court effectively upheld the Tenth Circuit decision in a 4–4 deadlock. Oklahoma could not fire the teacher simply for speaking about being gay.

Even after the favorable Oklahoma decision, gay-rights activists understood the Supreme Court to be enemy territory. It had never ruled that the Constitution affirmed gay rights in any way.[5] With the appointment of Sandra Day O'Connor, it had begun to steer in a more conservative direction. So had lower courts: At the halfway point of his two-term presidency, Ronald Reagan had already created 160 new seats on the bench and filled 753 vacancies—almost entirely with white Republican men, of which nearly a quarter were millionaires. Justice Harry Blackmun felt the seismic shift among his colleagues and let it be known. The court was "going where it wants to go," he said, "by hook or by crook."[6]

Retirements loomed among the older justices—primarily among those who had voted with the liberal bloc. If they left and if Reagan's nominees were confirmed, the nation might be on the cusp of an unprecedented reversal of a generation of accepted constitutional principle. The stakes for that year's presidential election were enormous. Voters might not be voting only for a president. They might also be voting for a future Supreme Court.[7]

Kathy Wilde had spoken with Hardwick only a few times when he called her in late 1984, agitated and concerned for his safety. He worried he might be singled out for his stand and that he might be arrested again. Atlanta had become too dangerous. He just wanted to leave. *My mother's scared to death for me,* he told her.

Hardwick had also grown impatient by the slow pace of the courts. He had been upset when the case was thrown out by the district court and grew frustrated when it took two years to reach the Eleventh Circuit docket. He had not attended that oral argument. He had no desire to be there and didn't need to be. With no depositions and no discovery, his was a "paper case," a matter of filing briefs, attorneys in court with judges, and a lot of waiting.

Wilde relented. He could maintain his status as a plaintiff if he were to move, she told him, but he had to come back if she needed him to appear in court. If it were found out that he was no longer in the state, it might somehow jeopardize his standing, though that seemed to be a remote risk. He would have to be discreet, but she wasn't concerned that he would be arrested again for either sodomy or possession of marijuana. The facts of the case had already been presented in court. Any transgression might have made the papers or television, but the case before the judges was the case they had to decide.

Hardwick assured her that he would return. Anything was better than the anxiety he lived with every day.

With Wilde's assent, he moved to a place more like home, back to the nightlife scene he knew well in Coral Gables, where he took a job bartending and catering at Uncle Charlie's. Dubbed "a beautiful place for beautiful people," Charlie's played the latest music videos on big screens while patrons imbibed all sorts of substances. Some scored them from a drag performer and trans woman who frequented the club. A chatty party girl, she sold drugs not so discreetly in the quieter corners of the room. Sweet and hilarious, she dedicated herself fiercely to the scene and to her work.

Miami brought Hardwick some familiar comforts, though it had grown more dangerous in its own way by early 1985. The city had become an epicenter of the global drug trade. Tourism in Miami brought in $5 billion a year—but cocaine trafficking brought in $7 billion, along with a wave of ultra-violence. On July 11, 1979, armed men had opened fire in a Miami shopping center at 2:30 p.m. at Colombian drug-trafficking figure Jimenez Panesso, one of the "cocaine cowboys," and his bodyguard Juan Carlos Hernandez.[8] Bullets flew through the mall parking lot during the "Dadeland Massacre," which left Panesso and Hernandez dead and two store employees shot. The Mutiny Hotel in Coral Gables, frequented by the drug kingpins, inspired Al Pacino's 1982 film *Scarface*, a film both hyped and reviled for the extreme violence that spewed from Pacino's Tony Montana and his AR-15 assault rifle.

Out on Miami Beach, Cubans and Haitians struggled to scratch out a living in a hostile place. They blended in with elderly Jewish retirees on pensions and Social Security who evaded the high cost of living in the Northeast, while they themselves evaded the crime that had become rampant throughout the town.[9] It had become dilapidated, particularly South Beach, where the city planned to demolish nearly four hundred Art Deco buildings to make way for a $1.2 billion network of canals they hoped would reinvent it as a latter-day Venice—even though Florida already had one Venice, on its Gulf Coast.

Straight tourists could imagine themselves inside a cops-and-robbers fantasy showered in the cool light of neon-lit Miami Beach. But for queer people, the AIDS epidemic had turned South Florida into "sort of a no-man's-land," where some feared to visit because of its popularity as a nightlife and sex hub. Gay businesses began to fail. Bathhouses closed, while others survived by shifting their emphasis to health. Miami's Club Baths turned to promoting safer sex and its beefed-up gym. Gay bars prospered in the meantime, with some places in Miami area emerging stronger in the epidemic because they formed a vibrant part of the community.[10]

Caution had become a medical tool too late. At an April 1985 conference, Dr. James W. Curran, head of the CDC's Federal AIDS Task Force, said that the number of people affected by AIDS likely would double in just the next year, from about 9,000 since it had been identified to nearly 20,000 by 1986. Queer men reported that they were engaging with fewer partners, but more of those people had already been infected by the virus. And while the CDC had already begun receiving progress reports on experimental drugs tested at both the National Institutes of Health in Bethesda, Maryland, and the Institut Pasteur, it could not predict when or if either team would be able to identify any effective treatments.[11]

Few outside of their triumvirate knew it yet, but by April 4, 1985, the Eleventh Circuit had decided in Hardwick's favor. Judge Kravitch had been the lone dissent. She wrote to Frank Johnson, who had tried to convince her that lower courts had undermined *Doe*, and that sodomy laws should be questioned anew. "Despite your very thorough and persuasive opinion," Kravitch wrote, "I am still convinced, after a careful stay of the cases involved, that my original position is correct. Therefore, with respect and admiration, I dissent."[12]

On May 21, 1985, the Eleventh Circuit Court of Appeals issued its decision. Judge Johnson had told his clerks to draft his opinion in the sharpest language possible: "write it strong," he instructed them, knowing that the decision would add to his firebrand legacy while it would also distinguish him in polite circles as the "sodomy judge."[13] They did as instructed. The opinion stated that the Georgia sodomy law infringed upon the "fundamental constitutional rights" of gays and lesbians.[14] Sexual activity between consenting adults was "beyond the reach of state regulation," and queer people had the right to "intimate association."

Georgia had not provided a compelling interest in regulating the sex lives of unmarried people, the panel wrote. Importantly, it found that the Supreme Court's 1976 *Doe* ruling had not been controlling. Those plaintiffs had never been arrested, and the Supreme Court itself had said in *Carey v. Population Services* that it had not "answered the difficult question" as to whether the Constitution barred states from enacting laws that regulated private consensual behavior between adults.

The panel agreed that Hardwick had the right to fear he would be prosecuted, but it dismissed the Doe couple's challenge. The married couple had never been prosecuted and had never requested a hearing to determine if they would be prosecuted.

Wilde reveled in the decision. "This is the first time an appeals court has recognized a constitutional right of privacy in the area of private consensual sexual conduct between homosexual adults," she said. "This ruling is a milestone in the protection of individual rights."[15]

The Supreme Court did not strike down the sodomy law, however. It sent the case back to the U.S. district court for trial—"at which time the state must prove, in order to prevail, that it has a compelling interest" in regulating the sex lives of anyone who participated in oral or anal sex.[16] Still, the decision had "set the highest hurdle possible" for the state to jump.[17]

The Eleventh Circuit decision would not be the last word. On June 12, 1985, the attorney general's office in Georgia asked for an en banc rehearing of the case, which it was denied. It believed that the Eleventh was "dead-ass wrong on the law," and that homosexuality was "unnatural," "wrong," and "aberrant."[18]

"Appeal it," Bowers told a staffer when he heard of the decision.[19] His response would ensure the case was among the hundreds each term that would be vetted for a place on the docket of the U.S. Supreme Court.

On Monday, October 7, 1985, the Supreme Court feted the fiftieth anniversary of its home. Completed on April 4, 1935, the neoclassical building paid homage to Greek and Roman ideals. The style subsumed the court's actual substance, given its real duty was to play traffic cop between the executive and legislative branches, to iron out their messy differences and to find meaning in law written hastily by partisan interests.

Its power lay in its role as an arbiter of democracy. When it focused its gaze on the rightful expansion of liberty, the court could provoke sweeping change for just cause, as it had done in *Brown v. Board of Education* and *Griswold*, *Eisenstadt*, and *Roe*. Those Warren court decisions reversed some of the damage the court had inflicted upon itself in the years between the Fourteenth Amendment and *Brown v. Board of Education*.

But when its gaze was averted by political concerns, the court exercised nearly unchecked power to reverse progress. Far from being the protector of liberty and equality, the court had a much longer track record of invalidating worker protections, authorizing extraconstitutional confinements, and granting overreach into the personal lives of citizens. Its infamy lived in cases such as *Dred Scott v. Sanford*, which stripped people of their humanity and goaded a willing nation toward civil war, and *Plessy v. Ferguson*, which codified second-class citizenship for and sanctioned hatred against Black Americans.

The court could at times wield near-total power over the lives of the citizens it served. What the court could not do was be impartial. It had always been a political creation—not expressly partisan, naked and unashamed of its agenda, but political in its incorporation. Justices were nominated by elected presidents and, most often, were confirmed in bipartisan congressional votes. Whichever party held the office of president was likely to benefit from the frequent but still unpredictable prospect of an empty chair on the court's bench.

Of those nominated to the court in the twentieth century, only seven were denied the seat. Richard Nixon failed twice to fill the seat vacated by Abe Fortas, who had resigned under a cloud of ethical concerns. Clement Haynsworth and G. Harrold Carswell, Nixon's first two choices, both failed to win enough votes for confirmation due to prior decisions against school integration and other civil-rights issues. Nixon's third nominee was Harry Blackmun. Born and raised in St. Paul, Minnesota, Blackmun had attended Harvard Law School, where he paid for school by working as a janitor.[20] Married in 1941 to Dorothy Clark, he became counsel for the Mayo Clinic before President Dwight D. Eisenhower named him to the U.S. Court of Appeals. Nominated to the Supreme Court on April 14, 1970, and confirmed unanimously, Blackmun dubbed himself "Old Number Three," a self-deprecating recognition that sometimes things didn't go as planned.[21]

Notably conservative in early decisions, Blackmun evolved quickly on the bench as he became deeply concerned with the decisions of the court and how they affected the people governed by those decisions. His majority opinion in *Roe v. Wade* had been informed by his time at the Mayo Clinic. As a neighbor to a gay man who lived in their Arlington apartment building, Blackmun had been suitably unimpressed when his wife tried to prevent Blackmun's discovery of the queer neighbor's sexuality.[22] Soon, he began to acknowledge the distinct disadvantage the law placed upon gays and lesbians.

Thurgood Marshall, born in 1908 in Baltimore, was the only justice who had been subjected to the ignominy and hatred of Jim Crow. A college classmate of Langston Hughes, Marshall married Vivian Burey in his time at Lincoln University, then went to Howard University for law school, where he began to work with the NAACP and became a titanic figure in the legal strategy to dismantle Jim Crow. He argued *Brown v. Board of Education* at the Supreme Court in 1952—and again in 1953, when the case was reheard, after which it was decided in favor of desegregation.[23] One of Marshall's critical writings during the Warren court era came in the 1969 *Stanley* case. Writing within the penumbra of Orwell, Marshall had found that "whatever the power of the state to control public dissemination of ideas inimical to the public morality, it cannot constitutionally premise legislation on the desirability of controlling a person's private thoughts."[24] A casual, witty, and earthy presence behind the scenes, Marshall would greet Chief Justice Warren Burger informally: "What's shakin', Chief baby?"[25] By 1985, hampered by glaucoma and no longer the fearsome orator of his youth, Marshall knew about the rumors of his imminent retirement.

Justice William Brennan, a Newark native and former World War II army colonel, moved through the New Jersey court ranks before Eisenhower named him to the Supreme Court as a recess appointment. Brennan had become one of the most vocal critics of those who would turn back the Warren court's progressive decisions. In 1985, he had told an audience at Georgetown University that Attorney General Ed Meese and the general bent of conservatives for originalism was in reality "arrogance cloaked as humility." It was the court's mission to read the Constitution broadly, he said, and to protect the rights that emerged out of basic "human dignity."[26]

Liberal justice John Paul Stevens's wealthy Chicago family lost their hotel business during the Great Depression. A navy codebreaker during the war, Stevens clerked with Supreme Court Justice Wiley Rutledge after Northwestern Law School and served on the Seventh Circuit Court of Appeals until President Richard Nixon named him to the Supreme Court in 1975 to take the seat of Justice William O. Douglas, who had written about the rights of privacy for the majority in *Griswold*.[27]

Chief Justice Warren Burger led the conservative flank inside the court. Burger grew up in Minnesota, where he went to the same elementary school as Harry Blackmun and became friends with him, even going on double dates at a later age.[28] He stayed for college and law school, and to practice. A grass-roots Republican who helped deliver votes to Eisenhower in the 1952 election, Burger became an assistant U.S. attorney general for the Department of Justice, then was appointed by Eisenhower to the Court of Appeals for the District of Columbia, where he served until named and confirmed by Nixon as chief justice of the Supreme Court in 1969. He replaced Earl Warren, who had presided over a court that delivered some of the most progressive decisions in history.

Byron White, a former football player from Colorado, had been nicknamed "Whizzer" for his talent as a halfback. The Rhodes scholar played pro football before he joined the navy as an intelligence officer. With a Yale law degree earned after the war, White clerked for Justice Fred Vinson. President Kennedy first named White to the Department of Justice, before he nominated him to take Charles Whittaker's spot on the Supreme Court in 1962.[29] White had concurred with Justice Marshall in *Stanley*, writing that "to condone what happened here is to invite a government official to use a seemingly precise and legal warrant only as a ticket to get into a man's home, and, once inside, to launch forth upon unconfined searches and indiscriminate seizures as if armed with all the unbridled and illegal power of a general warrant."

Sandra Day O'Connor, an El Paso native raised in Arizona, had graduated from Stanford law school in two years. A state senator, then Maricopa County judge, she left the Arizona Supreme Court of Appeals after two years when she was named by Reagan in the first year of his presidency.[30] Nominated as a moderate conservative, O'Connor took charge of the Supreme Court's annual Christmas party, for which the vending machines in the court offices would supply the funds, with some donations by the justices themselves—a suggested tithe of $25 per justice, payable to Supreme Court Marshal Alfred Wong.[31]

William Rehnquist, the hardline conservative scion of Milwaukee, had preceded O'Connor at Stanford by a few years. He clerked for Supreme Court Justice Robert Jackson and wrote a memo that argued Jackson should decide against *Brown* and that *Plessy v. Ferguson* had been decided correctly.[32] A former deputy attorney general under Nixon, Rehnquist took the seat of John Marshall Harlan II on January 7, 1972. He would be one of the two votes in dissent in *Roe v. Wade*.

Rehnquist had experienced personal difficulties during his tenure on the bench. In 1981, he entered George Washington University Hospital in D.C. for an addiction to the sleep-inducing hypnotic Placidyl. Given the drug for chronic back pain, Rehnquist had been taking up to three times the prescribed amount while his wife underwent cancer treatment. When he tried to go cold turkey and went into withdrawal, he checked himself into the hospital, where he tried to run away while dressed in nightclothes, convinced that the CIA had plotted against him for an unknown nefarious reason. It took him a month to go through detoxification.[33]

Seated on the bench the same day as Rehnquist, Lewis F. Powell spoke with a soft Tidewater accent that translated even through the Dictaphone that he used to communicate with other justices and with his clerks.[34] A native of Suffolk, Virginia, Powell attended Washington and Lee University and studied law at Harvard. Married in 1936, Powell had done intelligence work during the war and returned to Virginia to practice law in Richmond. His district had been named in one of the consolidated *Brown* cases, and like Rehnquist, Powell did not think the court had decided it properly. It would be 1960 before Black students were permitted to register in white schools in his state's capital. In 1971, Nixon named Powell as the replacement for Hugo Black.[35]

The court seated in the fall of 1985 would be one of the older ones on record. Five of the justices were in their seventies. All but O'Connor had been eligible to vote for Franklin Roosevelt in at least one of his terms as president, if not all of them. They shared the law as a common religion. What was the law, after all, but another belief system that conferred some order on ungovernable life?

The justices formed a dysfunctional, fractious family of opposing viewpoints, some maintaining warm friendships and others, aloof distance. Each had their own agendas and blind spots. Among the liberal justices, a palpable and discomfiting sense of change had arisen. A progressive era had concluded, and more rigidly conservative dogma had taken root. The first conference of the term would be on Friday, October 11. Many cases that involved civil rights clamored for their attention. One would rise above the rest.

Over the summer, on July 25, 1985, Attorney General Michael Bowers had petitioned the Supreme Court to uphold Georgia's sodomy law, saying that the Eleventh Circuit's decision in the *Hardwick* case earlier that year had conflicted with a decision in a case from military court, *Dronenburg v. Zech*, which found that military personnel had no right to engage in sodomy, and that the Eleventh Circuit had dismissed the *Doe* decision incorrectly.

Kathy Wilde had replied in a brief that the law upholding sodomy statutes had become unstable, and that for the case to proceed, the state must demonstrate how its sodomy law was so essential as to supersede understood concepts of privacy. Also, Wilde wrote that the case was not "ripe" yet for the Supreme Court, since *Dronenburg* had relied not on civilian but military law.

A grant of certiorari in the *Hardwick* case would be momentous—and timely. Sodomy laws were being challenged across the country, and it might be only a matter of time before the court faced a conflict it would be compelled to decide. The court might be pressed to hear the *Baker* case from Texas. Other suits against sodomy laws were in progress in Louisiana, where like in Georgia the law applied to unmarried couples, as well as in Nevada, Texas, and Missouri, where the law applied only to homosexuals. With its three elderly liberals, the 1985–1986 Supreme Court might offer the best and only chance to overturn laws against consensual sex between adults.

The justices brought preexisting views to the conference table, where twice weekly they discussed cases and chose those they would review. Among them, the conservatives—Justices White, Burger, and Rehnquist—voiced suspicion of what they believed to be the due process clause's tortured evolution into extraconstitutional guarantees of privacy. Gay rights were nearly absent from their concerns. Liberal justices believed that the right to privacy in consensual conduct between adults to be a natural extension of decisions through and including *Roe*, which had been under pressure from the day it was decided.

Each justice had clerks prepare briefs on the cases that clamored for their attention in what promised to be a busy year. The court had become a factory for decisions that rolled down a conveyor belt of justice. When they met in conference, justices had enough information to decide whether to hear the case or to let the lower-court ruling stand. Rarely did they have much knowledge of the people intimately involved in the cases or how a decision might affect them.

Before the year's first conference, Blackmun clerk Helane Morrison recommended in a memo that her justice vote to grant certiorari to the *Hardwick* case, given the conflicts between the Fifth and Eleventh Circuits, but Blackmun was not convinced that the case could win.

William Stuntz, a Powell clerk, believed it should fail. On September 28, 1985, Powell received a memo from "Bill," who outlined the case as decided by the Eleventh Circuit, noting that Judge Kravitch had "authored a persuasive dissent" and argued that the 1976 *Doe* decision controlled sodomy law. The court could deny Hardwick and wait for the district court to try the case based on the instruction of the Eleventh Circuit, to demonstrate how the state could govern privacy to that degree.[36] The Supreme Court could also issue an opinion regarding *Bowers v. Hardwick* that laid out how and why *Doe* had been decided correctly and find in favor of Georgia without any oral arguments.[37]

On October 11, 1985, the justices voted 7–2 to deny certiorari to *Bowers v. Hardwick*, with White and Rehnquist in favor. Failing in the conference and eager to set precedent, White politicked to get the case on the court's docket. He wrote a memo in dissent that noted that the Eleventh Circuit's decision conflicted with other rulings, as courts had affirmed the Texas sodomy law and *Dronenburg*. Rehnquist signed on to the White dissent, but Powell remained unconvinced. In a second vote to consider the case, Justice Marshall joined in the vote to hear it. He believed the questions raised by the case would not go away.

In a shock to his clerks, Justice Brennan signed on to White's dissent, which gave the case the four votes it needed to be granted certiorari. Brennan may have believed at first that a fifth vote to overturn Georgia's sodomy law existed. When disabused of that notion, he reversed his vote.[38] But Marshall would not change his. He felt that not every decision on a case should be strategic.[39] With three votes to grant certiorari from Marshall, White, and Rehnquist, Chief Justice Burger added his name, giving the case the four votes it needed to move ahead. *Bowers v. Hardwick* would be heard.

When the Georgia attorney general's office appealed the *Hardwick* case to the Supreme Court, Hardwick's attorneys began to talk about who might argue it. Should it be Kathy Wilde, or an experienced Supreme Court litigator like Laurence Tribe—or should it be a queer person?

Wilde had already been stung by the opinions of queer leaders who felt a straight woman should not oversee such a monumental gay-rights case. The day Wilde had filed the lawsuit in 1983, Arthur Warner of the National Committee for Sexual Civil Liberties called her to bellow, *Who the hell are you and what the hell do you think you're doing?* She had shattered a carefully planned strategy that advocates had hoped would one day put the right case before the Supreme Court—after a slow, step-by-step slog through state courts. She began to feel pressure to have her case dismissed and then to step aside so that those carefully crafted strategies could be resumed.

Instead, Wilde joined a group started by Lambda Legal attorney Abby Rubenfeld. The Ad Hoc Task Force to Challenge Sodomy Laws had quickly evolved into a think tank, one that calculated how to argue Hardwick's case and carve out a win from a conservative-majority court. Many on the committee thought Wilde was a lesbian; why was never clear to her.[40] She felt compelled to clear the air, though she did not want to lose the support of the group. *Oh God*, she thought, *how do I do all of this?* She decided to have quiet conversations over a committee dinner with the people around the table. It bewildered her that people would think that only a gay person would be interested in arguing such a case, when she had devoted nearly three years of her life to it.

During the summer of 1985, the committee brokered a deal to which Wilde agreed. She would stay on the case as co-counsel, but the legal team would invite Laurence Tribe to write the briefs and argue the case should it make the Supreme Court docket.

Tribe had been born in China to parents of Belarusian Jewish heritage. His father had left China for the United States for a few years and had worked as a car salesman and line cook. He became a U.S. citizen then.[41] He returned to China, where Japanese forces interned him in a prison camp during the war. While detained, his father kept an American flag hidden in a false-bottomed trunk, knowing that it could get him killed.[42]

After the war, the family emigrated to San Francisco, where a junior high school teacher took note of Laurence's artistic talent. With his parents' permission, the teacher arranged for studio time and a teenage Tribe drew nude figures from live models. He attended Harvard for math and worked in the kitchen serving food and washing dishes but was drawn to the law and the study of the Constitution. Within its elegant but spare outline for democracy, the Constitution's silences fascinated him. Where it did not have clear meaning, it left a gap to be filled. He wondered how the founders meant for that silence to be heard.[43]

After graduation from Harvard Law, Tribe clerked for Supreme Court Justice Potter Stewart and worked on a case that contemplated the legality of electronic surveillance. Stewart thought the court would not sign on to an opinion that would require a distinct search warrant for electronic surveillance. Tribe had written otherwise.

"You're new here," Stewart told him. "This is not going to go this way." Tribe offered to write the memo, which became the prevailing opinion in *Katz v. United States* (1967).[44]

Tribe's clerkship was also during the era when pornography and obscenity became legalized concepts that commanded judicial attention. In the basement of the Supreme Court, a projector played films that might be banned or were in contention. Justice Harlan, at the time losing his sight, would watch the films as research while Thurgood Marshall provided commentary.[45]

In 1968 Tribe became a professor at Harvard Law School. As a professor, his lectures evolved from outlines to thousands of words of notes. Those notes turned into a 1978 book, *American Constitutional Law*, which turned Tribe into the Supreme Court counsel of first resort. In the book Tribe wrote that discrimination against gay people was like that of racial or sex discrimination—fundamentally wrong. That thesis proved to be highly controversial. He had written his treatise on a range of questions, including the freedom of consensual sex. It was a startling, advanced piece of theory that included a section on the freedom of the mind, in which he argued that mind-altering drugs were indistinguishable from literature. People had every right to induce whatever mental state they wanted, so long as they did not harm anyone else.

Teaching let him watch as ideas took shape in a student's mind, and the satisfaction and pride in that connection could not be replaced or even budged. But he enjoyed arguing cases before a court that demanded his universal, unblinking attention to detail. Because of his professorship, Tribe could restrict his cases to those in which he believed in the legal principle or argument. It freed him from the pressure of having to argue a different point of view and gave him a fearsome weapon when he took the lectern: confidence. Any opposing counsel who tried to lure him into a legal or verbal trap would rue their gambit.[46]

Once Hardwick's case had been granted certiorari, the ad hoc task force convened to plot out its responses to the initial brief to be sent by the Georgia attorney general. On November 15 and 16, the committee met in New York, at the ACLU offices on Forty-Third Street in New York.[47] The latent hostility had abated. The national ACLU had not been a part of the case to date, in part because the ACLU of Georgia's Judd Herndon had been angry that a straight woman was handling Hardwick's case. Along with Kathy Wilde and Abby Rubenfeld, the group included California attorney Jay Kohorn, Nan Hunter from the ACLU, Nancy Langer from Lambda Legal, and Jim Kellogg from the ACLU of Louisiana. Tribe and his co-counsel, fellow Harvard professor Kathleen Sullivan, would attend the Saturday meeting.

The Friday session drew heated opinions about the two cases that could be argued in front of the Supreme Court. Hardwick's had been granted certiorari, but some on the committee believed that it would bolster the chances for the overturn of sodomy laws if it were heard in tandem with the appeal to the Fifth Circuit's decision in *Baker v. Wade*. Though litigant Don Baker had spoken with Tribe and considered retaining him as his attorney for a petition of certiorari to the Supreme Court, concerns grew that the Baker case had been in motion too long. To argue both, it would be necessary to get *Baker* granted review, then have both cases delayed until the 1986–1987 term. Still, *Baker* had advantages that were missing in *Bowers*. It had a strong equal-protection argument, since the Texas law punished only same-sex acts, and that might appeal to Justice Powell.

"Privacy and equal protection would be a strong combination," Baker told the group, "and Tribe wants to do both." Kohorn admired Tribe's breadth of knowledge, but believed that the court "will not now, and possibly never, shove gay rights down the country's throats as they did with the racial issue." Either argument path was viable—and sufficient on its own, he felt. He argued passionately that the group should not throw too much at the court at once. If it wanted to decide against gay rights, it would do so, and could take down all available avenues for justice with one spiteful decision.[48]

On Saturday, November 16, the ad hoc task force resumed its agenda, joined by Tribe and Sullivan. Tribe had argued a 4–4 decision in *Oklahoma* earlier in the year, which left the lower-court decision intact but was a dead end in terms of precedents it might have set. He had called the ACLU in the summer of 1985 to offer his services in *Bowers*.[49] Tribe championed the cause of equality and fought discrimination because he felt it was his duty to the country that had taken in his family after World War II.

On July 31, 1985, the ACLU of Georgia formally asked the national ACLU to bring on Tribe as co-counsel with Wilde, to argue the case jointly and prepare briefs jointly for the Supreme Court. Like most local affiliates, the ACLU of Georgia operated independently without a lot of support from the national organization. They couldn't afford all the case's travel expenses and litigation costs, and they knew it needed someone with expertise in handling the Supreme Court's unique performative needs. At the time, there were no openly gay litigators who had Supreme Court experience, though brilliant legal scholars such as Mary Dunlap were discussed.[50]

Tribe had accepted the role to argue *Oklahoma* because he had friends and colleagues who were queer. Most were closeted and stigmatized and were at risk for being harassed or even arrested. On November 13, he accepted Hardwick's case, with Wilde as co-counsel.[51] Tribe said he would include Kathleen Sullivan as co-counsel—he considered her the finest student he had yet taught—as well as a recent graduate of Harvard Law School, Brian Koukoutchos, who worked with both in the Oklahoma free-speech case earlier that year.[52] Koukoutchos loved to recite Auden's poetry. It was one way in which he infused himself with a respect of his queer friends that turned into advocacy.

The Supreme Court was not and would not grow friendlier to gay civil rights, Tribe knew. The best paths to ease it toward a favorable decision were equal protection and privacy. "Unfortunately, gay sex poses special problems," he said. "We must deal with closed minds." Some on the court, Stevens and Powell in particular, were "even more uneasy with advocacy than they are with privacy."[53]

Tribe initially favored the *Baker* case for its merits, then warmed to the *Hardwick* case for its privacy argument. Equality had a superior moral dimension, but privacy had its roots in property. Tribe believed that even the most liberal justices, Brennan and Marshall, would be more comfortable if the case were argued along the lines of privacy and liberty. Tribe believed that Marshall would be circumspect about any connection between Hardwick's civil rights and the still-evolving cause of racial justice.[54]

He had at first thought it better to pair the cases. Now he felt *Hardwick* would offer the better prospects alone—if he could convince the court that Georgia's law should be subject to some degree of scrutiny, since the government sought to disrupt the home in order to judge Hardwick's sexual preferences. If the court could not be persuaded that privacy applied to queer sex, then he held little hope that it would find in favor of equal protection.

It all came down to one justice. "Burger and Rehnquist are 100 percent impossible, White is about 90 percent impossible, O'Connor about 75 percent impossible," he said. "Blackmun and Stevens we have a good chance of winning, Brennan and Marshall we can count on." As for the remaining vote, "the biggest question mark is Powell, and so we must aim for him." It would be a challenge to frame the case in a way that would attract Powell's vote—but that would be the only way to win.

A "Homo 101" brief—one that brought justices up to date on the current cultural, medical, psychological, and ethical beliefs about queer life—would be essential for a favorable decision, but Tribe was wary of any attempt at a public relations campaign. "We're trying to move a conservative Court beyond its instincts, and any whiff of stirring up public opinion in order to pressure them will backfire."[55] The case had to lean into descriptions of Big Brother's intrusion into private lives. They should not present Hardwick "as the Dred Scott of the gay movement." Judicial homophobia, regrettably, was a real force to be neutered. The court could be reminded that Georgia's law was motivated by bigotry, but Tribe said, "it's not a good idea to remind them that they are bigots."[56]

On December 19, Michael Bowers's office filed Georgia's brief with the Supreme Court. In it, the state argued that the Eleventh Circuit had failed to follow binding precedent established by *Doe v. Commonwealth's Attorney*. "Moreover," it wrote, "the court below seriously erred in judicially creating a fundamental right of privacy to engage in homosexual sodomy, and by finding constitutional protection for this perceived right." Only those rights that were considered "fundamental" or "implicit in the concept of ordered liberty" were to be respected by the law.

The brief bristled at the idea that the sex acts implied in the sodomy statute would be compared to the intimacies of marriage. "No universal principle of morality teaches homosexual sodomy is acceptable conduct," the brief argued. It implicated that homosexuality naturally led to "sadomasochism, group orgies, or transvestitism," and that because as practiced in public parks, gay bars, gay baths, and restrooms, it led to multiple anonymous partners and therefore could be linked to AIDS, gonorrhea, hepatitis, and other diseases, placing it in the category of public health and welfare. In deciding the right to practice consensual sex, the Eleventh Circuit had "demoted traditional marriage to an alternative lifestyle," that it had "ignored the traditions and collective conscience of this nation."[57]

The Hardwick team assembled amicus briefs—legal opinions by outside organizations that could amplify or lend nuance to the common cause—with Abby Rubenfeld of the Lambda Legal Defense in charge. The first female class president at Princeton, Rubenfeld had dreams of becoming a senator and even of becoming president, but she came of age in the 1970s, when no out, queer politician had been elected to national office. She was out before she graduated from law school and took on cases of queer Southerners who needed help extricating themselves from legal straightjackets while keeping custody of their children.[58] The ad hoc task force had been her idea, but she had let a male colleague run it, simply to cut quickly through sexual politics to begin to dismantle sodomy laws.[59] Some of the men involved in the case thought it had been timed badly and that the court was not yet primed to deal with queer sex. But Hardwick had wanted to challenge the law, and it was his choice. The perfect case might not always come at the perfect time, Rubenfeld believed. Sometimes you had to take what the universe offered.

In their amicus briefs, the American Psychological Association and American Public Health Association sketched the contemporary sexual landscape for the justices, which largely confirmed Hardwick's sex life to be utterly natural. Most Americans had engaged in oral sex, and the emotional lives and health needs of gay men weren't all that different from those of straight people. Sodomy laws conspired against public health, the APA wrote, "by driving the disease [AIDS] underground where it is more difficult to study and by impeding the flow of information about prevention from public health experts to the population at risk." Meanwhile, the National Organization for Women (NOW) wrote that Georgia's sodomy law violated the equal protection clause, and that gays and lesbians should be considered a legally protected class because hostility toward them rendered them powerless.[60]

At Lambda Legal Defense, Rubenfeld's newest hire, Evan Wolfson, drafted much of their amicus brief. In it, Wolfson wrote that the Constitution did not protect families because of tradition but instead because the intimacy of those relationships formed the essence of individual identity. And, he argued, those relationships performed the same role for queer people and were just as important to them. If the nation relied on tradition and tradition alone, birth control would still be illegal, and the country's schools still would be segregated.[61]

Meanwhile, Tribe finished and circulated his brief on January 31, 1986. In it, he argued that the Eleventh Circuit had not invalidated the *Doe* decision. It only had remanded the case back to district court for the lower court to determine how the law had a compelling state interest. In other words, what business did Georgia have in the bedrooms of consenting adults? "All that is at issue here is the appropriate standard of review," he wrote as he aimed for an easier path to victory, "not the validity of the statute."

The state, Tribe argued, was trying to extend its reach into the bedrooms of private citizens without a good reason. The state offered only that a majority of Georgia's legislators disapproved of sodomy. The Eleventh Circuit's decision only said that the state had to explain why it had an interest in patrolling and regulating consensual, noncommercial sex. Georgia wanted to "freeze the right to be let alone by government" to include only married people and to bar anything else, or at least to hold it under a microscope.

The Supreme Court had already decided that private consensual activities were constitutionally protected in their rulings on contraception. Sex was implicit in those decisions. With those decisions the government had "drawn a firm line at the entrance to the house." Hardwick's privacy, Tribe argued, was the same as any other person's privacy, queer or straight, single or married, male or female. The argument would later be described by Sullivan as "a love song to Lewis Powell sung in the key of Justice Harlan."[62] It was an affirmative argument for privacy for all genders and all sexual activity—and gutted the arguments of those who believed there was some moral consensus on sodomy.

To Tribe's brief, the Bowers team answered that sodomy had never been included in the "zone of privacy" normally accorded inside the home. Tradition still held sway in almost two dozen states, it countered, and the trend to repeal sodomy laws abandoned that history.[63]

While the legal teams composed themselves for oral arguments, the justices prepared themselves to question the attorneys in court. They heard from their clerks, vetted their opinions, mulled over the core issues, and sent out feelers to colleagues on what they were writing. In most Supreme Court cases, memos were circulated within each justice's chambers and between justices, with the questions of the case laid out and sometimes answered far in advance of the actual arguments. The oral arguments served more as a sounding board for the conference and for eventual concurrences and dissents, and as a final chance to flummox one side while flattering the other.

Visitors were allowed inside the courtroom during oral arguments, but they were not allowed during these back-room sessions. Nor were all justices diligent at keeping records. Much of what transpired between them was done behind closed doors, with a paper trail only when they felt it made sense. Their conferences were all but off limits, even to their clerks. The court held its own privacy sacrosanct.

While the case was percolating among the nine justices, Brennan penned a memo stating bluntly, "we should affirm." The case was about conduct that was—here he wrote on separate lines, for emphasis—"consensual," "between adults," "undertaken in the privacy of the home," and "intimate and private." *Griswold* and *Eisenstadt* were firmly implicated as such, as were two decisions, *Payton v. New York* and *Stanley v. Georgia*, "which recognize that the home remains a sort of a castle within our legal system."[64]

Asserting which cases controlled others—which held the currently prevailing legal theory—became something of a parlor game, an attempt at assembling convincing bits into a narrative that could swing the correct number of justices into one camp or out of one. Brennan admitted the case was complicated but simplified it in his notes. The state had to explain why the law existed beyond the distaste for some kinds of sex. "I simply cannot believe," he wrote, "that this would be a controversial result."[65]

Harry Blackmun assigned the Hardwick brief to Pamela Karlan, a Yale Law graduate who had expressed interest in the case, though she had not yet come out to Blackmun as bisexual. In her March 23, 1986, memo to the justice, Karlan dissected the Eleventh Circuit decision, the crux of which rested on Judge Johnson's opinion that the constitutional right to privacy involved only "personal rights that can be deemed 'fundamental' or 'implicit in the concept of ordered liberty' " as found in *Roe v. Wade*.

Karlan recommended that Blackmun vote to affirm the Eleventh Circuit's decision. The law was too broad, and it interfered with marital sexual intimacy, so Georgia had to have some compelling interest to have such a law on its books, considering its constitutional implications. The law gave the state the authority to invade the right to privacy in the home, and traditional religious beliefs alone were not sufficient to justify the law's existence. Georgia had to do more, she wrote, "than point to the immorality of practices about which there no longer exists any consensus."[66]

Justice Powell handwrote a note atop the March 29 memo—"well written as usual. Mike would find no fundamental right." His clerk Michael Mosman believed Powell should vote to overturn the Eleventh Circuit decision. Tribe's brief had written much about what the case did not affect, Mosman wrote. The case was not about the conduct of married people, he wrote. The state "practically concedes that the statute cannot apply to married couples." It was not about the way the law was enforced, since Hardwick had not been prosecuted. "For all the Court knows, he may be acquitted," Mosman noted.

Most important, it was "not a case about the 'sanctity of the home' . . . A man may fantasize all he wants in his home about using cocaine or battering his wife, but if he actually does either, the State is free to punish him notwithstanding the fact that the conduct took place in his home." Caution was paramount, Mosman said, because "the right of privacy is not intended to be the vanguard of changes in societal values. It is intended to protect those values that are imbedded in the fabric of our society, not to imbed new values into that fabric of its own force."

As he ignored the words of the Georgia law and the precedents set by *Eisenstadt*, Mosman affirmed that in his view, "the right of privacy as it relates to this case has been limited thus far to marriage and other family relationships, protecting the family and the right of potential procreation." If the court affirmed Hardwick's victory, it would no longer have a limiting principle when it came to any conduct inside the home.

"Personal sexual freedom is a newcomer among our national values, and may well be, as discussed earlier, a temporary national mood that fades," he wrote. The national "laboratory of experimentation" of different states "properly reflects the differing and sometimes changing values of our people." He added, "I would respect those differences. The right of privacy calls for the greatest judicial restraint, invalidating only those laws that impinge on those values that are basic to our country. I do not think that this case involves any such value. I recommend reversal."[67]

Yale graduate Daniel Richman discovered early in his clerkship Justice Thurgood Marshall's gift for storytelling and his playful relationship with his clerks. Marshall could rib and razz his clerks as well as he could take their verbal jousts. He had grown tired of being in the minority of opinions on the court and saw some of the gains that had been won being diminished or threatened, but his vote in the *Hardwick* case never would be a question. Richman knew Marshall had a long friendship with Bayard Rustin, the gay Black man who had organized the March on Washington in 1963, as a key ally of Martin Luther King Jr. He knew that would inflect the justice's thinking in the *Hardwick* case when he was assigned to it.

In his March 31 memo, Richman recommended Marshall affirm the Eleventh Circuit. In his view, the court didn't need to contemplate whether *Doe* still controlled the case. The court had decided to rule, and it could do what it wanted.

Richman knew the case was very much a case about AIDS, without the word being said or written. The court was culturally and socially disconnected from the queer community, and Richman felt it necessary to steel Marshall against the arguments about the imaginary ills that would come to society if a right to gay sex were recognized. He wrote to Marshall that the petitioner's hints about the AIDS epidemic had no place in this argument.

The Georgia law punished straight and gay people alike. "To repeat the point," Richman stressed, "which I'm sure many members of the Court will forget or ignore: THIS IS NOT A CASE ABOUT ONLY HOMOSEXUALS. ALL SORTS OF PEOPLE DO THIS KIND OF THING." He argued that Georgia had to first explain why it had any interest in the recreational sex of any private citizen. Its law had sanctioned some sex acts, including some that were "incredibly popular among a substantial chunk of the population," while it made others illegal simply because of the participants. That made no sense, Richman proposed. The state could try to argue how sodomy so damaged society that it required legal intervention, but then would have to demonstrate how it intended to patrol the behavior without infringing upon the right to privacy.[68]

The idea of home played greatly into the concerns of Lewis Powell as he mulled over the major questions posed by the case. In a final missive to Mike Mosman, dated March 31, Powell struggled with the idea that homosexuality was legitimate, prevalent, and worthy of legal standing.[69]

He referred to the case "that we should not have taken" as one in which "the facts are straight forward (if one can use that term in this case!)." But Powell found fault with the ruling from the Eleventh Circuit. "The question is now presented to us in the narrowest possible terms. Professor Tribe, with his usual overblown rhetoric, does focus his claim in the narrowest possible language: 'Whether the state of Georgia may send its police into private bedrooms to arrest adults for engaging in consensual, noncommercial sexual acts, with no justification beyond the assertion that those acts are immoral.'"

Powell latched onto Tribe's use of the phrase "sanctity of the home." The home was something created for heterosexual families, in Powell's worldview. "In view of my age, general background and convictions as to what is best for society," he spoke into his Dictaphone, "I think a good deal can be said for the validity of statutes that criminalize sodomy. If it becomes sufficiently widespread, civilization itself will be severely weakened as the perpetuation of the human race depends on normal sexual relations just as is true in the animal world."

That said, were he operating inside a state legislature, Powell wrote he "would vote to decriminalize sodomy," since in many places like San Francisco, the criminal statute was almost never enforced. Police were too busy for that—but none of that was his quandary. His task was to determine whether the sodomy law violated the Constitution, which was silent on the subject. Powell noted that the oft-cited dissent of Justice Harlan in *Poe v. Ullman*, "explicitly refers to homosexuality as not within the right of privacy that he found to exist with respect to the use of contraceptives." The question was whether there was a right of substantive due process—"within the meaning of liberty and privacy—to engage in private, consensual sodomy."

Powell had come to no clear conclusion by the day of oral arguments. He could see that the momentum was toward decriminalization. But he took deep umbrage at the use of the word "home." "I must say that when Professor Tribe refers to the 'sanctity of the home,' I find his argument repellant. Also it is insensitive advocacy. 'Home' is one of the most beautiful words in the English language. It usually connotes family, husband and wife, and children—although, of course, single persons, widows and widowers, and others also have genuine homes."

If Powell were to side with Tribe, to get over his disgust over the equating of gay people's houses with straight people's homes, where would the limits be? Would they be in a bordello, in a public restroom in a gay bar, or in a hotel room? Powell asked none of these questions of the straight couples implicitly sanctioned in the Georgia law for sodomy—but instead wondered if "sodomy is to be decriminalized on constitutional grounds, what about incest, bigamy and adultery." He saw all kinds of precedents set in recent cases, even in his own decision in *Moore v. City of East Cleveland*, which found a local ordinance unconstitutional because it intruded upon the living arrangements between a grandparent and grandchild. If that case's logic held sway, Powell would reverse the Eleventh Circuit and find in favor of Georgia and its sodomy law because Hardwick's case did not involve, or any way affirm, the sustenance of family.

"In sum, Mike, I am sorry you had to be burdened with this case. I probably will not make up my mind until after the oral arguments and Conference discussion. I would, however, like a summary memo as to how the case should be analyzed."[70] Powell initialed the memo, then had it distributed on the morning of March 31, 1986, the day Michael Hardwick strode into the Supreme Court cafeteria to sit in the pews and hear oral arguments in the case that bore his name.

Theater

On the day after Easter in 1986, Michael Hardwick walked across a 252-foot oval plaza toward white columns that graced the entrance to the U.S. Supreme Court. A motto inscribed above the west entrance doors read "Equal Justice Under the Law," while the six-and-a-half-ton bronze doors told the history of law, with figures from Achilles to Chief Justice John Marshall. Hardwick strode past statues by James Earle Fraser that flanked the building. To the right, a male figure embodied the Guardian of Law. To the left, a female figure depicted the Contemplation of Justice. On this visit, Hardwick would not kneel in front of her.

The building had been erected as an edifice to ancient wisdom and omnipotent knowledge—but had been completed only in 1935. It rose four stories tall, with ornate Corinthian columns, clad in marble from Vermont, Georgia, and Alabama, with furniture hewn from American oak. Its grandeur was intended to evoke awe.[1] Its muscular authority came as much from its physical reality as it did from the gravity of the court's body of work, from *Marbury v. Madison* to *Dred Scott v. Sanford* to *Plessy v. Ferguson* to *Brown v. Board of Education*.

Hardwick had flown up from Florida, where he had been living for the past eighteen months. He had remained off the front pages and out of sight from television newspeople. In the months between the case's Supreme Court grant and its oral arguments, reporter Nina Totenberg had come close to finding him in Florida. It might have jeopardized the case, or at least justices' private opinions, if it were made public that he no longer lived in Georgia.[2] Dressed in a gray suit, his hair grown long, Hardwick walked down the hall past portraits of former justices, including one of Frank Murphy, toward a small cafeteria where some of the legal team, including Evan Wolfson, had already ordered breakfast.

A young volunteer for Lambda Legal, Wolfson had been practicing law for just three years. He had joined the ad hoc task force and involved himself in the legal cause against sodomy before Abby Rubenfeld tapped him to write the Lambda amicus brief for *Bowers v. Hardwick*. He sat with Tribe and Koukoutchos, who had invited Wolfson to join them for breakfast, which was unusual. He'd been to arguments before but had never been invited into the inner circle. Wolfson glimpsed Thurgood Marshall, a personal hero, and he also witnessed Tribe withdraw into himself, visibly nervous, while others chatted and ate.

Wolfson looked across the room and saw Hardwick enter. *Who's that?* he wondered. Hardwick, with his good looks, was hard to miss. To Wolfson's delight, the man came to their table. He found Hardwick pleasant, calm, and smart, and already impressed by going to the court. As they moved upstairs to the courtroom, he and Hardwick stood in line together by what Wolfson thought was random luck and then took seats next to each other. On edge but excited, they made small talk while Hardwick was baptized into legal history.[3]

The courtroom chamber was 82 feet wide and 91 feet long, with a 44-foot-tall ceiling. A long, curved mahogany bench for the justices provided visual impact. Above the bench were elaborate regiments of blue laurels and white leaves against a red floral background. On the murals directly over the head of the Chief Justice, two half-naked men sat in judgment at the center of a frieze of bodies in various states of dress. The justices entered through parted towering red-velvet curtains, the stars in the performance of law.

In front of the justices' bench, the counsel sat at their tables near the clerk of the court and marshal of the court, flanked by red benches on either side for special guests and the press. The public sat behind a bronze railing. More than a hundred people could be admitted to observe oral arguments and decisions. They sat on long walnut benches carved in curlicued precision like church pews, studded by brass eyelets used to cordon off the aisles. Pomp was crammed into every corner of the room.

From the public pews, Hardwick had a close view into the workings of power. He could see every expression the justices made.[4] While Hardwick became more relaxed, Tribe grew tenser. Though he relished difficult cases, he did not consider his job entertaining in any way. He had argued ten cases at the Supreme Court prior to this one, but as usual, he was terrified. In the weeks before an oral argument at the court, he would grow anxious and stay that way.[5] Tribe would bring a sheet of paper to the lectern, filled with a blizzard of ideas written in multiple colors with notes and arrows and diagrams, a chaotic chart of legal theory. But he would not refer to the sheet while he presented his case. He read instead the justices' gestures, attention, and body language and focused on them, ignoring the notes he had scrawled.[6] Relief would come once the session began, when he could get into the flow of it.

Chief Justice Burger brought the proceedings to a start, with a call to the petitioner: "The Court will hear arguments first this morning in Bowers against Hardwick. Mr. Hobbs, you may proceed whenever you are ready."[7]

Michael E. Hobbs had inherited the case after Assistant Attorney General George Weaver left the state office for private practice. His nerves struck as he stood. Though he had experience in the federal circuit, this was his first appearance before the Supreme Court. Tribe's presence as opposing counsel amplified his nervousness. Hobbs had held two practice arguments, one in Georgia and one in D.C. He reminded himself what a colleague had told him: The justices conducted their inquiry in a conversational tone; it wasn't combative. That helped, but Hobbs still felt the butterflies when he took to the lectern. He knew Stevens, Marshall, and Brennan were out of reach for his argument. The rest likely would listen and be open to persuasion.[8]

Hobbs, whose soft Georgia accent was just enough to locate him culturally, and perhaps for Powell to identify with him more strongly, told the court that the case asked whether there was a fundamental right for people to engage in "consensual, private homosexual sodomy." He mentioned that the case had never been presented to a grand jury, which drew the first question.

"Was there a reason," Justice Blackmun asked, "that it wasn't presented to the grand jury?"

Hobbs explained that he only knew it would not be presented to the grand jury until further evidence developed.

"How many prosecutions have there been in the last year," Justice Powell asked in his drawn-out Tidewater accent, "or five years?"

Hobbs could not answer that but said that the law typically was enforced when it involved public behavior. The last time it was enforced in a private home, that Hobbs could recall, was in the 1930s or 1940s. He did not know of an instance when it had been enforced against a married couple in their home.

"It is our position," he added, "that there is no fundamental right to engage in this conduct and that the State of Georgia should not be required to show a compelling state interest to prohibit this conduct." In *Carey v. Population Services* the court had written that it did not hold a state must show compelling interest in every question of sexual freedom—and, Hobbs pointed out, "in *Moore vs. City of East Cleveland*, Justice Powell noted the difficulty this Court has sometimes had in defining fundamental rights under the due process clause of the Fourteenth Amendment and suggested, based upon numerous cases of this Court, that appropriate limits and guidelines for determining whether or not rights are truly fundamental can be found in the tradition, history, and heritage of this nation." The court protected the family because of tradition, he argued, and that was the appropriate limiting principle when it came to privacy.

In the audience was another Atlantan, the ACLU of Georgia's Buren Batson, who had been arrested in 1980 for solicitation of sodomy of an undercover Atlanta police officer. Batson later wrote that Hobbs was nervous, "with good reason." Hobbs broke and paused often, and to Batson, the case seemed weak and easy for Powell and others to poke at its holes.[9]

Justice Stevens interrupted Hobbs to ask whether the case could have been brought against a married couple. Hobbs thought it would be unconstitutional, given the court's prior decision, "based upon this Court's findings in *Griswold v. Connecticut* in which Justice Douglas stated the right of marital intimacy is older than our Bill of Rights."

"He didn't say anything about this kind of conduct," Stevens retorted.

"That is correct, Your Honor," Hobbs resumed. "The Court has previously described fundamental rights, whether they be under the general heading of a right of privacy or other fundamental rights, [are] those which are so rooted in the conscience of our people as to be truly fundamental. Principles of liberty and justice which lie at the base of our civil and political institutions, privileges which have long been recognized, a common law as essential to the orderly pursuit of happiness by free men. The simple fact is that homosexual sodomy, which is what is involved in this case, has never in our heritage held a place—"

"Is the record clear," Justice Blackmun interrupted, "as to whether the conduct was with a male or a female?"

"The record, I believe, Your Honor," Hobbs said, "the complaint indicated that Mr. Hardwick was arrested for engaging in [a] sodomitic act with another male." Then he parried the arguments that brought another Georgia case, *Stanley v. Georgia*, into the fray. *Stanley* had been Marshall's majority opinion. It found there existed a right to privacy to consume obscene materials in the home—and its author would be the only justice not to speak during the arguments.

"One wonders if he can," Batson wrote later. "He is so obviously ill. However, he makes his contribution by being here and by being."[10]

Stanley was inapplicable, Hobbs said, because there was no information or idea being expressed that could be defended by the First Amendment. What was at stake here was the redefinition of family to include all kinds of relationships, including nontraditional ones. "Respondent and some amici in this case have argued that perhaps the definition of the family should be changed so as to be extended to homosexuals," he said, "and other types of relationships which have not been recognized in our society thus far so as to accommodate the conduct which is prohibited and elevated to a constitutional status." The state, in other words, had the right to surveil relationships outside of the traditional family.

Justice Stevens asked about the difficulties of enforcing sodomy laws inside the home and pointed out that Hardwick readily admitted that he was frequently engaged in the act of sodomy. Georgia hadn't bothered to prove or argue that point and yet maintained the law. How could those two be squared?"

Stevens was "alert and calm," Batson thought, and would have the most pointed critiques of the state's law and enforcement.[11]

"To be quite frank," Hobbs answered, "I do not know what was in the mind of the District Attorney when he decided not to prosecute this case."

The state had been presented with a "silver platter," Stevens went on, and they declined to go forward. "It seems to me there is some tension between the obvious ability to convict this gentleman and the supposed interest in general enforcement."

Hobbs rerouted the inquiry to safer waters. "It is submitted that this crack-in-the-door argument is truly a Pandora's box for I believe that if the Eleventh Circuit's decision is affirmed that this Court will quite soon be confronted with questions concerning the legitimacy of statutes which prohibit polygamy, homosexual, same-sex marriage, consensual incest, prostitution, fornication, adultery, and possibly even personal possession in private of illegal drugs." Morality was a public issue, he said, and that "it is the right of the nation and of the states to maintain a decent society, representing the collective moral aspirations of the people"—disregarding the idea that those collective moral aspirations could include personal liberty.

From his vantage point in the crowd, Hardwick only heard Hobbs discuss the state's interest in his bedroom, "because it prevented adultery and retarded children and bestiality, and that if they changed the law all of those things would be legal." He thought Hobbs was an "idiot" who "made absolutely no sense."[12]

He was heartened when Laurence Tribe took to the podium. They had only just met, but he understood that Tribe truly believed in his case. Tribe thought Marshall and Brennan believed it profoundly wrong for the government to tell people whom they could love, what they could do in the privacy of their homes, and that they would write powerfully for that position. It was almost inconceivable that there would be five votes in Hardwick's favor, but Tribe had come to believe that it wasn't impossible. He had to believe that. Otherwise, the case would be marked by a sense of failure from the moment he stepped to the lectern.

In the weeks prior to oral arguments, Tribe paced his office, going back and forth, doing little if anything else. He wouldn't talk to anybody about the issues in the case. He wanted to preserve the energy, not drain it. He had convinced himself by the time he stepped to the podium that it might go his way. He had grown up as a lawyer in the brief Camelot of the Warren court and believed the court could bring the better angels of the nation's nature to bear.

"Mr. Tribe?" Chief Justice Burger intoned.

Tribe carried his cardboard primer to the lectern, only to then ignore it, and set out to argue not what Michael Hardwick was doing in his bedroom but what the police were doing there.[13]

"Mr. Chief Justice, and may it please the Court," Tribe began, "this case is about the limits of governmental power. The power that the State of Georgia invoked to arrest Michael Hardwick in the bedroom of his own home is not a power to preserve public decorum. It is not a power to protect children in public or in private. It is not a power to control commerce or to outlaw the infliction of physical harm or to forbid a breach in a state sanctioned relationship such as marriage or, indeed, to regulate the term of a state sanctioned relationship through laws against polygamy or bigamy or incest.

"The power invoked here, and I think we must be clear about it, is the power to dictate in the most intimate and, indeed, I must say, embarrassing detail how every adult, married or unmarried, in every bedroom in Georgia will behave in the closest and most intimate personal association with another adult."

Tribe almost immediately was stopped by Justice Powell. "Professor Tribe, is there a limiting principle to your argument?"

Powell wanted to know how the law could draw a line between consensual acts and those including "bigamy, incest, and prostitution that might also take place in a private home." Powell did not hesitate to ask questions never before asked in the court, in one of its first exposures to queer law.[14] Powell wanted to know whether the principle of privacy would include the backseat of a car, or a public toilet, or a motel room. To some in the room, it seemed Powell might be looking for a place to rule for Hardwick while not undermining laws against sex work, adultery, and bigamy.

Tribe believed he was connecting and making the right points to see a greatly written dissent; by perhaps Powell, he thought, as he grew more confident. If he could sway Powell, the whole world could be different.[15]

Two kinds of limiting principles could be at work, Tribe answered. One was the place—inside the home—but the more critical one, not already affirmed by *Stanley* and other cases, was intimacy itself. "I think it is somewhat broader to be candid, Justice Powell," he said, always careful to answer questions by replying with the justice's name. "I think it includes all physical, sexual intimacies of a kind that are not demonstrably physically harmful that are consensual and noncommercial in the privacy of the home." The state had the burden to prove its interest in legislating the kinds of consensual activity that could go on in the home, and in Hardwick's case, it could not articulate any harm. He reasoned and argued while, unbeknownst to him, Powell had written "torrent of words!" in response.

At this moment, the chief justice—who may have nodded off during the inquiry—jerked his head up and asked Tribe if he had answered the question about incest.[16] "Suppose it is parent and adult child," he prodded. "Those are two consenting adults then perhaps."

The state could reasonably understand how power worked in relationships, Tribe argued: that power could create the illusion of acceptance. Consent could be an illusion, but Tribe added, "there is nothing about this law that limits it to cases where consent is questionable or where there is some other relationship between the parties that makes this other than completely consensual intimacy."

Hardwick watched Tribe argue. He found it incredible and grew even more hopeful. He had never seen a person so in control of themselves and their mind.[17]

Justice Rehnquist parried with Tribe next, leaning back in his wood and black leather chair, hands braced behind his head in casual dismissal. He questioned Tribe with open hostility—and at one point, he left the chamber during Tribe's argument, only to return a moment later.[18] Rehnquist inquired whether the laws against polygamy would be invalidated if Hardwick won. Tribe responded that in Hardwick's case no existing relationship was being violated, thus avoiding that quasi-contractual question.

Would those questions be subject to heightened scrutiny as well? Justice O'Connor asked. Tribe loved being interrupted; he used every question to engage in a conversation about the principle, not to engage in verbal combat. To O'Connor, he said that the state could act on behalf of children and existing relationships with rational reason. It could act with heightened scrutiny were any of these to take place in the home and keep the law so long as it was shown to be in its compelling interest.

Powell tapped Tribe again for further explanation of the sphere of privacy. "I don't think I gave you an opportunity to answer." Would Tribe consider the public toilet, or the back of an automobile, to substitute for "home"? That was uncertain, Tribe answered, but the Fourth Amendment protection against search and seizure had been applied to hotel rooms. Powell then pivoted to *Poe v. Ullman*, the case in which Justice Harlan had specifically excluded sodomy from the purview of privacy.

In a moment of hubris, perhaps, Tribe told Justice Powell that he had "been troubled by parts of the Harlan dissent, in *Moore* which rather casually mentioned homosexuality, and for that matter abortion, in much the same breath." It wasn't absolute immunity Tribe argued for, he said, but heightened scrutiny. *Poe v. Ullman* had rightly recognized that intimacy was an evolving idea; the court had acknowledged as much in *Loving v. Virginia*, when it held that interracial relationships were not inherently immoral, despite hundreds of years of persecution through the law.

Wolfson thought Tribe had engaged with the court. He believed it to be an offensive case to begin with, but despite its tenor he thought it was going well. Wolfson and Hardwick gave each other looks or squeezed a knee when certain things were said. Their physical relationship had begun.

What had changed since *Poe v. Ullman* had specifically called out homosexuality and sodomy? Justice Rehnquist asked. Tribe didn't think Justice Harlan, if presented the *Hardwick* case, "would have decided to draw the line based on which body parts come into contact. I think he would have recognized that the power of the state in a case properly presented, the power of the state to have its own catalogue of how you can touch someone else in the privacy of the home is limited."

"Then he just wrote that part of his dissent in a fit of absent-mindedness?" Rehnquist had pierced Tribe's assuredness, to laughter in the courtroom. Tribe had second-guessed a highly respected jurist in front of a jurist keen on limiting the rights of privacy. The courtroom burst into laughter, perhaps some of it at Tribe's expense.

Tribe continued unabated. "No, I don't think Justice Harlan was capable of fits of absent-mindedness. But, this Court's doctrine about advisory opinions recognizes that even the best justices are at their best when they have a genuine case or controversy before them. And, I do think that we have one here."

While Tribe spoke, Blackmun leaned forward "with obvious relish, not for the issue, but for the debate."[19] He had often been threatened with physical harm since he wrote the *Roe* decision, but he had not backed down from controversial stances. If anything, Blackmun had grown more convinced that respect for the law did not come from punishment meted out through strict interpretation of its original intent. That respect came instead when law was used to end discrimination and to ensure individual autonomy.

Justice White took a turn and asked Tribe which constitutional provision he had relied upon for his arguments. In particular, Tribe said that Hardwick relied upon *Stanley*, as well as *Griswold* and *Eisenstadt* as they affected marital and nonmarital intimacy.

"How do you articulate this right or this process of declaring a—you say is a fundamental right or is it a—how should we go about identifying some new right that should give protection?" White asked.

Tribe began to feel even more encouraged. He had argued for the National Gay Task Force a year prior and felt intense pushback on his every point. As he discussed the *Hardwick* case with the nine justices, he didn't feel that degree of negative response—but he did realize White was openly hostile to the idea of protected privacy rights. White, he believed, thought the whole thing was crazy, that he would even be in front of them pushing the idea that there was a right to engage in oral or anal sex.[20] A long string of decisions, he answered, had established a generalized principle that the court would have to look beyond its ideas of family and marriage—which appeared nowhere in the Constitution—and instead shift its gaze to the individual and their rights to "solace, selectivity, and seclusion."

"If liberty means anything," he said, "it means that the power of government is limited in a way that requires an articulated rationale by government for an intrusion on freedom as personal as this. It is not a characteristic of governments devoted to liberty that they proclaim the unquestioned authority of Big Brother dictate every detail of intimate life in the home. . . . The principle that we champion is a principle of limited government, it is not a principle of a special catalogue of rights."

The chief justice returned to Hobbs for a final statement. "The State of Georgia is not acting as [B]ig [B]rother in this particular case," Hobbs concluded. "It is adhering to centuries-old tradition and the conventional morality of its people. . . . Each statute enacted by any state must be rationally related to a legitimate government purpose and it is submitted most respectfully to Mr. Tribe that this statute is related to the legitimate purpose of maintaining a decent and moral society. It is inherently intertwined with the state's concern with the moral soundness of its people . . . In summary, the liberty that exists under our Constitution is not unrestrained. It is ordered liberty, it is not licentiousness. If the Eleventh Circuit's decision is affirmed in this case, the State of Georgia and other states will be impeded for making those distinctions between true liberty, ordered liberty, and licentiousness. Thank you very much, Mr. Chief Justice."

"Thank you, gentlemen," Burger concluded. "The case is submitted."

Hardwick and the swarm of attorneys made their way outside to the front steps of the court, under the pediment where EQUAL JUSTICE UNDER LAW is inscribed, when the arguments concluded. Batson watched Hardwick as Larry Tribe took questions. Hardwick stood aside, mostly unknown, and avoided the spotlight. When Batson leaned in and asked him, "How does it feel, if only for a moment, to have the undivided attention of the entire nation?" Hardwick answered him only with a smile.[21]

The cluster of forty or more people on Hardwick's team then walked a few blocks from the Supreme Court to the American Cafe, upbeat if not jubilant. Most thought the case had been well argued; many thought it would result in a victory. Some on the team of lawyers foresaw a 4–4–1 upholding of the Eleventh Circuit's findings, one in which Justice Powell stood apart to argue that Georgia's punishment for sodomy constituted cruel and unusual punishment. Some exuberantly thought a 7–2 decision in Hardwick's favor could be possible. The ACLU began to prepare for the decision with draft statements and a possible national press conference, since a both a win and a loss seemed possible.[22]

Tribe remained circumspect. His hopes had been elevated, but he still felt as if they would lose the majority. His arguments and the legal team's work on Hardwick's case had given them the material for dissent from four justices that would prove inherently useful in the next stage of the battle for equality. If they didn't win this case, they had advanced the notion of equality during an especially fraught time for queer America.

Rubenfeld, meanwhile, felt sure they had won. Hell, she had put on a skirt for the case, she thought, and some people could hardly believe that. As they ate, she saw from the corner of her eye that Hardwick and Wolfson got up to leave together, saying their goodbyes. The queer members of the team chuckled to and between themselves. Tribe didn't seem to understand why they were leaving.

Larry, someone told him, *they're going out to do just what you fought for their right to do.*

Rubenfeld just smiled. Wolfson was her friend, and she was happy for him. Both he and Hardwick were single, the moment was ripe, and good for them.[23]

Wilde leaned close to Hardwick. "Don't get arrested again," she counseled.

It had been unusually warm and pleasant in Washington, and the cherry blossoms framing the Tidal Basin showered the men in pink petals. It was Washington at its most innocent, and its most enchanting. They walked the basin toward the White House, where they kissed in defiance as much as they did out of the joy and exhilaration of the day. Then Hardwick took off in a cab for the airport and his flight back to Miami, while Wolfson headed toward Union Station for the train back to New York.[24]

Reversal

John Paul Stevens scribbled in his almost indecipherable chicken scratch, while Harry Blackmun took careful notes in beautiful penmanship. The justices had waited until their regular meeting on Wednesday, April 2, to discuss the merits of *Hardwick*. The court preserved its own mystique by holding these meetings with no clerks, in front of no court audience, and with no cameras or recording equipment present.

Blackmun had spent much of the previous ten years fending off hostile opinions from citizens and fellow jurists alike. Though a constant flurry of cases had already threatened to overturn *Roe*, as of 1986, the right to have an abortion was as entrenched as it ever would be.[1] *Roe* was the opinion Blackmun felt would be his hallmark. "We all pick up tabs," he said. "I'll carry that one to my grave."

Roe had broadened his mind, and as he began to comprehend all the morally fraught and uplifting consequences of the decision, Blackmun became more progressive, dissenting as early as 1978 in favor of gay rights. He had met queer people when he was a child, and when he was being brought up, their sex lives had been anathema.[2] But he had changed. He had hired his share of queer clerks, and he held them as dear as he did the rest. He believed they were good people.[3] It was clear, in the *Hardwick* case, that Blackmun would vote to affirm the right to privacy and liberty.

He and Warren Burger had been childhood friends. What had gone so differently between them that their opinions would be so radically different? Burger would be a clear vote to overturn the Eleventh Circuit's decision, but only in the days and rapidly changing atmosphere inside the justice's chambers would it become clear how markedly the two Minnesotans had diverged in opinion and how far the chief justice would go to cultivate a decision in Georgia's favor.

Around the room were a generation of legal minds that had seen America emerge from one nadir of the civil rights for Black men and women, only to sit at the precipice of another, that of queer people. None had professed anything other than heterosexuality, but they sat in judgement of queer people nonetheless. The gravity of the case coupled intimately with the absurdity of the era. Culturally liberated in some ways but increasingly retrograde in others, America was a place where any adult could watch other adults have sex on movie or TV screens but could not do with their own genitals as they pleased.

Burger opened the April 2 conference by insisting the *Hardwick* case was about the right only to homosexual sodomy, which had been governed by law in Georgia since the early 1800s. Tradition limited the right to privacy, and in this case, no fundamental right to privacy existed. He cast his lot with reversal.[4]

White, whose very first dissent on the court in *Robinson v. California* had been one in which he argued against "judge-made constitutional law," struggled with even more basic concessions to the culture of modernity.[5] In the case of *Malley v. Briggs*, which was decided just before *Hardwick*'s oral arguments, White wrote for the court that the police could be sued if they made an unconstitutional arrest even if in possession of a proper warrant. White danced around the issue central to the case, an arrest for marijuana, and wrote out definitions as if the testimony needed translation: "doing her thing" was to him "rolling a marihuana cigarette."[6] The justice's spelling of the drug led to its own internal debate: was the drug spelled "marijuana" or "marihuana"? The former had become the norm, but the latter still littered court documents. The court persisted in many traditional ways while the rest of the world had moved on.[7]

By the time of the conference, Powell had begun to explore ways in which to affirm the Eleventh Circuit. But he could not identify with homosexuals or the pressure they now applied for civil recognition. If there were a justice for whom the "Homo 101" briefs were written, it was Powell who needed them the most. And yet, among the court's other justices and among the pools of clerks, it was widely understood that Powell had a unique advantage he didn't even realize: he had chosen a succession of gay clerks, and among his staff that year there was at least one gay man.[8] Powell had said during conference for the *Hardwick* case to his colleague Harry Blackmun, "Harry, I've never known a homosexual in my life."[9] In response, Blackmun said as he later related it to one of his clerks, "'Look around your chambers.'"[10]

Blackmun had made oblique reference to Powell clerk C. Cabell Chinnis, also from Virginia like Powell, mostly discreet about his queer identity although Powell had met his partner. Chinnis assumed Powell must have known he was queer. Why else would Powell have consulted with Chinnis about the particulars of gay sex? In his indecision over the *Hardwick* case, Powell had asked Chinnis in the presence of other clerks how gay men maintained erections, even though Michael Mosman and not Chinnis had been assigned to the case. Chinnis would come to believe that Powell had tried to protect him by feigning a lack of knowledge about queer people.[11]

Mosman had written a memo on April 1 to dissuade Powell from agreeing with Tribe's privacy angle, arguing that society had traditionally protected heterosexual marriage. He believed that saying gay relationships deserved protection because they resembled marriage would be "bootstrapping." It could lead to the suggestion that gay people could "adopt and raise children," and would naturally lead to the nullification of restrictions on gay people becoming public school teachers.[12]

Powell, in contrast, looked toward the Eighth Amendment as a compromise. If he voted to maintain Georgia's sodomy law, he could at least write that any punishment would be unconstitutional, as Georgia's potential twenty-year sentence for sodomy could be deemed cruel and unusual punishment. He queried Chinnis twice more as he struggled to find a rationale that could satisfy all his concerns and prejudices. Chinnis prepared to out himself to Powell and to explain how a decision against Hardwick could damage him and his relationship but felt that Powell had moved toward an affirmation of Hardwick's legal rights.[13] His instinct was proven correct at the first conference vote, when Powell cast his lot with Hardwick and with those who would affirm the Eleventh Circuit.[14]

They included Brennan, who found Hardwick's privacy rights in *Stanley*. Marshall, who'd authored *Stanley*, agreed. Blackmun voted in favor of Hardwick based on the logic held in his *Roe* opinion. Stevens voted to affirm and noted that if a married couple engaged in sodomy, they certainly had a right to privacy. Rehnquist, White, and Burger voted to reverse the Eleventh Circuit, as expected. O'Connor voted to reverse as well, on the grounds that the right to privacy was not absolute and that it did not preclude state laws like this one. The tally: 5–4, affirming the Eleventh Circuit's decision in Michael Hardwick's favor.

At the end of the session, the chief justice assigned *Bowers* to Harry Blackmun, who knew what havoc an opinion could bring upon his family. Someone had fired a shot into Blackmun's apartment in anger over *Roe* when his wife was home.[15]

Chinnis was elated by Powell's vote, and somewhat shocked,

since just days before the justice had told him that he had never met a homosexual. Flabbergasted, Chinnis had responded that couldn't be the case. Now Powell seemed to show a newfound sensitivity to the lives of queer people. Perhaps one day Chinnis might be able to reintroduce Powell to Chris, not as the "friend from New Orleans" who already had met the justice, but as his partner.[16]

Everyone on Hardwick's legal team knew Powell would be the critical vote in the case. Many of them also knew about Powell's gay clerks. Wilde tried to convince others that they should contact one of them. If they could connect, they might be able to convince the clerk to out themselves to Powell, in the hopes that it might sway Powell and win his vote.

The discussion went nowhere, as some thought it was too much to ask of anyone. Wilde didn't think so. It might be too much to expect a clerk to step forward and come out. Powell might consider it completely improper and out of bounds. But if they did not ask, they carried an even greater risk of losing the most important gay civil-rights case in history. In talks outside of Wilde's purview, the idea was dismissed.[17]

Once the conference ended, Chief Justice Burger lobbied Powell hard to change his vote. In an April 3 memo, Burger took aim at Powell's vacillation and at his contention that Hardwick could not be punished for his homosexuality, much as a drug addict could not be punished for their addiction. Burger, who held a degree in psychiatry, held this as nonsense.

"I have never heard of any responsible member (or even an 'avant-garde' member) of the A.P.A. who recognized homosexuality as an 'addiction' in the sense of drug addiction. It is simply without any basis in medicine, science, or common human experience. In fact these homosexuals themselves proclaim this is a matter of sexual 'preference.' Moreover, even if homosexuality is somehow conditioned, the decision to commit an act of sodomy is a choice, pure and simple—maybe not so pure!"[18]

Hardwick's team hadn't made this argument because it might subject Michael to some kind of compulsory treatment program, Burger wrote. He admonished Powell for promoting Eighth and Fourteenth Amendment arguments he found "extremely dangerous" because they might limit states' abilities to criminalize "incest, prostitution, or any other 'consensual' activity." Such a precedent could even sanction queer teachers or queer Boy Scout leaders. "In short, your argument would swallow up centuries of criminal law . . . Are those with an 'orientation' towards rape to be let off merely because they allege that the act of rape is 'irresistible' to them? Are we to excuse every 'Jack the Ripper'?"[19]

Powell scrawled notes in the margins of Burger's memo. "There is both sense and nonsense in this letter," he wrote, "mostly the latter." He circled Burger's statement about Hardwick's case being "the most far-reaching issue" of the chief's career: "Incredible statement!"[20] The Virginian, genteel and polite, did not hold Burger's intellect in the highest of regard. He called the balding chief "The Great White Doughnut" behind his back because the ring of white hair on his head framed nothing. He found Burger's invocation of incest, drug use, and gambling and the like to be "irrelevant" in this case: "the C.J. should know this." And yet, Powell decided to reverse himself. At the top of Burger's note, Powell wrote, "I have changed my vote to Reverse, but I adhere to my 8th Amend position."[21]

Blackmun believed he was writing a majority opinion until April 4, when Powell called to tell him that he was changing his vote in *Hardwick*.[22] On April 8, Powell circulated a memo in which he displayed deep regret over his initial decision to affirm the *Hardwick* case against Georgia. While he worried that a potential Hardwick conviction could have led to a sentence of up to twenty years, he did not believe that the right to privacy existed for behavior that "has been recognized as deviant and not in the best interest of humanity."[23]

In response, Justice Stevens reminded Powell he had another choice: he could issue an opinion that said the court was "equally divided" and neither concur nor dissent.[24] But his plea was in vain. Chief Justice Burger reassigned the majority opinion to Byron White on April 9. Blackmun began to turn his majority opinion into a dissent.

In cases where he knew he would not be in the majority, Blackmun wrote with muscular language, in the knowledge that his opinions might one day be used to give shape to the laws that would govern those who lived after him.[25] Blackmun had come to believe that judicial ideology meant less to him than the effect every case had on the people affected by it. No matter how great a legal philosophy seemed in writing, it failed in practice if justices forgot the humanity of the litigants.[26] Even so, Michael Hardwick had rarely entered the discussion about the case on a personal level. Not much, if any, time was spent inside the chambers thinking about Michael Hardwick at all.[27]

White circulated his draft opinion on April 21. Blackmun thought it was the worst opinion he had ever written. It was *ipse dixit*—in other words, "this is what the law is or ought to be." In essence, without any analysis whatsoever.[28] He hoped that when White read his dissent, he might propose some changes to the majority opinion, but that did not happen. The two would remain like "two ships passing in the night."[29]

The Supreme Court made mistakes, but they tried to make as few as possible, even when one justice changed their mind.[30] Blackmun thought White had missed the point entirely. Blackmun didn't want Big Brother in the bedrooms of America. He didn't want the knock on the door late at night. The Fourth Amendment existed to protect against that; the Fourteenth Amendment implied that. Blackmun would be distressed to learn his own children had committed sodomy, but who was he to choose for them?[31] What was held as a sin was not always a crime, and vice versa.

Queer people would find little dignity in the Supreme Court, and even less in the public sphere when the subject turned to AIDS. They were forced to decide whether to be tested for the virus and to be branded by their status if it were disclosed, or to remain silent and wait out their death sentence.

But hope was in the offing. On April 11, the experimental drug Compound S—also known as azidothymidine, or AZT—was announced to have gone through a Phase One study at Duke University and the National Cancer Institute. Most of the patients who had been given the drug saw an increase in T cells and the remission of other symptoms. Encouraging results meant the testing of the drug would move to a second phase. A protocol location had been established in Miami.

While those infected waited for effective treatment or even a cure, those farthest on the political right raised the prospect of mass quarantine. In a March 18, 1986, column in the *New York Times*, conservative commentator William F. Buckley Jr. advocated for tattooing all people with AIDS—whom he mistakenly conflated with those infected by HIV—and said it needed to be done "in the upper forearm, to protect common-needle users, and on the buttocks, to prevent the victimization of other homosexuals," thereby implying that all acts of sex between queer people involved the buttocks. The tattoos were vital to protect the health of everyone else: "A generation ago, homosexuals lived mostly in the closet. Nowadays they take over cities and parade on Halloween and demand equal rights for themselves qua homosexuals, not merely as apparently disinterested civil libertarians."[32] They were roaming freely, in Buckley's worst nightmare.

Buckley was not alone, or even novel in his call to strip medical privacy from those who might be afflicted. In April of 1986, California political radical and frequent far-right presidential candidate Lyndon LaRouche had put forth a state ballot measure that would label AIDS patients as "suspects" and would call for their quarantine. Anyone who had AIDS and those "suspect" of having AIDS (which included gay men and needle-drug users) would be reported to local health bureaus and could be confined or isolated. People with AIDS would be prohibited from working in the food-and-beverage industry and could not travel outside their area without permission from local health officials. LaRouche followers obtained nearly 700,000 signatures—nearly twice the required 393,833—to place the initiative on California's November ballot.

During the time between oral arguments and the reading of the decision, advocates were hoping that the Supreme Court would issue a strong affirmation of the right to privacy and of the dignity of queer people. On April 16 on the Gay Cable Network, Evan Wolfson said that the argument had gone well, and that "the court seemed respectful, interested, genuinely wrestling with the issues of this case." He felt that the state had argued for a traditional view of morality and hadn't offered any other reason to have a sodomy law. He hoped the court would uphold the Eleventh Circuit and require that Georgia go to trial to demonstrate why it had the right to "step into citizens' bedrooms and tell them how to live their lives."[33]

Others were sanguine about the prospects for a win, and about what a win might mean. The ACLU's Nan Hunter said that gay rights had become an irrevocable part of the discourse, in part due to AIDS, and in part due to Hardwick's case. She hoped that he would win, even if it were a narrow decision, but didn't expect any "sweeping judgements on the morality of lesbian and gay relations." If Hardwick won, the movement would seek to eradicate all remaining sodomy laws—"all hell will break loose on that issue"—but if he lost, it would signal "a major retrenchment."[34]

Tom Stoddard, executive director of Lambda Legal Defense and Education Fund, wondered at the possible outcome that could be announced any day. "Who would have guessed 15 years ago," he said, "that *Newsweek* would do a cover story on growing up gay? Who would have guessed that a midwestern state [Wisconsin] would adopt a gay rights statute? Fifteen years ago, we were still trying to convince people that we existed. I am optimistic about the future—it will be ours."[35]

Justice Byron White read from his majority opinion on June 30, 1986, as the Supreme Court issued its decision in *Bowers v. Hardwick*, against Michael Hardwick.

"This case does not require a judgment on whether laws against sodomy between consenting adults in general, or between homosexuals in particular, are wise or desirable," he said, then proceeded to affirm exactly that kind of decision—that sodomy laws should exist, based solely on precedent. "No connection between family, marriage, or procreation on the one hand and homosexual activity on the other has been demonstrated, either by the Court of Appeals or by respondent."

Sodomy had been forbidden since colonial times, White said, and all but five states made it illegal in 1868, when the Fourteenth Amendment was ratified. Almost half of the states still made sodomy illegal and because of that, "to claim that a right to engage in such conduct is 'deeply rooted in this Nation's history and tradition' or 'implicit in the concept of ordered liberty' is, at best, facetious."

White warned that the Supreme Court had erred in its expansion of the rights implied by substantive due process, and that it ventured toward illegitimacy when it approached "judge-made constitutional law having little or no cognizable roots in the language or design of the Constitution." If it found a right to consensual sodomy without limits, he wrote, it would be difficult to limit the prosecution of incest and adultery, among other crimes. The law was built on contemporary ideas about morality, and if the due process clause could invalidate them, "the courts will be very busy indeed."

In a stinging rebuke to the gay-rights movement, Chief Justice Warren Burger wrote in his concurrence that Georgia had made "crimes against nature" illegal since 1816 and that, as descended from English common law, crimes against nature were considered worse than rape. "Condemnation of those practices is firmly rooted in Judeo-Christian moral and ethical standards," he wrote. "To hold that the act of homosexual sodomy is somehow protected as a fundamental right would be to cast aside millennia of moral teaching." In Burger's worldview, the state not only could be the voyeur in the queer bedroom, it had the moral charge to do so.

Justice Lewis F. Powell intimated in his concurrence that, had Hardwick been convicted and jailed, his view would have been different based on Georgia's onerous twenty-year maximum sentence. "In my view, a prison sentence for such conduct—certainly a sentence of long duration—would create a serious Eighth Amendment issue," he wrote. He agreed, however, that there was no right under the Fourteenth Amendment to engage in sodomy.

In dissent, Justice Blackmun argued that "the Court's almost obsessive focus on homosexual activity" could not be justified with so broad a law, especially one enforced almost exclusively against gay men.[36] Blackmun took the unusual step of reading his dissent from the bench. Once a year or so a justice would do that; Justices Harlan and Black had done so against Blackmun when he read the majority opinion in *Roe*.[37] Blackmun felt strongly that his message should be preserved in more than a dissent buried behind the poorly argued screed. As he spoke, the words that would suffuse the gay-rights movement for the difficult years to come echoed throughout the room.

> *I have filed a dissent in this case and it is joined by Justice Brennan, Justice Marshall, and Justice Stevens. Justice Stevens has also filed a separate dissent and is joined by Justice Brennan and Justice Marshall.*
>
> *The five Justices making up the bare majority recite more than once that what the case involves is an asserted "fundamental right to engage in homosexual sodomy." Those of us in dissent feel that that is not so at all. This case is no more about such an alleged fundamental right than* Stanley v. Georgia *was about a fundamental right to watch obscene movies or than* Katz v. United States *was about a fundamental right to place interstate bets from a telephone booth. What this case is about is what Justice Brandeis called "the most comprehensive of rights and the right most valued by civilized men," namely, "the right to be let alone."*

The Court concludes almost without analysis, in our view, that the Georgia statute is valid essentially because the laws of many States still make such conduct illegal and have done so for "a very long time." The fact that moral judgments expressed by statutes like this one may be natural and familiar, however, ought not to conclude our judgment upon the question whether statutes embodying them conflict with the Constitution of the United States. Justice Holmes observed that it is revolting to have no better reason for a rule of law than that it was laid down in the time of Henry IV. He went on to say that it is still more revolting if the grounds upon which it was laid down have vanished long since, and the rule "simply persists from blind imitation of the past." I agree and believe that we must analyze respondent's claim in the light of values that underlie the constitutional right to privacy. If that right means anything, it means that, before Georgia can prosecute its citizens for making choices about the most intimate aspects of their lives, it must do more than assert that the choice they have made is what the Georgia Supreme Court has called "an abominable crime not fit to be named among Christians."

So far as the Georgia statute is concerned, the sex or status of the persons who engage in the Act is irrelevant as a matter of state law. The purpose seems to have been to broaden the coverage of the law to reach heterosexual as well as homosexual activity. Thus, Hardwick's standing may rest in significant part on Georgia's willingness to enforce against homosexuals a law it seems not to have any desire whatsoever to enforce against heterosexuals, despite the statute's obvious application to the latter.

Our cases long have recognized that the Constitution embodies a promise that a certain private sphere of individual liberty will be kept largely beyond the reach of government. What is at issue here is what is done in the bedroom in one's home. The home is the place to which *the Fourth Amendment attaches special significance. Justice Jackson in the flag salute case decided in 1943 observed that freedom to differ is not limited to things that do not matter much.*

That, he said, would be a mere shadow of freedom. The test of its substance is the right to differ as to things that touch the heart of the existing order. It is precisely because the issue raised by this case touches the heart of what makes individuals what they are that we should be especially sensitive to the rights of those whose choices upset the majority. That certain religious groups condemn the behavior at issue gives the State no license to impose their judgments on the entire citizenry. This statute has a religious base. Its very name, derived from the city of Sodom, illustrates this.

It seems to us that Georgia and the Court fail to see the difference between laws that protect public sensibilities and those that enforce private morality. The mere fact that intimate behavior may be proscribed when it takes place in public, as everyone concedes it may, cannot dictate how States can regulate intimate behavior that occurs in intimate places.

This case involves no real interference with the rights of others, for the mere knowledge that other individuals do not adhere to one's value system cannot be a legally cognizable interest, let alone an interest that can justify invading the houses and the hearts and the minds of citizens who choose to live their lives differently. It seems to us in the dissent that depriving individuals of the right to choose for themselves how to conduct their intimate relationships in private poses a far greater threat to the values most deeply rooted in our Nation's history than tolerance of nonconformity could ever do.[38]

Blackmun remained seated next to White, as usual, when he finished. They acknowledged each other and remained cordial. Blackmun watched reporters get up immediately to leave the courtroom and write their stories.[39] The decision was one of hundreds the court would issue that term. It was time to move on to the next one.

Blackmun had done his best to change minds. A court messenger brought him a note that hinted at Thurgood Marshall's still collegial but now weary tone.

"You was good."[40]

Rick and Kitty Hardwick met at a Miami Beach USO dance, and within a decade had four children. Top photo, circa 1955: Alice, Rick, Michael, Susan, and Patrick. Lower photo, circa 1958: (*Top row*) Alice, Patrick, Kitty, and Rick. (*Bottom row*) Michael and Susan. (Photos courtesy of Susan Browning-Chriss)

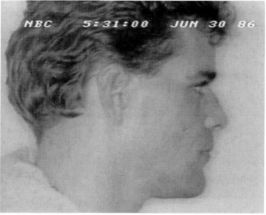

In the days before his August 3, 1982, arrest for sodomy and marijuana possession, Michael Hardwick had been involved in a fight—with three men, he said, unknown to him. (Still video frames from Vanderbilt TV News Archive, via NBC News. Atlanta's police department declined to provide the original mug shots.)

Police arrested Mobile native Dwight Sawyer along with Michael for sodomy and possession of marijuana. (Photo by Joseph Potter)

Opposite photo: During the summer of 1986, protesters decried the *Hardwick* decision by taking to the streets. On July 17, 1986, in San Francisco, protestors picketed an appearance by Justice Sandra Day O'Connor: RESPONDING TO YOUR DARKEST FEARS . . . AMERICA'S 30 MILLION QUEERS, read one banner. (Photo by Tom Levy / *San Francisco Chronicle* via Getty Images)

Hardwick spoke before thousands of protestors who amassed at the Supreme Court on the morning of October 13, 1987, at the conclusion of the march on Washington. (© JEB [Joan E. Biren])

Police arrested some 600 people, including Hardwick, during the Supreme Court protest on October 13, 1987. (*Washington Blade* photo by Doug Hinckle)

After his loss at the Supreme Court, Hardwick became a well-known designer and artist in the burgeoning Miami Beach nightclub scene. Pictured: Susan Browning-Chriss, Michael Hardwick, and Jasmine Browning outside Hardwick's Miami Beach studio at 550 Meridian Ave. (Photo courtesy of Susan Browning-Chriss)

Hardwick's artwork included an "atomic garden" of crepe flowers and a wire-mesh angel that hung over the bar at Jack Kearney's nightclub, Squeeze. (Photo courtesy of Susan Browning-Chriss)

Michael spent the last six months of his life with family in Gainesville, Florida, before he died of complications from HIV/AIDS on June 13, 1991. (Photo courtesy of Susan Browning-Chriss)

RESURRECTION IV

Backlash

Michael Hardwick rose from bed early on June 30, 1986, and at about nine in the morning, he walked to Uncle Charlie's to occupy himself with side work. He hadn't been able to sleep. The looming decision had given him a nervous gut for weeks. He jumped at the sound of the phone. Not due at work until eleven, he had gone in to prep the complimentary buffet the bar served during happy hour.[1]

A friend rushed into the bar, in tears. *I'm so sorry.* He had seen a report on CNN and, not finding Hardwick at his apartment, went to Charlie's.

For a moment, Hardwick tried to calm his friend down. He was bewildered and could hardly understand what his friend was telling him. The case had been decided, his friend said. *Michael, you lost.*

Hardwick wept for the next few hours. He had been so optimistic after going to Washington and witnessing what he thought would be a turn in history. He sat stunned in disbelief.[2]

The decision demeaned queer people. It relied heavily on tradition and on the Bible for its pronouncements. Hardwick had been convinced he was right, and that he had the perfect case, but the Supreme

Court could not get past its own prejudices. He lived in a country woefully unprepared to honor its commitment to liberty.

God, he thought, *it was all for nothing.*[3]

Abby Rubenfeld dialed the Supreme Court office, as she did every day the court issued opinions. The 5–4 was in—and had been written by Justice White. "Are you sure you have the right case?" she asked. She choked on her own emotions. How could they lose? What would they do now? Was she an outlaw too?[4]

Before Abby could reach her, Kathy Wilde got a call from an Atlanta reporter who asked abruptly, "What's your comment?"

"What's the question?"

"You just lost in the Supreme Court."

"Oh shit, I'll call you back."[5]

Wilde tried to wait until Hardwick's normal work hours to call, but by eleven o'clock, she had received a maelstrom of press requests. She felt sure he must have found out about the decision, but they hadn't spoken since oral arguments in March.[6] They would not speak for at least one more day.

Laurence Tribe felt kicked in the gut when he learned of the decision. He had not expected to win but was appalled and dumbfounded that the court would decide the case in the language and for the reasons they chose. It smacked of puritanism. He was devastated.[7] The law was indifferent toward the plight of gays and lesbians. "The privacy of the home, and the inner sanctum of the bedroom, is not secure from Big Brother," he told the network news. "It's really hard to know where the power of government stops."[8]

Evan Wolfson was still in bed that morning when his friend Roz Richter called to tell him. He had been so excited during the oral arguments and thought Hardwick might have won. He felt betrayed by White's opinion, that queer people's claims to equal rights were "facetious." That day, he walked to the Oscar Wilde Bookshop and purchased a pink triangle pin, which he swore to wear until the court overturned its decision.[9]

Kirk Slusser sat with his family when he heard the news on TV. He didn't say anything to them, but disappointment stabbed him. He went to the library and tried to read coverage of the case in the newspapers. He didn't know how to reach Hardwick. He didn't even know if he still was in Atlanta.[10]

Dwight Sawyer heard it on television and read about it the next day in the *New York Times*. If he and Hardwick had been caught in Piedmont Park, maybe the arrest would have been justified, he thought—but when a police officer walked into a home and arrested consenting adults, that wasn't the law. That was an intrusion upon queer people's lives, one that used the law as convenient cover.[11]

From his Atlanta office, Georgia attorney general Mike Bowers told an ABC News reporter that "The Supreme Court, in upholding our statute, has said that public morality is a legitimate basis upon which to make distinctions."[12] The reporter noted the ruling "may discourage those who have AIDS from coming forward to seek treatment," then was followed by an update on the development of AZT and other drugs used to treat AIDS.

On CNN, an exultant Jerry Falwell claimed a "moral renaissance" for the country on *Larry King Live*, one in which the church and the government would unite to exorcise the "soulless hedonism" of queerness from America.[13] Indifferent to the loss of political status for queer people and the implications for equality that the decision would draw in bright relief, Falwell cheered while gays and lesbians were deemed second-class citizens.

Hardwick tried to work the rest of his normal shift that day, but the funereal procession of friends who came by to grieve with him distracted him instead. Those who knew him and knew of his case kept offering their regrets. All he wanted was silence.

When he couldn't get it, he asked to be put behind the bar, so he could tend to customers and forget the whole thing had happened. He did that until about eight o'clock, when a reporter from WFOR-TV channel 4 burst into the club with cameras rolling, a horrifying reminder of the days when bars were raided.[14]

The reporter wanted an interview, but Hardwick fled upstairs to his manager's office to wait him out, trembling with fear and on the verge of tears once more. The reporter eventually left after the bar manager told her that Hardwick would have no comment until the next day. Hardwick wrote a short statement to be delivered to any other reporter who found him, then went home and went numb.

Hardwick's case buoyed the conservative movement. "The highest court has recognized the right of a state to determine its own moral guidelines," Jerry Falwell said as he applauded the decision, "and it has issued a clear statement that perverted moral behavior is not accepted practice in this country."[15] Conservative commentator Cal Thomas believed the Supreme Court had seen "the darkness proceeding out of the rapidly increasing number of AIDS cases. . . . Had the court legitimized sodomy throughout the country by striking down the Georgia statute, it would have sent the wrong signal at a time when caution and even celibacy among homosexuals ought to be what is being called for. This is a time to focus, not on 'gay pride' or on 'gay rights,' but on 'gay wrongs.' "[16]

Queer activists erupted in outrage. "We believed in the Constitution," California lesbian activist Pat Norman told *Newsweek*. "Guess what? It doesn't mean us."[17]

"Not since the Supreme Court declared in the Dred Scott case that slavery was legal and blacks were not citizens has there been a high court ruling as seeped in prejudice as this one," queer author John Rechy wrote in an op-ed. Issued on the eve of Independence Day, the ruling had eroded queer trust in the justice system. Younger queer people felt betrayed, while older queers saw the "potential return to the violent repression of years past"—which included "prison sentences of up to life; suicides; blackmail resulting from arrests; roundups out of gay bars and into waiting police vans."[18]

Before a day had elapsed, the community responded in what was becoming their usual manner: protest. The first sign of the conflagration to come erupted in New York and San Francisco on the evening of June 30. In San Francisco, hundreds of angry protesters went to Harvey Milk Plaza to rebuke the court that had revoked their citizenship, attacked them, interfered with their private lives, and denied their equality.

One of the leaders of the protest read Hardwick's official statement to the crowd:[19]

It is inconceivable in this day of enlightenment that our highest court should express and demonstrate a mentality that would be more suitable for the hierarchy of the Spanish Inquisition, not the Supreme Court of the U.S. . . . This is not specifically a homosexual issue as the court would conveniently have us believe. This is a human rights issue and is a flagrant violation of all peoples' constitutional rights. We did not lose today if this arcane decision by the Supreme Court emphasizes how important it is for us to be visible. The decision by the Supreme Court places individual freedom back 200 years. It endangers the freedom of every adult in the United States.[20]

Amid signs scrawled in haste—THE SUPREME COURT CAN SCREW FAGGOTS, SO WHY CAN'T I?—attorney Mary C. Dunlap took a copy of the decision in front of the crowd and ripped it to pieces. It was her coming out, in a legal and professional sense, as she tossed the pieces in the air and let them rain down over her.[21]

Nancy Langer stood huddled with her girlfriend while protesters shouted in agitation and confusion. The associate director of Lambda Legal, Langer had attended the November strategy meeting for the *Hardwick* case. On the morning of the decision, she went to work at the ACLU building in Manhattan, armed with her usual cup of coffee and muffin, headed for the tiny office where Lambda worked on queer cases. The long holiday weekend was coming, and only a few people had shown up that day. No one picked up the press line when it rang, so Langer did. It was Kathy Wilde, in tears, calling to relay the news of the decision.

As she spoke with other colleagues throughout the day, Langer learned that a permit to protest had been issued. After work, she and her girlfriend, Allison Sue Smith, went to Sheridan Square to join the hundreds of people who angrily massed as night fell. The crowd spilled over Seventh Avenue, chanting, "It's time for militancy!" and "No more nice guys!"[22]

Speakers took to the mic to protest. The court's decision, said

Douglas White, New York State Commissioner of Human Rights, was "in keeping with Gestapo or KGB tactics . . . any person suspected of variant sexual activity would be fair game for overzealous police officers and spiteful neighbors."[23]

Smith urged Langer to announce a protest march. *We can't take this sitting down.* Outraged, Langer grabbed the mic and told the crowd, "We all know what's going to happen July 4th—Warren Burger will be in town." A massive celebration to rechristen the Statue of Liberty had been planned for the weekend. Burger's appearance would be the perfect backdrop for protest. People raised their fists in the air. Some filmed it, as much for posterity as to preserve a video record in case the police grew overzealous.[24]

Langer had taken the gay leadership present by surprise. A protest was not the plan. The plan had been to head to the Hamptons or Fire Island and spend the lazy summer weekend at parties, not to plan and stage a huge protest. Langer didn't care. She went to a copy store near the square with a young gay man from the crowd, drew up a handwritten flyer announcing the protest on July 4—it encouraged protesters to "disrupt traffic, snarl subways and show our rage"—had a couple hundred copies printed, and dove back into the crowd to hand them out.[25]

After ninety minutes of speeches, another activist, Buddy Nor, instructed the crowd to stage a sit-in along Seventh Avenue. Police detoured traffic around the squatters, and after half an hour the group had filled the block to the east along Christopher Street, toward Sixth Avenue. Standing up to move, they sang "We Shall Overcome" as they flowed toward Greenwich Avenue and sat again, shutting down traffic for nearly four hours until they finally dispersed after midnight.[26]

Tom Stoddard called Langer into his office the next morning. *This isn't what Lambda Legal Defense can do,* he explained. *We have to take cases in front of the court. You cannot make statements like that about the court*. Chastened, she thought she would be fired. Instead, Stoddard told her she'd be in charge of organizing the legal observers for the rally she had precipitated out of the summer air, as she lit the fuse for what would become a summer of protests.

On July 2, in Washington, D.C., gay-rights supporters formed a circle outside the Supreme Court, as nearly 200 people listened to Eleanor Smeal, president of the National Organization for Women, dub the Supreme Court decision "neo-fascism." Another 200 people cheered on gay-rights activist Rick Buchanan, who told a crowd gathered at Cincinnati's city hall, "We will not go back into the closet" while others offered to work on sodomy repeal in next-door Kentucky. Ohio had repealed sodomy laws in 1974. A crowd of 500 protested at city hall in Dallas, where the Texas sodomy case *Baker v. Wade* had begun.[27]

In Atlanta, more than 200 protesters stepped onto the sidewalks near the Richard B. Russell Building on July 3, in the last tailings of sunlight. "We are here because we are angry and hurt," Kathy Wilde told the crowd of supporters. "Everybody's right to privacy is in jeopardy, whether married, single, straight or gay. . . . We are determined that this court decision cannot stand."

As Wilde spoke, police threatened protesters with trespassing charges and arrest—in particular, one man who argued with a police officer and tried to lower the American flag to half-staff, a sign of mourning. The officer demanded it be left up. The crowd hustled the man away before he could be arrested.[28]

At noon on July 3, 1986, the bells at St. Patrick's Cathedral rang clear in the humid ninety-degree air while fireworks lurked on some forty boats floating in New York Harbor. Concerts would soon blare from the city's parks: Placido Domingo would sing, and Itzhak Perlman would play violin in a free Central Park concert while tall ships drifted around New York Harbor as though history had been reversed.

Chief Justice Warren Burger had given the oath of citizenship to 270 people gathered at Ellis Island, where they swore themselves to America and its ideals—all before President Ronald Reagan used a laser device to point to the Statue of Liberty, freshly unveiled from its two-year, $66 million facelift. The spark of liberty lighted the torch once more, promising freedom to all. Reagan's eyes grew wet at the orchestrated patriotic festivities dubbed the "party of the century."[29]

For queer people, the sight of the Statue of Liberty reminded them of the jarring decision in *Hardwick* earlier in the week. The country had banked so much goodwill on its symbols of liberty and yet they were belied by that hateful decision.

While Reagan clambered onto the USS *Iowa* to review a fleet of twelve domestic and twenty-one foreign warships and then viewed Operation Sail 1986—a procession of twenty-two tall ships—protesters gathered in Greenwich Village at midday in Sheridan Square and listened as speakers vented about the decision. "The torch that is lit today had best cast some light on the dark, dank chambers of the Supreme Court," said Raymond Jacobs of the Gay Men's Health Crisis. "We will not allow America to accept the lies and bigotry of this ruling. And I truly believe America will not allow it either."[30]

At 1:30 p.m., crowds swarmed down Manhattan streets chanting, *Out of the closet and into the streets!* Some carried handwritten signs, others painted sheets, which they waved in the air as flags trumpeting gay and lesbian liberation. Signs read MISS LIBERTY? YOU BET I DO and PRIVACY: A BASIC AMERICAN RIGHT.[31]

They marched toward Wall Street, close enough to the stage of America's self-congratulatory exercise.[32] Counter-protesters screamed, "Fuck gay rights!" In Little Italy, Nancy Langer was marching near one young man, along with other legal observers, when a group of bystanders leapt on him, punched him, and broke his cheekbone.[33] When Langer ran toward the injured man, his attackers stepped back and allowed an ambulance to arrive.[34]

The caravan swept down Seventh Avenue toward Foley Square, where the city's government buildings were. There more speakers derided the Reagan administration's hypocrisy. Reagan had stood against John Briggs and 1978's California Proposition 6, which would have banned gay teachers from classrooms, when he said that a law banning gay and lesbian teachers was "just too much government," after all.

Steven Carlson, age thirty-two, of Los Angeles, wore a black baseball hat with the red letters NY REPENT. He clicked a bullhorn to life and told the crowds that Judgment Day would be full of fire and brimstone for those in the gay rights camp. He said God would "make Chief Justice Warren Burger look like a Campfire Girl."[35]

The crowd swept past him toward blue barriers, where police, hundreds-deep, assumed a defensive posture while marchers chanted "Shame!" and "Freedom!" A wall of uniformed officers formed, some chuckling at the mass demonstration that had erupted around them. Some protesters swayed and continued to sing "We Shall Overcome," while others climbed the statue of an eagle as the Statue of Liberty shone in the background.[36]

"Civil rights or civil war!" someone shouted.[37]

The group passed Trinity Church on Broadway, after being shouted at by a few bystanders who chanted, "Homos go home!"[38] Others shouted for the protesters to stay calm. They wanted liberty, not bloodshed.

As they neared Wall Street, police officers brandished nightsticks and formed a barrier in front of wooden barricades, halting the march at about 3:00 p.m. before it could reach Battery Park and a planned rally. After fifteen minutes of tense sparring with the police, protesters swarmed around the barricades and made their way to the park, where they regrouped.

"We've had enough," a speaker told the crowd, "and we're not going to take it anymore!"[39]

The group pointed at the Statue of Liberty, then raised fists in anger at it: "Shame, shame, shame, shame!" they cried.

The next day, July 4, while the nation celebrated independence with the biggest fireworks display ever seen in the United States, all Nancy Langer could do was think of the young man who had been brutally assaulted. She had found out his name and the hospital where he was taken. The next day, she went to see him. He never would have been harmed if it hadn't been for her call to action. She tried to comfort herself but could not as she sat with him in the hospital, not knowing whether he would regain sight in the eye that had been kicked until it bled.

For two days Hardwick worked in near silence. It was a case about privacy, Wilde told reporters on his behalf, "and that's the way he wants to keep it." She admitted that the decision had left him "very discouraged and saddened." He still was in danger of prosecution. The statute of limitations for his case would not expire for another month, and though the Fulton County district attorney's office said they had no plan to take further action, Hardwick worried the whole thing could happen again.[40]

The day after the decision, the *Miami Herald* had found him and asked him about the case. "It's frightening," he said. "I just can't believe that, in 1986, they can make a ruling like that."

"I thought I would win. I didn't—we didn't. You can change all those I's to we's, for all the consenting adults in America. . . . They're turning this whole thing into a homosexual issue. It's not a homosexual issue—it's a human rights issue."[41]

For his contribution to the gay-rights movement, Hardwick had even been sent a bill by the Supreme Court for paperwork costs, which totaled $778.30.[42]

Now it was time to put it in his past. "I feel like I've done my part," he told the reporter. "It's time to get on with my personal life."[43]

When he and Kathy Wilde finally spoke, she told him that a *Newsweek* magazine poll showed 47 percent of Americans opposed the decision and 57 percent thought that states should not have the right to bar consenting private homosexual behavior.[44] Then she told Hardwick that Phil Donahue had called to invite him to appear on his TV talk show. It would be the best way he could get his message across to the millions of Americans who knew little about him or the case. It was a great opportunity to turn the disaster into something useful for the gay-rights movement. He went on a Miami-area talk radio show appearance to feel out the situation, then agreed to go on *Donahue*.[45] As his mentor Meher Baba had taught, the darkest nights could produce the brightest stars.

In the summer of 1986, Phil Donahue hosted the number-one talk show on daytime television in the United States. On any given weekday morning, more than a quarter of all people watching TV were tuned to his show. Donahue's canny mix of provocative questions, knowledgeable guests, and in-depth discussion of hot political and social issues had spawned a new generation of rivals—Sally Jesse Raphael, Geraldo Rivera, and his ratings peer and afternoon rival, Oprah Winfrey. Shows and hosts like Donahue cast aside conventionally manufactured celebrities. Instead, they cast ordinary people as the stars for the moral dilemmas they endured. Donahue was responsible for inoculating daytime television with a radical new agenda, and for fostering a new brand of stardom.

Donahue often booked guests for frank discussions of intimate issues, conducted with graphic specificity. On this July morning, he would need to explain the ins and outs of sodomy to his audience.[46]

"I'd rather not be the person with [the] responsibility of sharing [it] with you," he offered, somewhat disingenuously. After all, he had final approval of his guests and led the discussion. "Sodomy—for the purpose of law and as described in pursuant to this matter—sodomy is anal or oral sex." At Donahue's table sat Kathy Wilde and, next to her, in a dark blue blazer and red tie, Michael Hardwick.

"Consider this," Donahue said in his stentorian voice as he relayed the basics of the case, Hardwick's ticket, and the fateful morning of his arrest.

"When is the knock coming to your house?" Donahue intoned.

"I think basically what we've got is a court that said that morality is something that we are willing to have be a legitimate state interest," Kathy explained while Donahue began to stalk the audience for opinions, "and I think that's very sad."

Among the audience members, and those who spoke out over the phone lines piped into the studio, most people thought Hardwick had been wronged.

One caller with a light Southern twang grew more upset as he wound toward his point, linking it with the privacy protections the Supreme Court had granted in 1973's *Roe v. Wade* as well as the civil-rights movement. "I am an angry, taxpaying homosexual decorated Vietnam War veteran from Florida," he said. "I have had the same lover for nine years, we practice monogamous sex. And that if this country did not learn in the '60s with the Blacks and what they tried to do with them and restricting their rights, believe me, as a homosexual in Florida, they will learn in the '80s."

From the audience, Donahue executed his classic maneuver, a swooping dive toward someone, microphone extended, eyes wide behind the enormous rounded lenses of his glasses. "And who's first? What do you think?"

"I think that it's wrong and the law should keep out of it," said a dark-haired woman in a navy skirt suit. "And oral sex or whatever type of sex engaged by two homosexuals or whether the pair be straight, should be their own private matter."

One audience member wanted to know about the linkage between the *Hardwick* case and the HIV/AIDS epidemic, whether that crisis had elevated the sodomy ruling into the realm of the notorious.

"Good question, good question," Donahue said, pivoting to the star of that day's show. "Does the AIDS issue loom here, in your view? We should say that AIDS, no reference to disease, was made at all in this ruling, but obviously more than a few folks are wondering whether that's not behind this."

When Hardwick spoke, he linked his story with that of the epidemic for the first time.[47]

"Of course it's affected it," he agreed, with a slight curling smile that betrayed some nerves, though he spoke calmly on-camera to an audience of millions. "There's no doubt about it. But the point is that this is not a homosexual issue; we're talking about a human rights issue that has nothing to do with AIDS, it has nothing to do with being promiscuous, it has to do with the privacy of your own bedroom."

Donahue had first pitched Hardwick to be on a show with Jerry Falwell, but Hardwick declined, since he didn't believe it to be a religious issue. When Donahue called back, the host said that Falwell would not appear with him and that Hardwick would be there by himself.[48]

Hardwick told the audience about what Donahue said must have been "a pretty nightmare experience." The decision "shocked" him, the young man said. "I never expected it to go this way. I just, I can't believe in this day and age that they would issue a decision like that. I wasn't expecting it at all." The host, reading from Justice Harry Blackmun's dissent, underscores that the minority of justices found that the state had no interest that could "justify invading the houses, hearts, and minds of citizens who choose to live their lives differently." Wilde called it a "sad" and "dangerous" ruling.

Some of Donahue's callers were indifferent over the precedents that had been ignored in Hardwick's case. "I support the Supreme Court's decision 100 percent and I agree with the Georgia law," one said to Donahue. "The fact of the matter is that the ACLU's arguments are ridiculous because according to their logic, you shouldn't have prostitution laws, you shouldn't have laws against drug abuse, because as long as you do them in your home, there should be nothing wrong with them."

"That's not what's at issue here," Wilde interjected. "The question is whether, in fact, if you have no money, no minors, no force, no harm to anyone in your own home, the state can't criminalize what you do without bothering to give you a better reason than public morality."

How would the caller react to a law that banned heterosexual oral sex? "Would you like them to control it?" Hardwick asked the caller. "To tell you who you can sleep with? When you can sleep with them?"

"Do you support this kind of enforcement against heterosexuals?" Donahue drilled away at the caller. "Would you support a law which made it illegal for a married couple to engage in oral sex?"

"No," a meek response came, "I would not."

"I think we've made it a sexual issue, but the part that I find very frightening is that this is an erosion of my privacy, and it takes us one step closer to Big Brother," Hardwick said. "The laws we're talking about are part of ancient history. It is time to change, and this is a resilient nation. We have to, well, get together and help out."

After a final commercial break, the show came back to a stage and seats pitched into semi-darkness. A half dozen flashlights began to peep into the privacy that the darkness had afforded them. Audience members laughed and waved their torches in the air.

"I just want to see if your flashlights work," Donahue chuckled, then set the audience into action. "Point them to the camera. Let's see. You are deputized now to make citizens' arrests. Now, get out there and stamp out this behavior!"

Bowers v. Hardwick marked a low point of the gay-rights movement. On the legal front it meant queer people could be denied legal custody of children, property rights, even social space, even in places usually friendlier to them. The decision thrilled New York City councilman Noach Dear. It would help his attempts to overturn New York City's gay-rights ordinance that prohibited discrimination in housing and employment, he said, because "it said homosexuals are not equal to heterosexuals."[49]

On questions of morality, it proved even more reprehensible. Queer people were still dying. So were some married people who had sex with other infected partners, and so were people who had received blood transfusions in hospitals. Some found a way to have their treatment records falsified so that they would be marked as dying from meningitis or pneumonia, anything that would not inspire or incite the hysteria that AIDS would. The decision crystallized the sense of anguish and helplessness that AIDS had wrought.

The next phase of the gay-rights movement had begun to precipitate out of the *Hardwick* decision. The first step would be to keep the repeal of sodomy laws in motion. The laws were vulnerable to state constitutions that proscribed any legislation that inhibited the right to privacy. *Hardwick* steered activists toward state houses and state courts. It nudged them toward economic pressure; several gay-rights groups discussed a boycott of Coca-Cola until the company stepped in to help get the Georgia sodomy law repealed.[50] Wanting to keep the issue in the forefront, they planned a protest in California to coincide with an appearance by Justice Sandra Day O'Connor. "There is an incredible anger out there—people are really prepared to come out and fight," said National Gay and Lesbian Task Force executive director Jeff Levi.[51]

Before they could organize nationally, activists would learn from the *Washington Post* on July 13, 1986, that Justice Powell had initially cast his vote in Hardwick's favor, but later changed sides.[52] Switches such as Powell's had occurred in the past, but rarely were the machinations leaked to the public. The paper reported Powell's sentiment that he had been loath to recognize "more special rights not spelled out in the Constitution."

Hardwick's legal team would appeal the case. They rushed to petition for a rehearing before the Supreme Court ahead of a July 25 deadline.[53] Though it was far from even a remote chance, they had no other alternative. While they wrote, protests against the decision still went on.

On July 16, 1986, a crowd of 3,000 protesters surrounded by 100 police officers in uniform and a dozen plainclothes U.S. marshals were outside the San Francisco Hilton chanting and taunting the first female justice as she spoke to 1,000 local corporate executives. O'Connor told the executives that the work of the court naturally brought it into the political fray, "in the headlines and sometimes near various picket lines." Some must win and some must lose, she added coolly, and said, "there will always be someone unhappy with a ruling."[54]

The queer-friendly crowd outside had the better of the ripostes: "Hey, hey Sandra Day, support our rights or go away."[55] And, "What do we want? SODOMY! When do we want it? NOW!" Or "What Does

Mr. O'Connor Like to Do?"[56] And "Loosen Up, Sandy Baby"—a reference to the line uttered by drunken Washington football running back John Riggins when seated next to O'Connor at a formal dinner.

They wore their slogans with pride and blared their slogans from a set of speakers perched on a flatbed truck. The protest carried with it a new sense of danger. It was time to fight back. "There are only so many times we will assemble peacefully," said John Wahl, former attorney for Harvey Milk. "But if they keep oppressing us it is possible something else may happen."[57]

That Friday and Saturday, a group of two dozen activists met in New York to plan the successor to the 1979 March on Washington, which had been inspired by the assassination of Harvey Milk. Abby Rubenfeld greeted the group with a note that said the Ad Hoc Task Force to Challenge Sodomy Laws had felt the need to expand its focus post-*Hardwick*. They would continue to work the courts for challenges to sodomy laws but would now also work on political and legislative pathways for change.

To effect any change, ad hoc task force member Jay Kohorn thought it would take a commitment among queer people to reclaim their own morality. Cast as outlaws, some found the label romantic and lived as if that were the only way their lives could be organized. But if they claimed their lives as lawful as well as worthy, it might compel others to do the same. It could shift the conversation on a national level, which would give a future Supreme Court permission to change its mind.

For now, they simply had to put aside what *Hardwick* had wrought. "Finally, and this should go without saying, the purpose of this meeting is to prepare for the post-*Hardwick* world," Rubenfeld wrote. "We have a heavy agenda and no time to discuss the past, suggest 'blame,' or otherwise emphasize 'I-told-you-so's.' We should all be proud of our collective record on sodomy law reform efforts, and secure in the knowledge that we did all that we could to win the Hardwick and Baker cases. We need now to pull together, reassess our strategy, and proceed in a unified fashion to accomplish the goals for which we came together three years ago."[58]

A sense of urgency took over the meeting, which gelled rapidly around the idea of a nationwide event in the fall of 1987. The group decided to convene in New York that November to plot out the structure of what they hoped would be a massive, multi-day protest based around the ideas of the march that had been held in 1979. Within weeks of the meeting, state representatives announced their own meetings to coordinate what was already being dubbed the National March on Washington. The theme would be "For Love and For Life," with the tagline "We're not going back."

The location still had not been decided. Some thought it should take place in Atlanta, because "after all, it is the scene of the crime."[59]

At Liberty

In the weeks after the decision, Michael Hardwick went to weddings, worked long hours slinging drinks, and catered happy hours. He resumed his normal rhythm of life as much as possible. On August 3, 1986, the statute of limitations expired, and he could no longer be prosecuted.

On August 4, *Newsday* published the first of a series of profiles of Hardwick, who agreed to be interviewed provided that the pieces appeared after his case had died. Journalist Marilyn Goldstein had tracked Hardwick down in Miami after the decision and interviewed him while he worked, prepping chicken pot pie for a buffet, slicing limes, and piercing bright red maraschinos. He wanted people to know him as a person, not just as a court case that had brought him a mix of infamy and celebrity.

He also spoke with the *San Francisco Sentinel*, the *Advocate*, and for fourteen hours, with the *Washington Post*'s Art Harris as he came out yet again in his life, this time as a person who "never had to stand up for my sexual preference or my beliefs before but, now [have] to do it on a regular basis."[1] He presented the most ingratiating version of himself, attractively dressed, shirt opened to nightclub level, flirty and outgoing while also warm and intimate.

He still had the lean beach-boy look, but also now had long hair and an earring that paid homage to the glam-metal bands on MTV. He blurred his sexual identity, to a point. He had been, he told Goldstein, "actively heterosexual until I was 21." While speaking to Harris, he arranged bouquets of flowers—birds of paradise, lilies, and heliconias—and chatted with women who passed by, flattering them with light conversation and longer gazes.

"Who doesn't enjoy getting cruised by beautiful women?" He winked. "I'm a flirt. It makes them feel good."[2]

The arrival of a former flame queered the picture for readers. "I was 18 when we met," Jorge Vazquez said. "He [Michael] was 21. It was a major romance. We were goo-goo-eyed . . . We were together 18 months, then became best friends," Vazquez said. "That's unusual in the gay world, (where) people usually don't speak to each other after they break up."[3]

When he moved to Atlanta, Hardwick explained to Harris, he spent most of his time partying when he wasn't working, but also enjoyed canoeing. He had never planned on being an activist. He didn't even understand sodomy laws existed, he said. "I was a good-time boy. All I wanted to do was party, party, party," Hardwick told Goldstein. "I had no political affiliation." Still, he mused that gays were not far above drug addicts in the way society treated them.[4]

Vazquez called Hardwick "rebellious," but by and large a "happy-go-lucky guy." Still, he had changed: "He's gone from a good-time guy to Joan of Arc of the gay world," Vazquez said. "He's much more serious than he used to be."[5]

Hardwick spoke in a darker tone when asked about the future. When he first went public, he said, he thought some "crazy fundamentalist was going to blow my head off."[6] He remained in danger. Now anyone could find out who he was. The world knew he was gay.

To come out to the world as gay, "in this day with AIDS is a hard thing."[7] He already had seen ten friends die of the disease. "I hate to say it, but AIDS has had a positive effect," he said. "People in gay society are developing relationships, becoming more monogamous. It's simply because they're afraid."

The case had instilled in him a sense of confidence, and he felt strength from coming out and talking about the trauma he had endured.[8] He thought about sodomy laws still on the books, and how most people thought the situation would just go away. So long as they were on the books, gay people especially were in jeopardy. "All I can say is, wake up!"[9]

He still would do it all over again—he said "[I] could not feel very good about myself if I walked away from the whole thing"—but he felt vulnerable. When people asked how it felt to be famous, he said he didn't feel like a star. He felt naked.

He had dreamed three times the night before his *Newsday* interview that he had been jailed again. "I tried to explain to everyone that I wasn't supposed to be there," he said. "I dream about going back to court, I dream about going back to jail a lot."[10]

Harris also spoke with Officer Keith R. Torick that summer. The former Atlanta police officer had resigned from the city's police department in 1983, then left police work to open a driver-education school, a dozen miles away from the scene of the arrest.

During his time with the Atlanta police, his former supervisor confirmed, Torick had attracted a list of complaints from citizens—a few about his attitude, others that alleged brutality.[11] "He was a hardworking cop, but he was badge-heavy," the supervisor told Harris.

Years later, Torick felt Hardwick had extracted the most attention from the public that he could, taking the case to the Supreme Court— "Is he making any money off T-shirts yet?"—but told the reporter also that he regretted the arrest. Torick also laughed off some of Hardwick's public assertions, such as the idea he had watched Hardwick and Sawyer having oral sex for a half-minute. Torick claimed he watched only a few seconds and found it "gross." He countered that he had nothing against queer people, and had worked as security for Bulldog Lounge, a gay bar in Midtown Atlanta.[12]

Torick said Atlanta's tough police beat led him to leave for his father-in-law's cab company. He then worked for the Roswell, Georgia, police force, when during a lie-detector test, the examiner asked him if he'd ever broken the law. Torick thought of sodomy, and paused, then asked the examiner that the question "be rephrased as 'a serious undetected felony,' like robbing a bank."[13] He answered and passed.

Six weeks after the decision, protests still roiled cities with big queer communities or outsized roles in oppressing them: New York, San Francisco, and Washington. On August 11, 1986, about 400 protesters picketed on the plaza in front of Lincoln Center in Manhattan against Warren Burger, who was addressing the American Bar Association in the last speech of his term as both a Supreme Court justice and chief justice. At a luncheon at the same ABA conference, Lewis Powell told assembled attorneys that the Burger court had not reversed any of the critical landmark cases of the Warren court, such as *Miranda*, and that it had expanded other rights. He did not think that any "radical changes" were coming to the court, either, but admitted that the "cutting edge of some of the dissenting opinions was a little keener than in other years."[14]

The jurists were able to speak blithely about the case in elliptical terms because the legal options for the Hardwick team had all but died. On September 7, Hardwick, Wilde, and Rubenfeld appeared at a meeting of the Atlanta Business and Professional Guild. The group of queer business owners, some of whom knew Hardwick as a friend, heard the message that so long as the sodomy law remained in place it could affect any of them.

"It's not my fight, it's all our fight," Hardwick reminded them.

The battle had gained the interest of congressional candidate John Lewis, who had marched in Selma and now ran for Georgia's Fifth Congressional District. Lewis told the audience that he would stand up when he saw discrimination in any form, whether it was based on the color of skin or the sexual identity of a person, because, he said, "we are all a part of the same family that is the human family."[15]

Wilde spoke about the remote chance for a rehearing. She admitted that it was a "shot in the dark," but that the legal team had sent it to the Supreme Court anyway.

Days later, on September 11, 1986, the court denied the request.

"I guess you've heard by now, the Supreme Court denied rehearing in *Hardwick* on September 11," Tribe wrote to Wilde. "Apart from the apocalypse, how're you doing?"[16]

She hadn't told anyone, but Wilde didn't think Hardwick had looked well.

Bowers v. Hardwick licensed discrimination. In the months that followed the decision, although records weren't kept on incidents, some detected an increase in anti-queer violence—from a string of murders in Minneapolis and people being burned with lighter fluid to attacks on activists such as Cleve Jones, who was gay-bashed on the street in San Francisco. Many remained unmoved. Atlanta *Journal-Constitution* columnist Dick Williams told the CBS Evening News that "homosexual rights isn't a movement here" as he chortled and sneered that "it's considered something of a plague."[17]

But the fall of 1986 also brought a glint of hope in the fight against

HIV/AIDS. In clinical trials, the drug azidothymidine, or AZT, had brought down many patients' viral loads and cut the incidence of opportunistic infections. It gave them time.

Hope flickered in the words of theater star Harvey Fierstein, who confided to a gathered crowd at a Human Rights Campaign fundraiser September 27 that "the thing that has made me so incredibly giddy is that in about 36 hours from now, the first ray of hope, the first drug that we can give somebody will start being given out to 6,000 people in 36 hours," he said. "The worst part about finding finally a cure for this disease is the incredible pain we will have to go through when we think again of all the people we lost. Hopefully, 36 hours from now—I know it's not going to be exactly true, but hopefully 36 hours from now—it's an end to losing anybody ever again."[18]

Yellow-tinged lights threw a bright glow on a lectern at Thomas Paine Park in Manhattan on the evening of October 6, 1986. Protesters had gathered to mark the first day of the reign of Chief Justice William Rehnquist, to remind America that the Supreme Court's cold calculus had isolated queer people for no just reason. Evan Wolfson had recruited Michael Hardwick to speak at the event, along with political activist Bayard Rustin. Wolfson hoped the event would recast the case to create a defiant vision for a new America.[19]

Hardwick brushed away his fear once more as dark fell over the park. Its namesake, Paine, the author of the *Rights of Man*, had written, "My country is the world, and my religion is to do good."[20] Hardwick had endured speculation about his private life with grace, but now the case had put him under a literal television spotlight that revealed something else: a thinner, more angular jawline than he'd had just a year or so earlier, and what appeared to be a lesion on the side of his nose.[21]

"A lot of people have made comments on the courage for opposing the sodomy law," he said, pausing a moment to widen his mouth, warding off what appeared to be a sob. "Until you find yourself in that position where you find a police officer in your bedroom—God forbid you don't—you can't really make a decision as to how you would act."

Rustin then spoke with clarity on the issues that now confronted the gay community. He had decided during the height of Jim Crow that he had to be as affirmative of his homosexuality as of his Blackness. Linked to the Communist Party during the 1940s, Rustin had been arrested for lewd conduct in January 1953 in California as Hoover's FBI tailed him. "It occurred to me shortly after that, that it was an absolute necessity for me to declare homosexuality," he said, "because if I didn't, I was a part of the prejudice," he said. "I was aiding and abetting the prejudice that was a part of the effort to destroy me."[22]

People mocked him as queer even as he helped to orchestrate the major protests of the Black civil-rights movement. A committee had investigated whether as a queer man he could safely continue to work in public roles in the movement.[23] But Martin Luther King Jr. held Rustin in high regard and charged him with coordinating what would become "the greatest demonstration for freedom" that America had ever seen: the 1963 March on Washington for Jobs and Freedom.[24] Rustin had promised 100,000 marchers would come to the National Mall, commanding dignity and demanding it from others—and when that day was over, more than 200,000 had stood together.

Resplendent in a gray wool blazer and magenta bow tie, Rustin affirmed the horror of the *Hardwick* decision and its consequences. "If the average American citizen does not fight for the privacy of those they do not like, let us say homosexuals or Jews or Blacks," he said, "they are not able to fight for their own privacy when the time comes because they have already given away the initiative to the wrong people.... Now we are all one, and if we don't know it, we will learn it the hard way." Rustin ended his speech, then moved toward a cheering Hardwick standing behind him.[25]

The next day about sixty people took to Supreme Court Plaza in Washington to protest *Hardwick* once more, toting signs that read SODOMITES UNITE and to chant, *"Hey, hey, ho, ho, sodomy laws have got to go!"* Hardwick attended and reminded all who listened, "We're mad and fighting . . . we are getting organized. This is the beginning, not the end."[26]

On October 7, 1986, Hardwick's legal team disbanded. The team of more than forty lawyers had achieved a rueful consensus: they should not press ahead for a trial on the equal-protection implications of Hardwick's case. Rubenfeld held open the chance that Larry Tribe might disagree but began to close the matter. "While it is certainly difficult to accept defeat in this case, and to give up the best fact pattern we will probably ever get in a sodomy law case," she wrote, "I do agree with my colleagues that the risks involved in further pursuit of the case far outweigh the slight possibility of success under the present circumstances."

Those present circumstances had now placed Antonin Scalia on the high court in Warren Burger's place. In 1978 Scalia had written that the Supreme Court had "found rights where society never believed they existed . . . there is no national consensus about those things and there never has been. The courts have no business being there."[27]

Gay-rights activists had reserved other paths for future constitutional arguments through the principle of equal protection, and needed to carefully groom a case to pose the question in a way the court would uphold—either that or wait until its members changed. As Rubenfeld wrote, "Equal protection is too important a concept for us in too many areas outside of sodomy law reform to risk losing it through *Hardwick*. You and Larry did a great job on the case, and someday we'll all be proven right."[28]

Wolfson came to Florida around the holidays that year to visit family and met up with Hardwick. Hardwick invited him to the club where he worked in Coconut Grove. They later went to Hardwick's studio on Miami Beach, where he showed his works of art in progress, both paintings and large sculptures. He flipped through panels and canvases stacked on the floor, proud of the work, which was rife with neon-colored alien creatures and black-and-white geometric puzzles that bent the eye and the mind. They then went to Hardwick's house.

Wolfson left Miami unsure when he would see Hardwick again. Wolfson had hesitations about him: *He's smart, he's good-looking, talented; why is he living the life he's living?*[29] He felt that the walk under the cherry blossoms that spring, when all had seemed to be filled with potential, had been the high point of their relationship. They had parted then, Hardwick to the airport and Wolfson to the train back to New York. Now, as then, they were moving in opposite directions.

Plans for the next National March on Washington blossomed into committees, statements, missions, objectives, regional structures, fundraisers, newsletters, and the like—organizational bureaucracy that could kill off lesser ideas. Some 250 advocates met from November 14–16, 1986, in New York, to put the event together. They were greeted by a letter that writ the agenda large: "We're here to do no less than make history—to build an event and a national movement to right the rising tide of anti-gay and anti-lesbian bigotry and to make our community visible and valued."

They drafted mission statements and demanded a repeal of all anti-queer laws, a comprehensive lesbian/gay–rights bill, a ban on sexual-orientation discrimination in the government and military, as well as in custody cases, and protection for lesbian and gay youth from the discrimination that had produced *Hardwick*.

Some wanted "The Great March," as it became known, to take place in Philadelphia in 1987, where former Supreme Court Chief Justice Warren Burger would preside over a ceremony celebrating the 200th anniversary of the Constitution. Others lobbied for a Georgia protest instead of Washington, D.C., where protests might be dismissed as more of the usual.[30] The organizers finally zeroed in on D.C., on October 11, 1987.

While the mass protest moved forward, inch by democratically debated inch, pop-up rebellions kept public attention focused on the twin disasters of the AIDS epidemic and the *Hardwick* decision. A group called the Lavender Hill Mob broke up official proceedings at a CDC conference in Atlanta in February 1987 with a series of protests. One twenty-eight-year-old man stood outside a conference room in a gray uniform that echoed those worn by Holocaust prisoners. The man, who said he had AIDS, wore a pink triangle—the symbol that the Nazis made gay people wear—to call attention to the "holocaust of AIDS" that had enveloped the queer community.[31]

Then at the conference's last plenary session, members of the group yelled that AIDS needed more money for treatment and research.[32] "It's a coverup!" they shouted as they raced to the front of the room. "Why are we talking about testing now? What about saving people's lives?"[33]

The Lavender Hill Mob felt the scientists in attendance would not wake up to their needs without a dramatic intervention. America's system of political power had for decades conspired to drive gay lives underground. In doing so, it had created the atmosphere in which HIV thrived and had enabled the epidemic. In the Lavender Hill

Mob's assessment, the government, its scientists, and its doctors were responsible for a genocide.

Hardwick had put together a life in Miami. Never far from him, his dog Jumbo sat by his feet, mellow and laid-back like his owner. Jumbo earned his name from his huge paws and his nearly one hundred pounds of mixed-breed shepherd and retriever. He had become Hardwick's steadiest companion, the one who walked with him on the beach in the dim hours of the advancing day, where Hardwick would call him away from the used needles and condoms strewn on the sand.

Safe inside his darkened studio, sometimes with a Cuban coffee without sugar, other times with a tightly rolled joint, Hardwick worked tirelessly with a fellow artist on the sixteen-foot-tall statues that soared toward the ceiling and nodded toward his Eastern-tinged beliefs. His art had earned the notice of the high-rolling dance clubs that sprang up on Miami Beach's disused corridors. Now he carved Buddhas and Bodhisattvas with saws and knives from flat panels that were originally massive blocks of Styrofoam in the studio space that he, at last, could afford.

The statues were destined for Club Nu, a new mecca for nightlife that had been birthed out of a depressed block of Miami Beach when businesses had all but deserted the place.[34] A trio of brothers—Robert, John, and Tom Turchin, all sons of Robert L. Turchin, who had developed the Doral Hotel—spotted a gem in the rubble. Inspired by New York's Palladium, Nu had a glassy ground-floor restaurant, a huge dance floor with a state-of-the-art sound system, a 40,000-watt lighting array, and a mezzanine level where celebrities could watch the mortals at play.

When it opened on April 18, 1987, Club Nu had tamed a place

described as a wild and dangerous, and styled it an avant-garde blend of sex and space, tinged with a "pervasive sense of chaos." It began its inevitable decline from the moment it opened, as most nightclubs do, but at its opening peak, it gave Hardwick the place to announce himself as an artist on the scene.[35] According to his new cadre of friends, Hardwick clearly enjoyed his life and lived in his studio happily alongside his work, watching Miami Beach renew itself.[36]

While he dusted himself with the snow of freshly chain-sawed Styrofoam, Hardwick burnished his political celebrity. On May 14, 1987, he flew to Philadelphia to participate in a panel discussion entitled "Sexual Privacy and the Constitution," a part of a project dubbed "The Constitution and You"—a dozen town-hall style meetings held in Philadelphia neighborhoods to discuss constitutional issues of the day, some of them televised. Hardwick appeared on the panel, held at a law school in the gay neighborhood of Center City, along with Nan Hunter, the director of the ACLU's National Gay and Lesbian Rights Project, and Steve Parkman, assistant attorney general for legal policy.[37]

Then, Hardwick went to New York, to record an interview with Bill Moyers as a part of the public television series *In Search of the Constitution*. Hardwick made no apologies about his life as a "practicing gay."[38] Still capable of flashes of anger over the case, Hardwick told Moyers that he believed he had been a target for harassment simply for being queer, and reiterated as he had all along that the police officer came to his bedroom and stood in the doorway for at least a half a minute. If he had been with a woman, "probably it would have been a knock on the door and, 'Excuse me, Mr. Hardwick' type of a situation. But because of what it was he kind of took it and ran with it."

Hardwick repeated for PBS the harrowing story he had told from the start of the case—how he had been treated by police officers, who made sure the other inmates knew he was there for sodomy and told him that " 'I should be able to find what I was looking for in there.' "

"It was a nightmare," Hardwick said, with verbal and physical harassment, "pushing me around and stuff. But fortunately, I wasn't raped or anything like that."

He admitted that, at the time, he didn't even know what sodomy was, but told Moyers that the Georgia sodomy law had infringed on his rights as a human being, and that given the chance to do something about it, he chose to go forward. His mother worried she might never see him alive outside of prison again. He framed his decision as the frustration over a police force and court system that could use the sodomy statues selectively: as long as the law was on the books, he said, "they can enforce it whenever they choose."

"Society is not offended except when there is a majority that finds, for religious reasons or other reasons, what you are doing an assault on its sensibilities," Moyers countered.

"Yes, but then they understand that I'm not trying to assault their sensibilities. I'm simply trying to fulfill my purpose," Hardwick lobbed back. "I'm simply saying, 'Leave me alone to live my life the way I feel I need to fulfill myself.' That's all I'm asking. I'm not trying to offend anyone."

He reminded Moyers that, despite the chatter about his case revolving implicitly around AIDS, that "this issue has nothing to do with the spread of AIDS, because that is up to the individual. And that's in heterosexual or homosexual communities, that it doesn't matter. It's time that everyone get wise to what the disease is and that there is a plague. And that there's ways of going around it. You know, you don't have to, like, totally stop having sex and go into celibacy. You simply have to be careful and you simply have to know what is known about the disease. Unfortunately, there's not enough known about the disease yet. But I think it's time everybody pay attention to what is known and take responsibility."

"Was homosexuality a choice you made?" Moyers asked.

"Yeah, it was," Hardwick answered. "I've been heterosexual and am now currently homosexual. And the reason for that is simply because that is my needs. . . . It's not an immoral act. For me to love anyone else is not an immoral act. I mean, if I'm in the privacy of my own bedroom, with a consenting adult, which is what the case was, and we choose to, like, physically relate to each other, even if it's just touching, it doesn't matter what we're doing. It's nobody else's business. And as far as the morality goes, my morality says it's fine."

"Despite what happened . . . I know that the system works," he said. "And when I set out to do this, I never necessarily thought I was going to go to the Supreme Court. And I definitely didn't think I was going to lose at the Supreme Court. But I always had in the back of my mind that what I was setting out to do was to try to change the law. Not necessarily to change it though. Even if I could just lay a foundation for future change. And I think that has definitely been done."

"So when the Preamble of the Constitution says, 'We the people,'" Moyers asked, "it includes Michael Hardwick."

"It sure does. . . . and it still does," he agreed. "I am 'the people.' You know, I am part of 'the people.'"

Despite waning health, Thurgood Marshall had traveled to Maui to speak in front of a group of patent and trademark lawyers. Like his friend Harry Blackmun, Marshall's open irritation at the fluctuation of the court's moral compass could not be masked. In his May 6, 1987, speech, Marshall told the audience that the upcoming two hundredth anniversary of the Constitution and the planned celebrations were an occasion for pause. "The focus of this celebration," Marshall said, "invites a complacent belief that the vision of those who debated and compromised in Philadelphia yielded the 'more perfect Union' it is said we now enjoy."[39]

Marshall had been invited to take part in those celebrations but told the audience that he would not join. "I cannot accept this invitation, for I do not believe that the meaning of the Constitution was forever 'fixed' at the Philadelphia Convention. Nor do I find the wisdom, foresight, and sense of justice exhibited by the Framers particularly profound," he said. "To the contrary, the government they devised was defective from the start, requiring several amendments, a civil war, and momentous social transformation to attain the system of constitutional government, and its respect for the individual freedoms and human rights, we hold as fundamental today. When contemporary Americans cite 'The Constitution,' they invoke a concept that is vastly different from what the Framers barely began to construct two centuries ago."[40]

In the anniversary year, Marshall said, not every American would wave flags in a patriotic fervor. "Some may more quietly commemorate the suffering, struggle, and sacrifice that has triumphed over much of what was wrong with the original document and observe the anniversary with hopes not realized and promises not fulfilled."

As for the frail justice, fast becoming a relic of the progressive Warren court era receding into history, he said, "I plan to celebrate the bicentennial of the Constitution as a living document, including the Bill of Rights and the other amendments protecting individual freedoms and human rights."[41]

Marshall's sentiments were shared by A. Leon Higginbotham Jr., who sat on the U.S. Court of Appeals for the Third District. "When you look at the U.S. Constitution of 1787, not once do you see the word 'slavery,'" Higginbotham told *Newsday*. "In addition to sanctioning this brutal process of slavery, there also was an exercise of nondisclosure."[42]

Higginbotham sat onstage when the City University of New York held its law school commencement on May 29, 1987, at its Flushing campus. He would receive an honorary degree, as would Dan Bradley, a Florida lawyer and Carter appointee who outed himself and become a gay rights advocate, and Jo-Ag-Quis Ho, also known as Dr. Oren Lyons, chief of the Turtle Clan of the Iroquois Onondaga Nation and a professor of Native American studies at SUNY–Buffalo. Michael Hardwick also stood in the procession.

Hardwick could not be granted an honorary degree because he had not graduated from college. The school decided to honor him by including him in the ceremonies, and while Higginbotham spoke, Hardwick stood next to CUNY law students about to graduate. Some kidded with him: "Are you ready to take the bar exam?"[43] Hardwick had considered it. Since he was arrested, he realized how deeply the courts could impact someone's life. He knew that the president was packing the Supreme Court to make sure that his policies and conservative agenda would be held in place for the next twenty years or more.[44] Hardwick returned from New York, with his honor in hand.

On June 2, he checked into Jackson Memorial Hospital in Miami. Jackson had become the hospital of preference for patients with AIDS-related complications. Hardwick didn't have healthcare, and he might have been advised by many friends, or taught by their end-of-life experiences, to cloak his condition. But his only choice was to accept assistance from the Public Health Trust of Dade County.

He checked out of the hospital on Monday, June 8. His interview with Bill Moyers aired that Thursday, June 11.[45] He would find it impossible to maintain his medical privacy: On June 23, 1987, the state of Florida served him with a lien entered into the public record for unpaid services accrued at Jackson Memorial in the amount of $5,972.70.

By the summer of 1987, many Supreme Court watchers assumed Thurgood Marshall would be the next justice to retire. Instead, on June 28, 1987, Lewis Powell announced his resignation.

Powell's swing vote in *Bowers v. Hardwick* already had led to decisions that would reduce queer rights. Days after the *Hardwick* decision, the court refused to hear the Texas sodomy challenge *Baker v. Wade* that had been based on equal protection. At the end of the Powell term the court had decided in *Padula v. Webster* that the FBI could deny a job to Margaret Padula because she could not work in states where sodomy was illegal, and because her lesbian identity left her vulnerable to blackmail.

Senator Joseph R. Biden was among those who said that he hoped that the president would nominate a replacement in Powell's mold.[46] But the nominee who was chosen to replace Powell would be Robert Bork, who led the three-judge panel that had decided against the sailor convicted in military court of sodomy in *Dronenburg*.[47]

Bork heralded an even bolder gambit to move the court to the right. Were he confirmed, the Supreme Court might tackle more privacy rulings with even greater zeal. It might even seek to dismantle *Roe v. Wade*. Reagan, when he pronounced the nomination, admitted as much when he called Bork "the most prominent intellectual advocate of judicial restraint"—coded language that pointed toward the reversal of civil rights acknowledged during the previous two generations.[48] A long confirmation fight would no doubt be the order of the day, and it would be "serious," according to Biden, the head of the Senate Judiciary Committee.

While some held hope that Bork might grow moderate once on

the court, most saw nothing good in his nomination. He had been named acting solicitor general when President Nixon dismissed Archibald Cox as a Watergate special prosecutor in 1973, during the so-called Saturday Night Massacre. After two attempts, only the final Justice Department attorney he commanded would do Nixon's bidding: Bork. The critical question, to be answered in confirmation hearings, was whether "any president has a mandate to remake the Constitution in his own image."[49]

While the sides were drawn on Capitol Hill, organizers of the March on Washington were prepared with a response of their own. In the summer of 1987, the March on Washington Committee confirmed that an act of civil disobedience would take place in front of the Supreme Court Building on October 13. It would mark a protest of all anti-gay and anti-lesbian rulings, in particular, that in *Bowers v. Hardwick*. Training sessions for civil disobedience would be held on October 10 and October 12 at All Souls Church in D.C. to prepare and inculcate the principles of nonviolent protest in those who might want it to turn otherwise. Warnings were issued at the time of the confirmation of the event: there would be no clenched fists waved at police, hands had to stay out of pockets, and mouths had to stay shut. "Some Washington police officers are like some police officers everywhere; they seize the chance to lay a club across a demonstrator's head. Resisting arrest is in itself a crime."[50]

The planned act of resistance would take place during Bork's confirmation hearings. As sides were drawn, Laurence Tribe was pulled into the mix of those who might testify. When Tribe agreed to work with Senator Biden on a strategy to deny Bork the seat, friends such as political advisor Bob Schrum counseled him against testifying, saying it would burn bridges. Others, like sitting senators Alan Simpson and Orrin Hatch, let it be known that if Bork were confirmed, Tribe might get a seat on the court later himself.[51]

Tribe thought any testimony would make an enemy out of someone destined to be confirmed.⁵² Although he didn't want to have to argue cases in front of someone he had publicly castigated, he decided to testify and told the Senate that the very future of the Constitution was at stake. Bork had tried to modify his positions on civil rights and free speech, and claimed he would "respect judicial precedent" while he was twisting in the Washington wind. Tribe did not believe him. As a justice, Bork would "cast a vote that no higher court could correct."⁵³ If Bork were confirmed, history would not judge his deception. It would blame the Senate.

Bork's confirmation hearings had begun in September, while Judiciary Committee chair Biden's presidential campaign faltered over allegations that he had plagiarized part of a stump speech. Biden withdrew from the presidential campaign on September 23 and returned to the business of the confirmation hearings. He worked diligently with Duke law scholar Walter Dellinger and with Tribe to prepare for the hearings, reading up on constitutional theory.

With the help of Dellinger and Tribe, Biden built the hearings around the issue of privacy. "People understand how fragile their liberties are," he said. "I believe the American people have a genuine and justifiable fear of government intrusion in what they instinctively know is going to be an ever more intrusive world." ⁵⁴

On October 6, the initial vote in the Judiciary Committee to forward Bork's nomination with a favorable recommendation failed, 5–9. The second vote that day forwarded Bork's name with an unfavorable recommendation, on a 9–5 vote, to the Senate. The fate of the nomination seemed all but certain. The concerted effort to combat court packing had convinced just enough Republicans to choose privacy over party.

March

They marched because they were dying. They marched because the law said they were criminals. They marched because they no longer wanted to remain silent.

The only tool at their disposal was protest, but even as final plans were laid that summer, organizers still couldn't predict how many people might show up. The logistical challenge had nearly matched the daunting political vision. Organizers raised money in hundreds of cities around the nation. Thousands of volunteers had mobilized to prepare for the march. Protesters flowed into the city of Washington, D.C., by train, plane, car, and subway. U.S. Park Police would gauge the crowd at more than 200,000 people on Sunday morning; organizers would tally more than 500,000 of them by the end of the weekend.

More than a year of planning culminated on October 10, 1987, with the first public events of the march weekend. Subways disgorged lesbians and gays wearing pink triangles on the Mall, while runner Brent Nicholson Earle made a circuit of the Ellipse during the yearlong cross-country run he staged to draw attention to the AIDS epidemic.[1]

Across town, near the city's jail and the stadium that hosted its football team, a group gathered at Congressional Cemetery to place some of the ashes of slain gay-rights leader Harvey Milk. The idea had been that of Leonard Matlovich, a gay military officer who sued to be reinstated after his discharge for homosexuality. Matlovich, HIV-positive and in the last year of his life, had trekked to Paris to visit the graves of Alice B. Toklas and Gertrude Stein, and wanted to create something similar in the nation's capital—in the same place he had chosen to be buried. A box of Milk's ashes was placed with artifacts, including a rainbow flag, as planners worked on the design for a permanent memorial.[2] Matlovich had already installed his own marker at Congressional, which read, "When I was in the military, they gave me a medal for killing two men and a discharge for loving one."

At 2:00 p.m. that afternoon, more than a thousand couples met in front of the IRS Building for a mass wedding to affirm the moral righteousness of gay and lesbian couples in the face of sanctioned discrimination, a point driven home by the partnership between Karen Thompson and Sharon Kowalski. Hurt badly in a car accident four years into her relationship with Thompson, Kowalski had been ruled medically unable to care for herself and her father was named her guardian. "And now I have been kept apart from Sharon for over two years," Thompson told the crowd in front of the IRS. Thompson said that the last time she had seen her, Sharon typed out, "Help me! Get me out of here, take me home."[3] The presiding minister, Metropolitan Community Church's Reverend Troy Perry, told the couples to embrace and be affectionate in public; he reminded all, "It matters how we love, not who we love," and couples used chalk to write their names inside hearts they drew on the sidewalk.[4]

After a Saturday evening of concerts by gay men's choirs and nightclubbing at D.C.'s Tracks, the marchers regrouped Sunday on the Mall between the Capitol and the Washington Monument, to be confronted by the remarkable AIDS Quilt. Its originator, Cleve Jones, had asked marchers in candlelight vigils to carry the names of those lost to AIDS on posters. When those posters were affixed to a federal building in San Francisco, they resembled a quilt. Jones began to encourage people to make panels for a quilt that would be assembled for the first time in Washington.

The 1,920 panels were laid in place on the Mall with space for observers to walk between them on October 11. Jones was amazed. "I just couldn't believe that . . . I just couldn't believe how beautiful it was. And I wasn't . . . I wasn't prepared for [the] art of it. I wasn't . . . I was not prepared for the fact that . . . that mothers and grandmothers would sit down with [a] dead son's mother and spent every weekend through three months sewing together [to] create this work of incredible art, and then wrap[ped] it up in brown paper and sent it to a post office box in San Francisco."[5] Each panel told the story of a single person in graphic, handcrafted, painstaking form. It laid out in detail the devastation the quilters felt and how they wished their family or friends to be remembered. The memento mori recovered some of the dignity the dying had lost in the final moments of their lives when they might have felt frightened or abandoned.

At dawn on October 11, the names of the people commemorated on the quilt were read aloud. It took until midmorning to finish.[6]

The quilt focused media attention on the cause of the march. When asked if he believed if the quilt could touch "those cold hearts" in the Capitol Building, Jones stammered, "I hope so . . . I hope so. I can't begin to understand the administration's policies. I can't begin to comprehend them . . . maybe this will help." It created a flashpoint for anger too. Seething, Jones said, "I don't think I could speak rationally to the president. He has delayed and delayed and delayed as we died. He has done nothing." He estimated the quilt's display at the march would mean that people would create another thousand panels. He planned to put it on tour across the country, in part to counter the "epidemic of fear and misinformation and hatred. The quilt says very clearly and very simply how we should respond to the epidemic. We have to pull the country together. We have to unite. We have to reject division and we have to fight the disease."[7]

"One of the nation's oldest crafts, quilting, served the purpose it had always served: it brought folks together," ABC World News Tonight anchor Peter Jennings would remind viewers as he later named Jones as the Person of the Week. "It is also a good time to remind ourselves that AIDS is the nation's problem."[8]

Across the Potomac River, a group of gay and lesbian military veterans convened at the Tomb of the Unknown Soldier at Arlington National Cemetery to remember queer veterans before they joined their comrades at the march. Near midmorning, they merged into a swollen crowd that streamed down Seventeenth Street to the White House, then toward the Capitol Building's west terrace. Directly behind the veterans—prominently staged to give them visibility and to make sure they could get attention for their medical needs—people with AIDS came. It took an hour for people in the march to traverse twenty blocks.

They marched with silkscreened images of Ronald Reagan in yellow and black, with AIDSGATE stamped on them like a veto. They carried black banners with SILENCE=DEATH in white letters on a simple black background, and pink triangles with states outlined on them with slogans like "Minnesota—Out and Outraged." They beat snare drums, and some rolled along in wheelchairs, a visible sign of their complications from AIDS. Newly minted congresswoman Nancy Pelosi was among them. One of the few congressional representatives in attendance, Pelosi called the march a "great day," and said that federal legislation in the works would be the start of progress for the movement—bills on appropriating more money for AIDS research, a nondiscrimination bill, and a confidentiality bill. When asked to send a message to President Reagan, Pelosi addressed the camera: "I believe that President Reagan is in a position to do whatever it takes to fight AIDS. I beseech him to use all that is in his power, to take the medical advice of his medical advisers, and not make a political decision about AIDS. Too many people are dying, we need him in this fight, we beseech him to help."

While the march took over the streets in front of the National Gallery of Art, the Smithsonian National Museum of Natural History, and the National Museum of American History, it made its own history on the lawn's temporary stage, where politicians and performers spoke at a 1:00 p.m. rally about the dire straits America's gays and lesbians found themselves in. Civil-rights leader Reverend Jesse Jackson preached about the failure of American morality and pleaded for an end to violence against women, minorities, and lesbians and gays. Cesar Chavez, co-founder of the National Farm Workers Association, and Eleanor Smeal, a president of NOW and co-founder of the Feminist Majority Foundation pledged the support of their movements to gays and lesbians. Actor Whoopi Goldberg hurled fire and brimstone. "I would like you to just scream the words, 'How long?'" she demanded. "How long is it going to take before people get smart . . . we aren't talking about illiterate people, we're talking about senators and congressmen, and the fucking president!"

"I want you to hear this, straight America," said lesbian comedian Robin Tyler. "For years, for centuries, we have survived your mental institutions and your penal institutions and behavior modification. We have survived your hurting our families and our loved ones. Do you understand, America, that 12 percent of the little boys and girls growing up today are going to be lesbians and gays and they are not going to become faggots and dykes and queers and sissies?"

Directly refuting the entire movement claimed by Anita Bryant and other conservative activists, Tyler told the crowd, "We are going to save *our* children!"

The protest march and rally continued for nearly five hours. Organizers estimated as many as 3 percent of all gay and lesbian people in the United States had been there to demonstrate.[9]

Oral arguments were set to begin Tuesday morning, October 13, 1987, in the suit of *Hazelwood School District, et al., v. Cathy Kuhlmeier, et al.*, a case that held that a high school newspaper's journalism class could be considered a public forum for the purpose of the First Amendment. Students had written about the issue of teen pregnancy. Their principal deleted those pages before the newspaper was published.[10]

Months earlier, a group of march coordinators had studied the Supreme Court Building and its interior pews where visitors could enter for fifteen or twenty minutes at a time and watch the court proceedings. They had noted the brass eyelets on the ends of the wooden benches, which they thought would be perfect for securing plastic handcuffs so they could stand in silent protest in the room where the court had a year earlier decided they were second-class citizens.

Michelle Crone had taken charge of the protest and worked deftly to defuse that risky plan. She had gained grassroots organizing experience during the Seneca Women's Peace encampment in the early 1980s, which protested the placement of nuclear tailings near a Pershing missile transit point and army depot near Romulus, New York. Crone had attended the November 1986 meeting for the upcoming march on Washington with Robin Tyler when she first heard of a plan to storm the White House itself.

Oh my God, she thought, *that is so irresponsible. You can't do that. That's not how you do civil disobedience.*

She stood up and froze all talk of insurrection. She rattled off what could be done and what should be done—and what could not, absolutely should not, happen. There had to be training, there had to be affinity groups, there had to be lawyers ready to help. She spoke up and spoke out, and as usually was the case, she was put in charge of organizing it.[11] At the time she had been paired with Cleve Jones to work on it, but Jones had become too busy working on the Names Project and AIDS Quilt. Crone turned to the typical groups of activists who would be interested—queer-rights advocates and anti-nuke protesters—and set ground rules, including the training of all attendees.

Before taking part in the October 13 event, every person had to be drilled. Those exercises took place in churches across the country prior to the march weekend. Hundreds more convened in local churches for instruction during the weekend of the march. Some of the newly formed ACT UP groups attended.

Crone and the organizers of the action, in an unusual move, decided to approach people working at the Supreme Court, especially to understand what reactions its security people might have. Doing so was a radical breach of traditional activism. Crone, however, felt they had a responsibility to meet and prepare local law enforcement agencies for the specific needs of a queer-rights march, including the tactical reality of arresting people who had AIDS, needed medications frequently, and couldn't be detained for hours on end without them. She also wanted to make sure that they wouldn't be clubbed on the head by police.

It took an entire afternoon, but the leaders of the involved agencies, including the Capitol Police and D.C. Metropolitan Police, attended and came prepared with questions. Eventually a nearby bank was made available as a medical outpost during the action. Worried about coming into contact with blood from those with AIDS, the police believed they were the ones who would be putting their lives on the line.

Crone and the leaders of the action had settled on an initial plan to protest inside the Supreme Court. They would line up to be admitted to oral arguments and occupy all the available seats for that day's session. On cue, the group would handcuff themselves to the pews and raise signs protesting the *Hardwick* decision. They had tested that kind of action at a previous protest at the Statue of Liberty. But unbeknownst to them, the Supreme Court's marshal, Alfred Wong, had gotten wind of the proposed action and made the decision to close the building to all except those involved in the pending cases.[12] Crone and organizers had to pivot at the last minute to pool groups on the streets surrounding the Supreme Court Building, and to approach in waves, triggering arrests.

Crone worried about the execution of the protest until people began to sing and dance in a circle near the court as the sun rose at 7:30 a.m. Four thousand people showed up.[13] As they waited in their affinity groups, organizers used bullhorns to remind them that the law considered them criminals already. The action would affirm their anger at being denied basic human dignity. At 9:00 a.m., the first wave of dissidents crossed the plaza, where officers were posted to maintain law and order. The activists knew if they reached a line set by law enforcement, they would be trespassing on the Supreme Court's grounds and would be arrested.

Go! Go! Go!

Lesbians had taken the lead in planning the action, so a lesbian group stepped through barricades on to the plaza first. Police moved on them, leading them to buses parked nearby to transport them for processing. Each group had a name—Queer and Present Danger, and Hardwick's Sassy Sodomites, Safe Sex Sluts—and a support team to keep track of the each member's location, name, address, and legal status to ensure they were moved swiftly through the system.[14] Protesters outnumbered police, so some held back at times to allow the police to process and transport groups before the next group stepped forward. Occasionally the police brandished clubs to force the queer activists back.

Only sissies wear gloves! they chanted at the officers, who wore latex gloves to protect themselves against the perceived danger of AIDS. They sang, *This land was made for you and me*, and announced that they had come to the Supreme Court "to light a candle for justice."

Police were dragging the fourth wave of protesters from the plaza when Michael Hardwick emerged from the crowd, joined in a fifth wave by a group of lesbians from Atlanta and some men from California. Surrounded by a pack of rowdy protesters, Hardwick smiled when he saw news cameras pivot in his direction and addressed them directly: "We refuse to live a lie and we will not live a lie," he said, "because we have feelings, and we have a life."[15]

He crossed the steps next, with an affinity group named Michael Hardwick and the Sodomites.[16] The officer who arrested him handled him gingerly but smiled as Hardwick laughed along with him. It became clear on the news later that evening that the officer in question realized whom he had detained. Once in cuffs, Hardwick stepped to the side so that he was in front of the statue *Contemplation of Justice* and crouched down on the balls of his feet. He was being arrested for the third time in his life. In the joy of sacrifice, humiliation had turned into jubilation. The queer community cheered him on.

As the process dragged on—it would take seven hours in all for the waves of protesters to cross the plaza—some affinity groups broke their compact with police and attempted to enter the court building from the sides and the rear. The police redeployed to prevent the unplanned incursion. All day long, protesters refused to comply with their arrest. In classic civil disobedience style they were dragged off in plastic handcuffs or were carried; some slipped out of the cuffs' grasp; others gave fake names to the officers, like Sharon Kowalski and Michael Hardwick. They sat for hours on buses with no water or bathrooms, waiting to be transported and processed. Once at the jail or in an ad-hoc courtroom set up after officials realized the volume of arrests, many gave their $100 bond and left per the agreement with the courts, while others waited to make statements to a waiting judge in court, where a guilty plea would draw a $50 fine or three days in jail.[17]

Hardwick waited on the bus with his fellow Sodomites for their trip to the police academy at Blue Plains Drive. He sat near Karen Chance, an Atlantan who thought of herself as a garden-variety troublemaker. She hadn't known Hardwick until a few minutes before they walked across the court plaza in defiance. She had only found out about the protest the night before, and when she and the Atlanta contingent went for civil disobedience training, they found out Hardwick and his friends were looking for people to join them.

Karen had spent most of the day crying. It could be such a lonely experience to be a gay person. When she arrived in D.C. and saw thousands of other people like her, she cried again because finally it seemed real. The protest revolved around an epidemic and inequality, but at its core a community of joy was formed.

When Hardwick and the Sodomites crossed the line and sat down, the police had given them a choice of whether to get up and walk away, otherwise they would have to be dragged out. *Nope*, Karen had said, *you're gonna have to drag me, so drag me.*

When frisked by a female officer, she'd instinctively put her hands on the side of a staircase, only to be told, *You know, it's not a TV show.* She laughed. *It's nothing to be proud of*, the officer said.

Well, I am, she replied.

On the bus, an officer told the group that they were the nicest people he'd ever arrested. Karen planned to pay her fine and leave, while others insisted on being booked and getting a hearing before a judge. Those on the bus remained in high spirits until Hardwick spoke about the traumatic experience of his arrest and case, how it had freaked him out, and how he was taking a break from sex.

On another bus, the conversation erupted into a chant: *We are all Michael Hardwick!*[18]

He had become the movement's folk hero. It had needed one, in a time of shame and death. Much as the community had needed a star like Rock Hudson to span the gulf of empathy for those who were infected, the gay-rights movement needed Hardwick to show how inequality worked, how it felt, and how it affected ordinary people and their lives. He had done extraordinary service to a movement he had never politically engaged with before his arrest. Now with the march all but over, he could go home and let his name carry on.

The march bound together a generation of queer people. Some would return and come out to their families, no matter the consequences. Others would found the hundreds of local activist groups that would feed, house, and care for those clinging to life. Most would plunge back into a dreary and dangerous otherhood, in lives and hometowns where precious little had changed. Many would go home to die.

V

METAMORPHOSIS

Bliss

From the open door of his studio at 550 Meridian Avenue on Miami Beach, Michael Hardwick could swat at swarming dragonflies or hear the caws of the pandemonium of wild mitred parakeets that had taken up residence in the palms near the beach. They were art themselves, iridescent green with daubs of red and yellow. They chattered and bickered as they flitted from tree to tree in the park near his place.

Hardwick shared his space with a landscaper in a building that had been divided by a ceiling-to-floor chain-link fence. On the one side, the landscaper stored his equipment and raw materials. On the other side of the fence, in the front of the building, Hardwick's studio ran for the whole block on Meridian. A small patio in the back gave him a spot to work on taller pieces, or to have a Cuban coffee in relative peace.

Miami Beach lured artists with its inexpensive rents and its brilliant palette. In May 1983, Jeanne-Claude and Christo had wrapped eleven of the islands around the city and the beach with pink fabric that covered 6.5 million square feet. To prepare for the installation, the artists' teams of more than 400 people worked to pull out tires, mattresses, and refrigerators that littered the water, tossed in as an afterthought, turning the process of art into a recovery operation and reclamation. They turned Miami's archipelago into queer lily pads, an invitation extended in a most overt way.

The pink blended with green and aqua waters and buff sand to cement the palette that, when rendered in neon, had become a signature of Miami Beach—and of *Miami Vice*, the TV show that refashioned the city's gloss and drug violence into pop art. Advocates had been relentless in getting the city to recognize dilapidated Art Deco structures as historically significant and economically valuable. As *Miami Vice* filmed episodes, the show unwittingly embarked on guerrilla urban renewal. Crews would identify a faded, empty building, then clean and paint it to use as a sound stage. They reclaimed nightclubs, ballrooms, and swimming pools, and fashioned a Potemkin village that glittered under the sun and glittered at night under neon, then broadcast that image around the world as authentic. Slowly, then quickly, actual nightclubs began to fill the spaces and to attract more clubgoers, guests, and residents. The Miami Beach renaissance had begun. The lies Miami told about its glamour on television, bit by bit, became true.[1]

Queer and straight people alike flocked to the latest international playground. Photo shoots stopped traffic on Lincoln Road, and casual sex flourished in Flamingo Park.[2] The mix of elderly Jewish retirees and first-generation Cuban Americans shifted to the German photographers and their models who brought cadres of makeup artists and stylists. Bistros and bookstores followed. The sun-drenched beach and turquoise waters looked fabulous on film. It was almost a secret, another outpost in the queer archipelago, where one could run away and live cheaply and watch the world change.[3]

Hardwick immersed himself in this burgeoning art world, consumed by a passion unrelated to the political one he had just endured. "My life has nothing to do with that anymore," he said. "My life is my life now. And my life now is my art."[4] Then he had served a purpose.

Now he had one. He carried a small business card in a handwritten font that described him as an "optical alchemist." He stocked his studio with the pieces of mannequins that he transformed into art.

He tended bar on occasion, but less than he had in the years prior. He survived by selling his art. The sixteen-foot-tall statues Hardwick had carved for Club Nu made his name. On a smaller scale he explored ideas of futurism and nature. He shocked shoppers of one clothing boutique with nuclear-sized cockroaches that crawled up the walls. For another clothing store, Planet Beach, he drew mutant shapes like those from the *Alien* movies and fashioned what he conceived as a "board pod"—for surfers or alien refugees, it wasn't clear. One scaly aqua pod he drew looked like a particular Miami species of dragon fruit, studded by slim antlers and capped with pink-and-orange egg masses. It spoke to something that he tried to capture from his dreams. He drew a "New Frontier Octatarian," perhaps a reference to an ancient form, in the forms of a purple orb with dozens of blue and green tentacles sprouting from it and blue-bodied creatures with man-o'-war outlines and pink leg-like limbs. One striking piece that seemed ready to be printed on a T-shirt or poster was his rendering of Planet Beach's "Jetson birds," a geometrically reinvented bird-of-paradise plant, with a blue-green body and a red-and-yellow disc for its mouth.

After Uncle Charlie's, Hardwick had moved on to Club Cheers, which hadn't been named for the popular TV show. It had opened in 1983 as a video bar, with the goal of putting Uncle Charlie's and its owner out of business. A dance floor and DJ booth opened on February 9, 1985, where a soon-to-be friend of Hardwick's, Danny Tenaglia, worked on the lighting board while learning how to mix records from the club's resident DJ, Tommy Moore. By the time the third phase of the club opened, it had an outdoor patio, three bars, and a reputation. Cheers was a preppy bar for preppy people, a place where you came dressed as if you had shopped for the right clothes to wear. It was a high-octane, upscale nightclub that was busy from the moment it opened in the early afternoon until it closed, early the next morning.[5]

Video screens, fresh faces, drinks and drugs, and the bartenders created the illusion of happiness, putting on a show so that customers could put away their own lives.[6] Hardwick had appeared out of nowhere, bartender Lori Tanner thought, and fit in easily. He was a good time, so well-liked that the bar named a combo shot of Sambuca and aguardiente for him.[7] He and Tanner worked hip to hip at the bar, where patrons, flush with money and cocaine, threw dollars at them for drinks.

Like many people working in clubs, Tanner had friends who, when they grew ill, disappeared. She would find out they went home to live with their parents and knew what that meant.[8] Cheers owner Jan Harrold had warned the employees during a staff meeting: *This HIV thing is going to change all your lives. It's going to change the entire business too.* It didn't land with some of the younger staff, who were making a lot of money that disappeared in a flash of powder. Hardwick was different. He was older than most of the people there, and at this point he was kind of an old soul with a gentle demeanor. When the younger staff went out for beers at six or seven in the morning, he shied away. He told few people he was HIV positive, especially as his body was holding up.

With his art becoming known, Cheers hired him to outfit the bar with a new look. They refreshed the interior every few months. In one striking version of Cheers, Hardwick filled nearly every square inch of wall and ceiling with detailed black-and-white art that took more than two weeks to install. Inspired by taxicabs, he painted a road that went up the ceiling, a superhighway superimposed over skeletal tiles, squiggles, and giraffe print. A frieze of televisions ran in a band around the room. A skull-capped mermaid who wore black lipstick and a black zebra-striped top reigned supreme. He drew a solar system of streets and roads over the bar's neon lights, complete with little yellow taxicabs that appeared on the horizon and disappeared.[9] It mirrored his own life of the past two years, a procession of flights and speeches and appearances, taxi to plane, plane to taxi, to hotel, to home.

Hardwick had enlisted his sister Alice, who had returned to South Florida, to help plot and construct his designs. Alice dyed her hair a bright pink that she got from canned beet juice, offered unprompted advice, and generally consumed the attention of any room that offered it. Hardwick also had help from some of the other Cheers staff, including Brad Lamm, who had been hired at twenty years old, legally too young to serve alcohol. Lamm had grown up in a cloistered Quaker home with no radio, since the beat of the music was deemed too exciting. He had never been on a plane in his life when he flew to Florida to settle down with a lover. He promptly acquired a fake ID and applied for a job at Cheers. He told them he knew how to mix drinks and was hired. Brad was the perfect Cheers type, with his boyish good looks.

Lamm spent hours with Hardwick, handing him cottage-cheese containers of paint while Hardwick worked from scaffolding. He spent hours inches from the ceiling, doing his most elaborate installation yet. Every square inch of the bar would be transformed in his hands, into the throbbing patterns of traffic, complete with the tiny taxis hanging upside down overhead, or into geometric webs that embedded the Cheers videoscape into a textural exploration of Escher. The yellow paint he used would glow when the lights were turned off, as Danny Tenaglia's beats stole the oxygen from the room and filled it with the urge to get busy while the world was dying.

As he worked, Hardwick would talk to Lamm about queer life, about the ideas of sex versus love, and about making the latter the goal in a relationship. Sex was the easy part. He instructed Lamm to read Larry Kramer's *Faggot*. He told him to be careful, very careful, about whom he had sex with. He became a philosopher and teacher to his young student, as Baba had been to him in another life.

Hardwick was like no one else Lamm had ever met. He was a star in the Miami Beach firmament. Most people knew the story of his immediate past, and how it had broken him somehow. Lamm knew him more as the lovely, solitary soul he had a crush on, the man who had distanced himself from the culture that celebrated drugs, who would be at the club during the day but absent at the gray hours when it was really hustling. Who gave off feelings of anger and sadness only when he allowed himself to be known.

When he allowed for intimacy, Hardwick would talk about his swollen lymph nodes and about being afraid. He knew that other people were dying, and that he was headed there. Lamm still wanted to get closer to him. He wanted to show him love and attention in the way he knew best at that moment in his life, through sex. Hardwick was very gentle with him and said no. He told him it wasn't a good idea. He told him what they both knew to be true. *What's in me could kill you.*

Foucault held that "the exercise of power is strategic and warlike." *Bowers v. Hardwick* had birthed thousands of new activists who connected at the March on Washington and lurched into a wave of civil disobedience from sit-ins to die-ins to kiss-ins across America in the spring of 1988 to protest the government's policies on AIDS.[10] But without a set of marching orders, the exercise of power could be short-lived or misdirected. Those orders for the next phase of the gay-rights movement would be written down over a weekend in February 1988, where key activists gathered in a weekend of planning and maneuvers dubbed "The War Conference."

The War Conference took place weeks after Justice Anthony Kennedy took his seat on the Supreme Court. On October 23, 1987, the Senate had rejected Robert Bork's Supreme Court nomination, by a vote of 52–48. On October 29, Reagan nominated Douglas Ginsburg—but then on November 7, Ginsburg withdrew his name from consideration for a range of reasons, chief among them that he had admitted to smoking marijuana in the past. On November 11, 1987, Reagan offered California appellate judge Kennedy the spot.

In his thirteen years on the appellate court in California, Kennedy had voted against gay-rights plaintiffs in each of the five cases brought before him.[11] But a month after the *Hardwick* decision Kennedy had voiced some concerns in a speech before an ABA meeting at Stanford University in which he said that the decision was in direct conflict with the court's 1965 privacy ruling in *Griswold*. A notable voice spoke up in Kennedy's favor: Laurence Tribe. Kennedy, Tribe testified in the confirmation hearings that followed, "has recognized that the great protections afforded individual liberty by the Constitution cannot be defined by any scientific process or conception of the Framers' specific intentions but are bound up in a continuing examination of the principles of human freedom."[12]

According to its manifesto/invitation, War Conference leaders would gather at Virginia's Airlie House to assess the state of the gay-rights movement just after the March on Washington's success but still faced with a Congress that voted with Senator Jesse Helms's proposed restrictions on AIDS educational funding."[13] Organizers wanted to build a more diverse and stronger movement, one with a more unified strategy and better cohesion.

Invitees included Andy Humm, Joyce Hunter, Robin Tyler, Steve Ault, and dozens more who had been critical in the planning of the 1987 march. They connected over the long weekend to "combat what their leaders say is growing homophobia in America."[14]

The War Conference weekend resulted in "A Call to Action,"

which expressed the goals that the conference had resolved to pursue. "We came to say that no one is a second-class citizen," the document reads, "and that we shall be silent no longer." Some 3,000 of them had gone to the Supreme Court in protest, and it didn't listen. Among the goals agreed upon were to raise more money to fund more institutions defending queer health and liberty; to attract more leaders outside of the usual core group of organizers, to avoid burnout; to encourage people to come out; and to demand "accurate and affirming treatment of lesbians and gay men in all the media. Nothing less than a nationwide campaign to uplift the image of lesbians and gays in the media would be necessary.

Their determination was counterbalanced by a note of desperation: "We have lost so many of our number," they wrote. "We are fighting for our lives."[15]

It was going to be an "extraordinary evening," the fundraiser promised—one with "Liz Taylor and friends." The benefit that took place on March 13, 1988, steps away from Hardwick's studio, would be spread across fifteen private homes in the Miami area. A few hundred people paid $2,500 each to attend a dinner. In Coconut Grove, one host's house made of coral rock ringed its interior reflecting pool in orchids while guests sampled caviar and Champagne, and irises lay in repose on silver trays that held canapés served by waiters. The house had been built by William Jennings Bryan, three-time presidential candidate famed for his "Cross of Gold" speech, in 1909. Now a Rauschenberg hung in the foyer and served as a backdrop for the jazz group Manhattan Transfer as donors sopped up the coriander sauce in which lobster and shrimp swam. The epidemic was affecting everyone, though the fundraiser gilded over it. Transfer member Tim Hauser said, "It won't be long before everyone will have their lives touched by this disease."¹⁶ Each guest left with a purple amethyst in a lavender suede bag, in homage to the sponsor's famous eyes.

In the years since her friend Rock Hudson had died from the disease, Elizabeth Taylor had become a heroine and a guide for the straight world as it came to grips with the HIV/AIDS epidemic. Compassionate and sympathetic toward friends and strangers whose lives were decimated by AIDS, Taylor leveraged her roles as a Hollywood icon and Senator John Warner's wife to drum up funding for research. Stars like Taylor had been among the first to lose talented queer friends. They were the men who painted faces, choreographed dances, composed music, prepared food, styled wardrobes, and designed sets, while other queer people served their country, drove trucks, and worked desk jobs, all while they lived in anxiety if not outright fear.

AIDS donations still were a difficult appeal to those with the money to be charitable—and charity was a necessity even as federal funding for research began to grow. AIDS patients and HIV-positive people needed emotional support, but they also needed money for rent when they were fired from jobs. They needed meals when they could no longer cook. They needed help with their homes when they could no longer clean. They needed nurses when they could no longer sit up in bed.

Corporations were slow to step up to the plate. None would donate enough money to present Taylor with the oversized check that often signified major donations.¹⁷ The event had been announced late, and most big donations had been planned months before, but the subject of the fundraiser also kept many at arm's length. Some preferred to cloak their donations to AIDS causes in bigger organizations with AIDS initiatives, such as the Salvation Army. Or they would donate to pediatric AIDS care, which did not carry the stigma of a disease that affected sex workers, queer people, and drug users. To many, the epidemic still was someone else's problem. One organizer was asked bluntly: "Do you know one straight man or woman who has died?"[18]

Ticket sales had been slow. Organizers were forced to open the fundraiser's star-studded gala at Miami's famed Fontainebleau Hotel, to the paying public who could rub elbows with Cheryl Tiegs, Zsa Zsa Gabor, Peter Allen, and Ed Asner.[19] Even so, Taylor's efforts yielded just $2.3 million in donations during the Miami Beach offensive. The goal had been $3 million. "AIDS in is a transition state," marketing executive Dana Clay said. "By this time next year. it will probably be acceptable."[20]

On June 30, 1988, the second anniversary of the *Hardwick* decision was remembered with yet another protest at the Supreme Court. For this one, about thirty activists chanted, "Get the courts out of our bedroom!"[21] National Gay and Lesbian Task Force organizer Urvashi Vaid said the decision was a product of a "bigoted, racist, sexist, homophobic Supreme Court" and that sodomy laws should be dismantled in the twenty-five states and in the District of Columbia, where they remained on the books. Protesters dressed in black robes like those worn by the court's justices and performed as authoritarians disturbing couples asleep on the D.C. sidewalk, in an act of *protestus interruptus*.

Weeks later, two of the protesters arrested in the 1987 march action at the Supreme Court were sentenced to probation, community service, and a $100 fine after being found guilty of unlawful crossing of a police line and demonstrating without a permit. "The government simply decided that they had to make an example of these people," said Leonard Graff, attorney for Alexander Willis, who, along with Michael McDonogh, was convicted. "Considering the symbolic nature of the crime, the sentence was unnecessarily harsh." Fifty-one of the protesters had spent forty-eight hours in jail, while some women who protested were strip-searched and subjected to pelvic examinations.[22]

The decisions came as the city of Atlanta had put the finishing touches on its preparations for the 1988 Democratic National Convention for Michael Dukakis's presidential bid. The city had been on the front lines of the civil-rights era. Now it was on the front lines of the gay-rights movement during a week of speeches and demonstrations against the sodomy law and woefully inadequate HIV/AIDS policy. The convention included a clumsy speech by rising party star Bill Clinton, with ringing applause for Democratic politicians such as Texas governor Ann Richards and presidential candidate Jesse Jackson, who called the host city "the cradle of the Old South, the crucible of the New South." Nearly 40,000 delegates pumped $70 million into the city's economy. Television journalists toured Atlanta documenting it as a foreign land. They verified its Southern bona fides, from the usual *Gone with the Wind* tropes to the real-time existence of places like Aunt Fanny's Cabin, a suburban restaurant where young Black staff wore sandwich boards as menus and presented themselves to primarily white patrons.

The city spent $2.5 million to tidy up downtown, fixing potholes, planting flowers, and hanging red-white-and-blue banners; it provided reporters with shot lists of beautiful Atlanta skyline spots; Coca-Cola donated thousands of gallons of its namesake beverage; and a special "Dukakis Delight" ice cream was designed and serviced by Gorin's Homemade Ice Cream.[23] A "Super Bowl of civic pride, a high-wire prance between hospitality and hype put on for the benefit of more than 5,300 delegates and alternates, 13,500 journalists and 10,000 members of the political and corporate elite," the convention would be a warm-up round of exposure for what was to come in the next two years. Atlanta had been preparing a bid for the 1996 Centennial Olympics, and national politics were its dry run for global stardom.

Politicos tried to dissuade activists from turning the city's coming-out party into a platform for protest. "Having demonstrated all my life, I don't see a whole lot out there to motivate people to demonstrate," Atlanta mayor Andrew Young told the city's paper.[24]

On Sunday, July 17, the convention opened with a reminder of the stark difference between that Old South and the new one that Atlanta had tried vigorously and endlessly to create and promote in the media. At the convention's doorstep, a group from the National Movement, said to have pro-Klan sympathies, tried to set up a rally in the convention's "free speech zones," the city's Orwellian construct that determined where and when protesters could protest. Two parking lots on Marietta Street, each an acre large, could hold 30,000 people and were equipped with a sound stage and microphones. They had been created to keep traffic moving in and out of the Omni Coliseum, officials said. The National Movement group included J. B. Stoner, a self-proclaimed racist who brought a poster that offered the grotesque homily "Praise God for AIDS."[25] The white supremacists' march included police as guards and private security in camouflage fatigues.

While they marshaled at the nearby State Capitol for their 3:00 p.m. free-speech-zone slot, a group of counter-demonstrators led by ACT UP members had come to Atlanta for the convention as well as "assorted self-proclaimed anarchists."[26] Mississippi lawyer Richard Barrett, a National Movement leader, was among those in the middle of the tussle between his group and ACT UP comrades as police tried to split up the groups from a fight. Protesters spat and shouted at him, calling him a "yellow-bellied redneck." Atlanta Public Safety Commissioner George Napper, named in the original *Hardwick* lawsuit, was on-site, determined that there would be no "bloodshed on the streets of Atlanta."[27] Still, Barrett was forced to flee, and when skinheads attacked the counter-protesters as they reconvened at the free-speech zone, they beat and threw traffic pylons at them. The gay activists tracked some of the skinheads through downtown before a crowd of 500 counter-protesters flooded the free-speech zone. Atlanta police kept the 25 Klan members from getting closer than two blocks away. They couldn't guarantee their safety—even a preteen boy, who had been covered in spit hurled by the crowd. The crowd joined in with taunts against the Klan marchers. When one man shouted at Klan members, "Hey, honey, I'm gay, and if you come over here I'm going to kick your a . . ." two elderly Black women urged him on. When asked their names by a reporter from the local gay newspaper *Southern Voice*, the women declined to give their names, and said that they weren't exactly comfortable with gay/lesbian sexuality. But they added, anyone willing to " 'kick some Klan a . . .' had to be all right."[28]

ACT UP and other queer protesters took to the hot streets again the following day for an 11:00 a.m. "die-in" protest, which would turn into a "kiss-in."[29] The activists' determination—and desperation—to draw attention to the epidemic and their second-class status put them in danger on this 95-degree day, especially those who were medically challenged. The die-in of 150 people came first. Morris Kight and March On, an activist group from Los Angeles, led it, joined by independent presidential candidate Lenora Fulani. TV news crews recorded demonstrators lying on the pavement while someone drew their bodies in chalk, like a Keith Haring illustration. The name of a person who died from AIDS would be written inside each one and the names were read aloud in an homage to the AIDS Quilt.

Twenty to thirty people from ACT UP staged the impromptu kiss-in not long after, outside of the free-speech zones and right in front of CNN headquarters. Ira Frozen and Kevin Smith from New York started it off with a "long, passionate kiss before an attentive media audience."[30] Dozens of Atlanta police in riot helmets pushed the protesters out of the area with clubs and plastic shields, shouting, *Move! Move! Move!* They retreated, only to return in a picket line on the sidewalk. The police then forced them to leave. ACT UP member Michael Lowe said the group would complain after some ACT UPers were shoved into barricades. "We were just kissing for the right to display our affections like the rest of America, and you see what the Atlanta Gestapo has done to us. We were breaking no laws," he said.

Mayor Young would call the group out for being provocative, but apologized for the police intervention.[31] Later, Young was compelled to apologize for the apology he gave for at first blaming protesters for some of the kiss-in fracas. The reason he gave at first was that officers were forced to maintain order in 95-degree heat in full uniform. "I think it's easy to understand that somebody . . . operated on a short fuse." When asked if homophobia had been at play, the mayor answered, "Sure, no doubt about it. But we're working on it." ACT UP had got his ire up. "If you call yourself ACT UP, you're not going to get very far with me. If you come in here to act up at a time we're trying to elect a president, I'm not going to be very hospitable," he said. Chris Hagin, a state AIDS lobbyist retorted, "That was no apology."[32]

At the convention, the crowd outside of the Omni was drawn to a brief but powerful speech by Keith Gann, who took to the podium just before prime time. His was the first political convention speech given by a person known to have AIDS. Gann, a Minnesotan social worker and ACT UP member, opened his speech simply: "I'm Keith Gann from St. Paul, Minnesota. I am a person with AIDS."

"I rise to speak in support of the majority plank on the HIV/AIDS epidemic," Gann said, speaking directly to the determined supporters outside the Omni who questioned whether the Democrats running for the White House would do enough for their cause. Either Michael Dukakis or the Reverend Jesse Jackson would be better than the sitting president, Ronald Reagan: "I am outraged [by] the immorality of a president who sat idly by refusing to say the word 'AIDS' publicly for six years while thousands of my brothers and sisters got sick and died," Gann said in a gravelly voice from under his widow's peak of red hair, wearing a white shirt festooned with buttons in support of people with AIDS.

"I am frustrated with those who call me victim, stripping me of both my personal and political power," he continued. "I am not a victim. I cannot think of myself as a victim and survive. I am a person with AIDS. I am your brother, son, neighbor, friend, lover. I ask each of you to personally take responsibility for eliminating the word 'victim' from your discussion of AIDS. Do not divide the world into us and them. We must understand that we are all us. We are a people with AIDS."[33]

Gann, a Quaker native of Iowa, demanded an end to discrimination against people with AIDS and adequate healthcare for them in every state, and also called for an end to a two-year waiting period for Medicare assistance, which was forcing AIDS patients into poverty. He asked for more money for research and coordination, for an end to the discrimination "against gays and lesbians which has created this epidemic." As he closed, Gann told an audience distracted by party members greeting one another in the stands, "I want you to know that AIDS is a life-threatening illness but is not 100 percent fatal. There are already many long-term survivors. This is not denial," he insisted, "this is hope."[34]

The 1988 DNC also featured speeches by Rosa Parks and John F. Kennedy Jr., as it crested toward its conclusion. Dukakis, the former governor of Massachusetts, chose Texan Lloyd Bentsen as his running mate. Although a *Newsweek* poll after the convention showed Dukakis with a 17-point lead on Vice President George H. W. Bush, the election ended with a resounding victory for Bush, with 411 out of 535 electoral votes and more than 53 percent of the national vote. The clash on the streets of Atlanta had given queer protesters a moment in the spotlight, but it was the conservatives who continued to command the stage.

Hardwick redid the interior of Cheers eight times in two years, then felt as if he was repeating himself. He wanted a fresh challenge. Once he realized he had a talent, he said, he had let go of his fear and began to experiment wildly. What else had he been doing, he asked, out of fear?[35] Hardwick built a five-piece display titled *Silencing the Internal Dialogue*. Over the course of five canvases, a male figure gradually emerges from the flat surface into a standalone piece of sculpture in an act of gradual self-emancipation.

He took on a project for a new boutique, Hero. Hardwick decorated the store in yin and yang symbols, seated a polka-dotted mermaid in it, and committed the walls to flames that licked across skulls and crossbones. He doubled as bartender on the night the boutique opened, and served drinks to his friends Kim Stark and Andrew Delaplaine, among others on the Miami Beach scene.[36] For Delaplaine's birthday, Hardwick built an elaborate birthday cake from which local magazine editor Stark emerged in a red ball gown.[37]

Stark's publication chronicled the nightlife and celebrated art and theater and fashion, a timely choice given the influx of models and art from Europe. In one issue, she captured Hardwick in a full-page photo with a brief caption: "SoBe resident Michael Hardwick is responsible for some of the most dynamic designs in graphics and sets seen recently in Miami's new clubs and boutiques," it read. "A rarity, Michael was born and raised in these parts, typically Florida laid-back, Michael Hardwick lets his art do his talking."[38]

Stark thought Hardwick's work was primitive and naïve, interesting and beautiful. She admired his refusal to brandish his notoriety as social currency. He was without arrogance—which might not have been helpful in corridors where arrogance, or at least confidence, stood apart and stood out—and drew people to him with affable, low-gloss charm.

The South Beach queer party scene had begun to evolve into a high-wattage, celebrity-driven affair, one from which Hardwick steered clear. But the beach was also becoming a microcosm of the othered: poor immigrants, older retirees, models and artists, drug dealers, and HIV-positive men who migrated there to die. The beach owed its modern existence in part to Leonard Horowitz, who founded the Miami Design Preservation League with Barbara Capitman in 1976. By the spring of 1989, Horowitz had helped to save up to 150 buildings of pastel ebullience. He was forty-three years old and dying of AIDS.[39]

He was like many who came to the beach, where the sunset could mask some of the symptoms of HIV. Body culture encouraged them to work out, eat well, and get tan. Thousands of gay men moved in—and thousands of them were HIV-positive or had developed complications that classified them as people with AIDS. Some had far fewer than 200 T cells to count, another marker of the progression of the disease. A steady wash of pills could ward off death briefly—AZT and ddI would suppress the HIV virus, while antifungals and antivirals could suppress the opportunistic infections that set in as the immune system withered—but none could do it permanently.

Hardwick meditated, read, and walked with Jumbo down stretches of Miami Beach while he planned out his next works. He renewed himself spiritually and read to advance his mind while his body declined. He began to immerse himself once more in the teaching of Meher Baba, whose ideas reminded him that his life would take many forms, just as his "Internal Dialogue" had demonstrated. "The life of the reincarnating individual has many events and phases," Baba had written. "The wheel of life makes its ceaseless rounds, lifting the individual to the heights or bringing him down from high positions."[40]

Few, if any, of his new friends knew he was ill. He didn't have to come out to them. He was hardly sexual at that point. He had a straight male friend with whom he practiced breath-sharing Tantric training, which replaced penetrative sex for many HIV-positive people.

It had all become too normal a part of the everyday existence in Miami Beach. Men could work and play and hide their sex lives and hide their health condition until they visibly dimmed. They could survive on disability payments or on the proceeds from the sale of their life insurance policies—viatical settlements that gave them cash to live out the rest of their lives. Some would give in to the lack of T cells and take illicit drugs and party themselves into ash. Others sat at favorite cafés and sunned and contemplated the immediate future. To plan for more was to waste some of the little time they had left. They had come to Miami Beach to die. The community that showed itself so vibrantly on television harbored an intangible undertow that Kim Stark's magazine had documented in its very name: *Postmortem*.[41]

By March of 1989, Hardwick had given up his shared apartment in Coral Gables and moved into his sparsely furnished studio. He had been lured to work for a new club in Fort Lauderdale called Squeeze that would open on the city's waterfront, in place of the former Boat House restaurant. Lauderdale was trying to move past its "Fort Liquordale" spring-break image, and downtown was key, whether it was nightlife or food—or simply a respite from Miami Beach. Miami was like going to Europe, with $5,000-a-night DJs. Lauderdale was less costly, less fussy, but also less openly queer.

Squeeze pitched itself on the edge of a new musical and cultural edge. Times were changing, and the flashy Miami ethos of the 1980s was waning in favor of something darker, more experimental. Labeled a "progressive danceteria," Squeeze had as an early act a local duo dubbed Marilyn Manson and the Spooky Kids, who warned audiences that their howling heavy-metal tracks might be accompanied by flying chunks of cow heart or bodily fluids.[42] Fort Lauderdale had its own weird, beautiful underground of Goth creatures playing cutting-edge industrial metal. Squeeze would soon host the occasional fetish night, where one could watch a person sew another person's mouth shut with fishing line.

Owner Jack Kearney described it as "a constant metamorphosis."[43] He wanted something new all the time, whether it was live performances or artwork festooning the club up to the rafters. Kearney was an artist himself and had run bars in Boston and Philadelphia. He wanted someone to bring a different aura to what would be his new nightclub.

Kearney lured Hardwick to Squeeze after he bumped into him in downtown Miami. He knew Hardwick's sister Alice, who also was working as an artist. *Who the hell is this?* Kearney thought when he met her. She was small but all muscle. *She's either a witch or a genius,* he thought. Kearney asked Hardwick to come up to Lauderdale to look at his space. Jack loved him right off the bat. Hardwick was so entertaining, so alive. He noticed Hardwick's hands right away, how they would be in constant motion. He used them to talk, to convey ideas, to motion to Jumbo as he roamed the space that would be Squeeze.

The Squeeze building had twenty-four-foot ceilings so that, in its prior life, boats could be moved in and out. Hardwick described to Kearney what he saw in the Squeeze space—black lighting, neon outlines, an orgy of natural and geometric shapes—and Kearney could see what he was saying. Hardwick came back a few days later with a design and some sample pieces, and Kearney commissioned him.

Squeeze was a vast canvas, bigger that Club Nu, somewhere Hardwick could stretch out.

When Kearney saw Hardwick work, he saw him become an artist. Hardwick entered as a stranger, not sure what he was doing, then quickly focused on the space. He cased the joint. He made a quiet, undistracted study of the room. When he came into the club to lay out the space, the staff moved furniture out of the way for what they could tell would be an important work. When the space was ready, Hardwick locked himself inside to work alone for two days straight.[44]

Squeeze sat next to a courthouse and jail, and the kitchen stayed open to serve customers coming from those buildings. But Hardwick convinced Kearney he needed more space, so out came the kitchen. Hardwick laid it with geometric tile that turned it into an Escher stairway. The dazzling trompe l'oeil confused and freaked out patrons who believed they had made a physical descent, but it was all an illusion. He created a juice bar for the front of the building for underage clubgoers. He built a cage for two lizards that crawled up the wall, reviving childhood memories of "lounge-lizard" Halloween costumes that Alice had fashioned for the Hardwick kids.

Hardwick's gifts turned raw space into moods. He suspended mannequins from wires and decked some in red fur and others, armless, with wide white ribbons rolled into Medusa curls, splattered in neon blue and pink paint. An angel with wings ten feet wide hung over the main entrance. He kept his large-scale works inexpensive and fresh. Ideas from dreams would become real in his studio, then move into Squeeze to make room for their successors. He often took mannequins down from the ceiling and, at home, fashioned them anew—sometimes in pieces, just torso, arms, and legs. Hardwick's art assumed a world of instability.

Kearney sometimes saw him with a young man who idolized Hardwick and did a lot of work with him. Hardwick also spent hours with Alice, whose smaller works filled in empty spaces of the vast club. She made Kearney a voodoo doll of herself, complete with spiky hair, a leather jacket, and a look of incontrovertible horror. But Hardwick preferred to work at all hours of the night and by himself. He told Kearney that all he needed in life was a truck and a dog. As his work began to draw attention to Squeeze, Kearney gave him the money for an old red 1966 Chevy C10, like the ones in Coca-Cola ads. Hardwick could load up massive pieces of art from his studio and drive them up I-95 and A1A to install at Squeeze, with Jumbo riding on the bench seat next to him.

Kearney had seen Hardwick's studio in Miami Beach—it was a good space and had a ladder that went up to the second floor, where Hardwick slept on a mattress. He lived with his art. He fashioned a hand from chicken wire, covered it, and painted it Day-Glo green. He hung it over the bar, where it loomed large, visible from across the room. To Kearney, it signified Hardwick himself, a presence that gave Squeeze an essential if muted queerness.

As Hardwick's patron, Kearney tried to convince him to move into a studio space in Lauderdale. He offered to buy a warehouse he could get for next to nothing and set Hardwick up in it so he could keep Squeeze suspenseful, intriguing, and unexpected. But Hardwick didn't want to leave South Beach. He had made himself anew there, and he could work and meditate in relative privacy. He was happy, he told Kearney. *My hands are now busy.* That was enough.

You know, I'm not gonna be here that long, he told Kearney, *so I want to do as much as I can.*

Family paid visits to Hardwick in Miami Beach when they could. Susan and Mike brought Jasmine to town before a birthday cruise, and the women posed with Hardwick outside of his studio, his white painter's overalls splashed with neon paint, his chest plated by a pyramid studded by an all-seeing eye. They took another photo of Hardwick standing barefoot and posing in front of a queen palm.

Now a teenager and on the cusp of moving abroad, Susan's son, Robert, came to visit his uncle Michael and brought a friend. Jorge Alberto Perez knew Hardwick's sister Alice, as a quirky, utterly engaging woman who'd frequented a Puerto Rican restaurant in Gainesville where he waited tables during college. He'd noticed the chopsticks she had whittled herself and how she'd half-shaved her head and draped the rest, dyed red, over her face. She never put metal in her mouth, she told Jorge, and refused to use her Social Security number. She lived in a shabby place in the student neighborhood and jammed it with her wildly inventive art that reveled in the daily magic of life. Alice had introduced Jorge to her nephew Robert, and soon Jorge became part of the extended Hardwick clan.

Jorge and Robert spent a night in Hardwick's studio, not long after Hardwick had shaved his own hair into a mohawk. Jorge knew Miami Beach—he had lived there years before—but wasn't quite prepared for its latest iteration as a Wild West populated by drug dealers and elderly people. Hardwick's studio disoriented him too. Everything in it had the potential to be something else: halves of mannequins strewn about, Styrofoam carved into planets, fluorescent tube lights placed not as fixtures but as statements. It had a wildly inventive potential about it, as an archive of ideas waiting to be breathed to life. But it didn't feel vibrant. It reflected something of Hardwick himself, who Jorge found somewhat distant, albeit kind and generous.

Jorge and Robert met Hardwick's platonic lover, and they all went to dinner at an Italian restaurant nearby, where the server ushered Hardwick to his usual table. They soaked in some of the glow of Hardwick's local celebrity.

On previous visits, Robert and his uncle shared their common queer experience with each other—and Hardwick told Robert in detail what had happened during his arrest. They had become closer as family and as gay men, but Hardwick would not discuss what was obvious. In Miami, Robert noticed a lesion on Hardwick's neck that looked like a typical sign of AIDS. When Robert asked him about it, Hardwick gave him a non-answer and said he had become celibate. He hadn't gotten—and didn't want to get—tested.

From the omissions, Robert deduced his uncle was ill. When they left, Robert told Jorge that Michael refused to acknowledge that he had AIDS.

Hardwick was working on a new project when the latest reporter tracked him down at Squeeze, where he had mounted his new creation: a seven-foot phallus, in exuberant support of sexual freedom. Hardwick wanted humor in his art and wanted people to react to it, and he would laugh at them when they stared at it in embarrassment or incomprehension or awe. Jack Kearney called him the giggle maker.

When Hardwick had spoken out before, it had cost him greatly. Now when he spoke, it came from the unconscious place where he conceived of his art, in his dreams. He had dubbed himself an "optical alchemist," one who specialized in set design and sculpting. "An alchemist is someone who changes something of little value into something of great value," Hardwick said, his hair now long enough to pull back into a ponytail. He had painted the bar's front room with a sunset worthy of Maxfield Parrish. His art heroes were Parrish, Escher, and O'Keeffe, whose sensual and graphic displays of nature appealed to him. He had begun work on a room filled with what he called an "atomic garden"—tall blooms and eighteen-foot-tall birds of paradise that guarded the entrance.

He was solitary and intense but willing and happy to talk about his projects over the Memorial Day weekend with the journalist from the local newspaper. He was splattered with neon paint from shoes to shoulders, with craggy lines appearing in his face, hiding a ponytail under his hat, which only drew attention to the emerald earring in his ear. His hands were gnarled and scarred, cut by chicken wire and burned by toxic chemicals to which he was exposed on a regular basis.[45]

Over his head flew a creature that had come to him in a dream. He had imagined himself in the canopy of the rain forest, among the orchids, and saw a lizard grow as it unfolded wings from its back. He had sculpted the vision into a pterodactyl-like creature that roamed the sky inside Squeeze, wings spread wide, ridged belly exposed to the dancers below. It started off as a small creature on a mossy rock, but then it took its own form, growing larger and larger. He strapped the massive green-winged creature, some twelve feet long, into his pickup for the ride to Fort Lauderdale and hung it in the Lizard Lounge.[46] He had rigged it to click its transparent wings over the heads of partygoers via a motor timed irregularly. The wings moved in a lifelike way, so people could believe it to be real when it stirred.[47]

He had created his own garden, a fusion of electric psychedelia and deep-seated memories of childhood, in Jack Kearney's club, where in the black light the ceiling glowed with hallucinatory creatures. He exaggerated and distorted the scale of the sculptures to give the viewer a childlike perspective.[48] He wanted to stir the senses and put people off their footing, even if that meant transporting them out of their own space. At thirty-five years old Hardwick was beginning to plumb his own psychic depths, to find the joy that could rise from his trauma.

What he created with Alice was a new Eden in an old boat barn. Once the building's air conditioning system was in place, Michael and

Alice draped it with vines and then festooned the vines with flowers and buds ready to open. They worked on ladders pushed high into the ether. With crepe and paint, the Squeeze space grew into an electric orchid farm. He installed the buds first, then changed them out for flowers. A postapocalyptic vine with four-foot leaves and giant blossoms wound itself around the rafters, rendered in neon-colored hyperreality. The fecund environment had sprung from his fertile mind.

He worked fourteen-hour stretches without concern but knew that some people would only understand him as a kind of celebrity. His atomic garden told the story of the person he was in that moment. He could not ignore the radical civil-rights advocate who had fought at the Supreme Court, but he had tried to distance himself from that persona to create a new, lasting career, trading graphic sex for his graphic talent.[49] The loss in court had shattered him, then stirred an artistic spirit inside him.

He and Kearney sometimes spoke of the freedom of death. *It was almost as if he was in a state of bliss,* Kearney thought. *He was getting there, full of energy and full of love.*

Silence

"When people hear my name, they think of a radical cocksucker," Hardwick told the reporter in earnest while he toured him around his warehouse. "People don't know anything else about me."[1]

Hardwick had greeted a reporter from the *Advocate*, Robrt Pela outside of the warehouse space he rented to make his art. The paper's editor had sent the twenty-six-year-old Pela to Miami on his first assignment: write a cover story on Hardwick. Pela prepared himself to hunt down an elusive subject and for him to decline any further publicity. Hardwick had not been on television in more than a year, didn't even own a TV set, but had continued to speak with journalists about his art career and, begrudgingly, his Supreme Court case. Pela found him on the second day. Gallery owners had directed him to the warehouse where Hardwick worked.

Hardwick greeted Pela warmly, showing him various works in progress, including a mosaic bar top for a local nightclub. Though it was far from brightly lit, when he looked up, way up, into the dark recesses of the warehouse's ceiling, Pela could see that Hardwick had cut a hole in the ceiling to open a portal to the next level where he slept.

He was so very kind, Pela thought, to stop his work to help another young gay man get his career started. His overalls and sweatshirt bloused out around his body, paint splattering them as well as his hands and forearms. He had work to complete, but they agreed to meet the next morning.

On Sunday the Miami Beach street scene looked less louche, though it still had not given itself over entirely to the wave of developers who were plucking vintage Art Deco buildings from certain oblivion and rehabilitating them. When Pela clicked the Record button on his Walkman-sized tape recorder, Hardwick patiently relayed the details of his 1982 arrest to set the record straight once more. He told the reporter details he had related dozens of times. He knew that the Supreme Court had made him out to be some kind of sexual outlaw, but he refused to trade on that to sell his art. "I would feel pretty lousy if someone were to hire me because of my political name value," he told Pela. "I don't worry about that, though, now that my work is out there. I'm established as an artist, so I can afford to get back to talking about my politics."[2]

"I'm a strong believer in karma, and that had a lot to do with my decision to pursue the case," he explained. "I knew that the results—good or bad—would have an incredible effect on my life and my art."[3]

"I do some of my best work in my dreams," he told Pela, while discussing the sexuality evident in his work, like the large phallus erected at Squeeze.[4] As he spoke, the gears on Pela's tape recorder slowed down as the batteries began to fade, then stopped.

The next morning, Hardwick took Pela for a walk around some of the venues that housed his art. He had worked himself hard so he wouldn't be known only as an infamous cocksucker, and Pela could see it in the vibrant neon lines Hardwick had drawn in the Squeeze space, which housed Hardwick's most complete artistic vision.

Pela knew he had his story. Hardwick had been an easy interview, though the reporter carried the palpable sense that Hardwick had participated out of generosity. He seemed weary of telling of the same defeat but had done so one more time out of kindness. He didn't crave or need the attention, and he answered all the reporter's questions without antagonism and without animosity. He had done it out of a sense of duty, Pela concluded.

Hardwick had shown him the mosaic bar tops, which were less inspired but made him the money to buy the materials he needed to bring his grander dreams to life. He had made a point of taking him to see the giant East Asian–influenced statues he had installed nearby.

Far from being an attention-starved militant beyond control, Pela found Hardwick had been gentle and quiet. He was not one of those activists who needed to shout to hear themselves, or to be on the TV news to see their lives as complete. He had protested Anita Bryant in 1977 and had marched in Pride parades, but he had not considered himself an activist until that morning in 1982 in Atlanta.

With it all in the past, he didn't want to be a political pawn, or worse, a token.

"I do as much as I can," he said with a shrug. "I'm a gay activist, but I don't want to be used."[5]

Even when he could not be present, activists used Hardwick as a powerful symbol in pursuing the next stage of the gay-rights movement. Groups such as ACT UP injected themselves into the public sphere through TV, staging vivid theatrical protests that twinned the HIV/AIDS epidemic and the unfairness of sodomy laws to outline the inequality faced by queer people. They turned the cameras on America's hypocrisy. The watched became the watchers.

ACT UP had begun to plan a massive protest in Atlanta, a twofold action that would stage camera-worthy moments in two places. A protest against sodomy laws, complete with a brass bed as agitprop, would take place on the steps of the Georgia state capitol. A second would shut down traffic near the CDC while it underscored the lack of information and treatment for women with HIV.

Months of coordination would bring hundreds of activists from the New York group to Atlanta—but first, ACT UP would launch its most controversial and widely covered action to date, on December 10, 1989, at St. Patrick's Cathedral in Manhattan. ACT UP members entered the church for services with the church's implicit knowledge, including that of presiding cardinal John O'Connor, that they planned to protest the church's anti-gay stance and its protestations against sex education and condom-use instruction in schools. Outside, thousands of protesters held signs in anger, reading PAPAL BULL and other brief, catchy slogans. Inside, as ACT UP members handed out flyers to churchgoers and posed as ushers and attendants, Cardinal O'Connor began a celebration of mass with Mayor Ed Koch in attendance, along with dozens of plainclothes police officers in the pews. What had been planned as a silent protest turned vocal when Michael Petrelis stood and shouted, "You bigot, O'Connor, you're killing us!" The crowd erupted as ACT UP members tossed condoms to the crowd, lay down in the aisles in "die-in" fashion, and chained themselves to pews. It took hours to drag them all out. The health crisis was an emergency, and demonstrations of the conventional kind no longer worked.

"We're fighting for your lives too," Ann Northrop said into the din. "We're fighting for your lives too."[6]

When the group landed in Atlanta in January of 1990, it was understood that video would be a part of the action—it would be condensed into sound bites and clips, distilled messages that had been crafted by ACT UP members who worked in media and advertising. Filmmaker Ellen Spiro started videoing the moment the group landed at the Atlanta airport and walked through the terminal with protest signs held aloft—WELCOME TO GEORGIA, SODOMITES!—and chanted their slogan, "Fight AIDS, ACT UP, Fight back!" irritating passing travelers and airport employees. The next morning, they boarded a MARTA train for downtown Atlanta, waved their hands, and then broke into song and into the chant that would lead the day: *Hey, hey! Ho, ho! Sodomy laws have got to go!*

Even at midday, the forty-five-degree blustery weather did not chill the protesters' public acts of simulated coitus. The first day of the Georgia legislative session was just getting under way indoors at the state capitol while ACT UP mounted a raucous protest at their doorstep in a loud, obscene attempt to get the politicians to finally dismantle the state's sodomy laws—the laws that Hardwick had challenged at the Supreme Court and lost. Men made simulated love on an antique red quilt spread over a brass bed carried in by protesters, then two women engaged in a love tussle just below a placard placed near the headboard that read SODOMY: THE LAW IS THE PERVERSION, and above one at the foot of the bed that said THE SODOMY LAW SUCKS! The women then yielded the bed to two men, who indulged in clothed performances of analingus, then finally, inflatable love mannequins caught in flagrante took over the bed for the rest of the protest.

The protest spilled over into a nearby pro-life counterprotest at the church across the street, where some in a small group held signs reading GOD DIDN'T MAKE YOU GAY and GAY IS NOT OK.

"We went down here for our pro-life rally," one woman told a police officer. "The other side stands right here and screams at us the whole time, and they've never been asked to move."

"We're not going to do that no more," she was assured by the white-haired man, who also told her that a planned rally for January 22, estimated at 6,000 attendees, would not be disturbed.

As the dozen pro-life protesters turned to move on, ACT UP chanted in their direction, then infiltrated their ranks:

Racist, sexist, anti-gay! Your souls will burn in hell one day!

A black banner read SILENCE=DEATH, and another, HONK TO REPEAL THE SODOMY LAW. The protest lurched forward down Atlanta's main drag, marching, chanting, and agitating.

Keep your laws off my body!

Shrieks of police whistles and blasts of motorcycle sirens punctuated the chants as they grew more graphic.

Suck my dick! Lick my clit! Sodomy laws are full of shit!

Queer culture always had been a borderland, a frontier where the acceptable and the unacceptable are in constant negotiation, a perpetual intercourse between what is allowed and what is forbidden.

Protesters raised the brass sodomy bed on high, then lowered it to the ground as the chants shifted.

Legislators, can't you see? Georgians want their privacy!

The overworked inflatable dolls shifted positions from one oral pleasure to the next, while the anti-gay clutch across the street watched from their huddle. Activists waved a banner at traffic diverted from the main street—"Honk to repeal the sodomy law!"—and chanted more loudly.

Gay, straight, Black, white. Sodomy's a basic right!

Protesters laid handmade male and female symbols at the foot of a statue of Thomas E. Watson, a Progressive-era politician who promoted disfranchisement and violence against Jews, Blacks, and Catholics. They placed the bed in front of it too. They held up signs for the camera that connected political violence abroad with political subjugation at home: STOP U.S. INTERVENTION IN OUR BEDROOMS!

"Hello, all you sodomites!" self-professed butch dyke comedian Lea DeLaria bellowed into a mike that stood near the courthouse steps. "And all you straight people who like a more . . . *interesting* . . . sex life."

She continued: "There's some people down the street that got a big old sign, says gay is not good. Well, I hate to tell them and I know it's going to be a surprise to them, but I agree with them. Gay isn't good. Gay is fucking fabulous!"

DeLaria high-fived an intro to Sue Hyde, in a red beret and red plaid scarf, who brought "Greetings from Washington, D.C., the vortex of evil!"

"We are gathered here today," Hyde proclaimed, "to protest laws that criminalize private adults' consensual sexuality."

Shame! The crowd answered. *Shame! Shame!*

"We gather here today in Atlanta," she said, "to claim our freedom to differ, and to declare that all lives forever after will change the beating of the heart of the existing order."

The next speaker, Atlantan Sabrina Sojourner, told the rapt audience of about 300 that sodomy law had demoted queer people to a lower order. "We can lose our jobs. We can lose our homes. We can have our children taken away from us . . . Is this right?"

No! the crowd shouted.

"Is this justice?"

No!

"There are lesbians and gay men who disagree with this action," Sojourner said, touching on the worry in the Atlanta queer community that the hundred-plus New Yorkers from ACT UP and their more outrageous tactics would be a hindrance once the TV-friendly demonstrations were over. To those people, she said that had she and all

Black people waited until the laws changed to take pride in themselves, "we would still be waiting."

The demonstration built up momentum as it flowed from the Capitol steps to nearby streets. Then it spun out of control. Activists linked hands and shut down traffic across Washington and Mitchell Streets, where news cameras weaved and bobbed alongside helmeted police with bullhorns.

Hey, hey! Ho, ho! Sodomy laws have got to go!

"Move back, you're holding up traffic," a cop said into a megaphone, and the crowd cleared the street and retreated to the sidewalk, where Atlanta's first Pride protest had taken place nineteen years earlier.

Hey, hey! Ho, ho! Sodomy laws have got to go!

They lay down in the streets and enacted a pantomime of sodomy, trampled cutouts of the states with sodomy laws still on the books, until the first police wagon rolled in. They blocked another intersection, head to tail. Police tried to peel them off, one at a time.

The police lifted and pulled them out of traffic, still sitting with joined hands, and ushered them into a white van with white lattice laid over the glass. At least four arresting officers donned rubber gloves, while others wore them under winter gloves. The protesters cheered as they were arrested and stomped their feet on the van's floor.

Hey, hey! Ho, ho! Sodomy laws have got to go!

As the scene ended, one sandy-haired queer in a jean jacket sang a little song and grabbed a comrade in black leather and a black-and-white headscarf. *And I think we need to show you just what good gay sex can be,* he crooned as he embraced his friend in a long, ardent kiss at the foot of the steps of the Immaculate Conception Church.

"Where's your badge?"

"Excuse me?" The officer's mustache bristled, but when questioned by an ACT UP member, leather-clad Officer R. D. Fancher of the DeKalb County Police did not flinch.

"Where's your badge?"

"It's on my shirt," he answered as he and other officers made a show of putting on rubber gloves in front of the Centers for Disease Control.

ACT UP had coordinated this second Atlanta protest at the agency's headquarters on Clifton Road, and while people watched in amusement from inside the building, activists piled up outside the CDC entrance and spilled out onto the surrounding sidewalks. They chanted to call attention to the way the CDC tracked AIDS cases and deaths without tracking HIV infections and routes. Banners and signs labeled the agency the "Center for Death Counting," declared that "Women Die Twice As Fast," and accused, "CDC DATA: INACCURATE, INADEQUATE, INTOLERABLE."

CDC, can't you see? Lesbians get HIV!

The protesters lay down in the traffic circle around the agency amid more chants—*We die, they lie!*—until they were ushered onto the grass. Some dispersed, while others, armed with a megaphone, marched toward the building's doors. *CDC is killing women. Redefine AIDS!*

They plastered the front windows of the building with plastic sheeting painted to read CDC LEAVES OUT WOMEN: SEXISM=DEATH. Then the first of a group of women took to the bullhorn to embody the perilous health conditions of AIDS patients.

"I'm an HIV positive woman and I have cervical cancer," the first announced. "But I'm undiagnosed with AIDS."

CDC is killing women. Redefine AIDS!

"The CDC is killing women," Tracy Morgan said as she came forward. "I have AIDS. They don't know it. They don't define it. I can't get my Social Security. I can't get medical treatment and I'm dying."

CDC is killing women. Redefine AIDS!

"The CDC is killing women," said another woman. "I can't get the drug trial because they don't define me as having AIDS."

CDC is killing women. Redefine AIDS!

As they lay on the concrete outside of the front door, the crowd lamented. *Count the women! Get to work!*

People peered out of higher-floor windows. Two men appeared to laugh at the scene unfolding outside of their government offices.

Shame! Shame! Shame!

Across the driveway, the activists formed a protective circle around a flagpole as they hoisted a banner. They chanted and danced in a circle around the flagpole to the sound of police whistles. They raised their banner as high as the American flag—using it as a distraction while about a dozen of the ACT UP brigade hoisted a ladder and reached the roof of the squat building. There they draped a black banner that read CDC KILLS.

Police took activists at the base of the ladder into custody, while the activists shouted to those at the top, *Take the ladder up!*

Another protester climbed as the police tried to halfheartedly keep more from going up to the roof.

Arrest the real criminals!

After more than an hour, the police gained control of the scene. They warned protesters to clear the street.

"You going to have to move over there ma'am," an officer said as he clenched a gloved hand.

Act up! We'll never be silent again!

"Clear the street," he warned a second time. "You've got fifteen minutes. The CDC will prosecute you if you're on their property for criminal trespass."

CDC, you can't hide. We charge you with genocide!

The last gasp brought protesters to their knees, then to the ground, before they were dragged into custody.

Murderers! CDC has blood on its hands!

"Clear the roadway or you will be arrested," an officer boomed over his megaphone. "All people must clear the roadway or you will be arrested."

We die, they do nothing!
We die, they do nothing!
WE DIE, THEY DO NOTHING!

Hardwick received his copy of the *Advocate* and may have been taken off guard by the cover. He appeared as a thinner version of himself in his usual neon paint-splattered jumpsuit. On it the eye of providence stared out from atop the pyramid on his chest. His long hair was tied back, but a lock ruffled in the breeze. He gestured with a cigarette stub as he looked into the sun, skin shiny from the glare, eyes narrowed but with a wide smile on his face. Hard shadows cut behind his right cheek, and the bright and flat winter sunlight reflected the worst of the gray off the water below the pier. It made him look gaunt. Hardwick was "CAUGHT IN A NEW ACT," the cover blurb read, and had found a "fresh start in Florida." His photo shared the cover with news of ACT UP's protest at St. Patrick's in New York.

The most glaring problem with the cover photo was the blacked-out button pinned to Hardwick's overalls. The magazine had flipped the photo so Hardwick would be facing the cover blurbs, and that reversed the message on his SILENCE=DEATH button. The magazine's photo editor had tried to alter the photo so that the button would read correctly. When it couldn't be fixed, the editor blacked it out, a blot on Hardwick's overalls that would be reproduced in magazines across the country, sending an altogether different message to those it would otherwise have cheered.

When Hardwick flipped to the story, he took pen and highlighter and interrogated the words. Reporter Robrt Pela had gotten much of it right—his hesitation at coming out on national television, how he had felt that the process let him finally be himself. "Up until then, I'd been denying my own homophobia," he had confessed. "When I confronted the fear of coming out publicly, I recognized it as a form of internalized homophobia. I figure it's really a continuing process—I'll be coming out for the rest of my life."

He agreed with what was written about his journey since that day in March 1986, when he kissed one of his Supreme Court attorneys in front of the White House while President Reagan worked inside. It had been a moment of joy amid the years of emotional hard work and disappointment. He understood that if he could survive the untold public scrutiny of the Supreme Court case, he could turn it inward on his life, to try to find out what held him back from his true passion.

"I walked on the beach for hours every day, thinking about who I am and what I wanted," he had told Pela. "I realized that what I wanted most was to work in art, and the only thing holding me back was me."

It read truthfully, if also painfully, that he didn't need to worry about a partner or a lover. He had put romantic life aside for his preoccupation with art. He was alone but didn't always want to be that way. "Mainly late at night, after I've worked myself to death. I think, 'Why am I alone?'"

He could answer his own question. He could function in groups of people but had become acutely aware of his need and his desire for privacy. He had become more introverted, and still felt as if he were being punished. He walked the beach with his dog, Jumbo, didn't go out to drink or see movies, and didn't watch TV. Instead, he read incessantly, cover to cover, all the books on the shelf in his loft: from books on Tutankhamen and on art techniques to the works of his prophet Castaneda, who had taught him about the need to dream. When he dreamed, he would have visions of his next artworks, and would put his chemical-scarred hands to work when he woke to channel the visions that emerged during those fruitful, silent hours.

But he disagreed with some of the words in the story and checked them off in pen and in vivid yellow strokes. What had been reported wrong? The huge flowers and vinery he had installed at the Squeeze nightclub weren't Styrofoam, they were crepe. He denied parts about his sexuality flowering in his work and about being a gay artist. He hadn't dreamed about the Buddhas and hadn't said the police were homophobes or closet cases, or so he remembered. His memory had begun to fail sometimes.

It was unclear when he read it, but he had studiously avoided speaking with the magazine about his health, how tired he had become, the weight he had lost. He lived and created as if it didn't matter. Art was an expression of his identity, and it had also become Hardwick's palliative therapy.

"If I had to choose between living in the reality of the world dictated by our government and being a dreamer," he told Pela, "I'd choose to dream. I see people living in that other reality, and they're not happy. I am happy, particularly in my dreams." He could heal through his dreams and the art he gave to the world, just as he believed his art could heal him of the insurrection that had begun to mass inside his own body.

On the day the magazine was published, Hardwick traveled to Gainesville to meet Simone, his sister Susan's newborn daughter. He wanted to hold Simone in his arms, which had become thinner along with his face. His blond-brown hair still fell gently and framed his cheeks, but the bones shone through his skin.

The strains of classical music soothed him as he worked in those final months. The cellist Yo-Yo Ma coaxed notes from his instrument that spoke to Hardwick: Ma believed that his work, his culture, brought the world around him closer to an understandable scale. He felt it was his talent not to use nature but to see that he came from it and was a part of it.[7] Hardwick drew similar inspiration from the flotsam he warehoused in his studio.

On the rare occasions he spoke out publicly, Hardwick leaned into the ethereal and the spiritual. For one interview, he posed on a chair in front of a wall painted with flames and spoke of an imaginary seated group of women who had influenced his life.[8]

In the first chair, Hardwick had created the woman who read when he cleaned pools when he was eighteen and who had unleashed the idea of being controlled by his mind. In chair two, he seated Ann Forbes, the messenger of the Avatar Meher Baba, who whispered in his ear that he would stray many times but return. In the third seat was the dishwasher Blanche who told him he would speak to thousands about human rights one day. The fourth seat went to the unnamed woman who'd invited him to Atlanta and set his world spinning on a different axis.

It had been his karma. He was destined to do it, though he didn't understand why. It had worked out for the better—his travails had given him the power to develop his spirit, which he demonstrated in his art. Now, he told the magazine of an unknown fifth presence, "the spirit of Brightstar," who "entered the medium's body and spoke to him as an old friend."

He said he trance channeled, a meditative technique that relied on the innate ability of humans to alter their state of consciousness. Its adherents sometimes trance channeled to communicate with another dimension of reality, whether with spirits or the dead or other intelligent forms of life.[9] Hardwick said it had given him the ability to detach himself from the world around him and to let his mind create a picture of his future art, whether a room or a piece of furniture, always as an expression of beauty, something that made people feel good.[10] He used its power to picture his own hands in his dreams, to nurture his art by linking his conscious and his subconscious. He was not only able to picture his hands; he was able in his dreams, he said, to fly.[11]

He read deeply and looked to philosophy to guide him through his decline. Among the books in his loft—*Bonfire of the Vanities*, *The Aquarian Conspiracy*, *Stone Power*, and *The Courage of Their Convictions*, which discussed sixteen Supreme Court cases and how ordinary Americans had faced the court—he kept a paperback copy of Camus's *The Plague*. It may have attracted him with its dueling statements of absurdism and nihilism, as the townspeople of Oran are in the grip of a deadly disease, which condemns its victims to a swift and horrifying death only after fear, isolation, and claustrophobia usher them into quarantine. Some of those with plague resign themselves to fate. Some seek blame. A few like Dr. Rieux, the book's closest approximation to a hero, resist the terror as best they can.

Hardwick had read all seven books by Carlos Castaneda three times each. In *The Power of Silence*, the Castaneda book that sat in his loft as he worked on his last completed art project, Don Juan had identified Castaneda as a *nagual*, or a spiritual leader—as Meher Baba had been. Castaneda spoke of a warrior philosophy, of the weakness and uselessness of pity. Castaneda's writing instructed readers how to separate from reality, how to free oneself from personal history, and how to erase the past. Hardwick never professed to know the answers to the questions life had imposed on him, but he believed fervently in pursuing answers. Castaneda had taught him how to harness his dreams and import them into the real world he struggled to make sense of. While other philosophers, from Foucault to Camus, predicted lives like his more precisely and incisively, it was Castaneda who offered Hardwick a truth he could accept.

Aside from the joints that boosted his appetite, Hardwick depended on trance channeling to alter his mental state. With threads from the nineteenth-century Spiritualist movement, and with clear antecedents in Eastern religious philosophy, trance channeling permitted the individual to connect with entities that had supernatural aspects. It could become a personalized, curated religion of one, in which the world's workings were revealed to the practitioner on an intimate spiritual level.[12] Unlike speaking in tongues, drum circles, or ayahuasca journeys, trance channeling could consist merely of the individual closing their eyes and altering their breathing to put themselves into a trance.

One of the uses of trance channeling was to alter one's psychological state and to detach from trauma. To the casual observer, it could present as psychosis—a common experience of those with HIV, who often experienced paranoia and aural and visual hallucinations.[13] But to those who believed, channeling granted the power to translate an ideal world into their real world. It accessed new vocabularies of words and images that had remained otherwise out of reach. It could be used to seek a higher wisdom that could help the channeler to deal with the trials of physical illnesses such as AIDS.[14] It could give pleasure—a sort of high and the sensation of physical satisfaction and release—and it likely gave Hardwick meaning in his remaining time.[15]

Hardwick depended on Alice to help him stagger through projects. She kept him on track with AZT and ddI, medications that required exquisite timing in their administration, to ward off resistance to them for as long as possible. He suffered side effects from the drugs and from his infection. His hands began to shake. He was having full-blown hallucinations.

Alice took over some of the work that they both knew Hardwick could not complete. She wrought a darkly poetic end for her brother's atomic garden. His Eden bloomed in a riot of color and life, but Alice saw death in its beauty and beauty in its death. As Hardwick began a final retreat into his inner self through his art, Alice planned to release caterpillars into the grove he had manicured. The insects would feed on the flowers, then spin themselves into shells where they could gestate. They would emerge as butterflies, then fly away.

The billboard over the Atlanta freeway read GAY AMERICA LOVES YOU. Put in place for the summer of 1990 by the Billboard Project, it stood through Pride in June of that year.[16] During that time, two people were arrested for trying to vandalize the billboard.[17] The nation had halted the trend toward the decriminalization of gay sex, and the AIDS movement had moved civil rights down the agenda to caring for those with HIV/AIDS. Some hope had appeared: a few hospitals had begun allowing same-sex partners into hospital rooms and the courts were starting to look at partners as caregivers and surviving beneficiaries. There still was a long way to go.

AIDS continued to consume a generation, including queer people and some of those at the forefront of the art and political worlds. Robert Mapplethorpe, the gifted photographer of portraits and sensual and provocative queer sex acts, had died on March 6, 1989. Painter Keith Haring, whose ebullient outlined figures Hardwick had admired and mimicked, died in February of 1990. That May, Keith Gann, who had spoken just months before at the Democratic convention in Atlanta, died of AIDS in a Minnesota hospice facility, Grace House.[18]

Gay rights and HIV/AIDS had become a visible part of the American experience. That visibility, in all walks of life—in television in particular—would become "another sign of changing times—and attitudes," as viewers were told by the stentorian-voiced anchor Garrick Utley on the *NBC Nightly News* on June 24, 1990.[19] "Today was the culmination of Gay Pride Week across the country. There were rallies, marches, and speeches throughout the land. Hundreds of thousands of people took part," he said, smiling slightly as the video switched to New York.

The blatts of motorcycles filled the feed, with Dykes on Bikes trundling down the main drag of New York's Gay Pride Parade. A sea of protesters included ACT UP members and a spectacularly costumed drag queen in flaming red, riding high on a float. "We raise children, we get dogs, we run libraries, we run Fortune 500 companies," said protester Janice Thom. "We are your milkmen ... obviously the world has survived just fine with 10 percent of the population being homosexuals."

In Atlanta a picnic at Piedmont Park marked the celebration. In San Francisco a massive parade commemorated the twenty-one years since the first anniversary of the Stonewall rebellion. But still, Utley reported, a recent poll of Americans found only 29 percent favored gay rights.

"We haven't come as far as maybe people in the straight community think we have come," activist George de Bolt tells reporter William Schechner, "and we still need to go a lot farther."

"The goal is equal rights," Schechner concludes.

Visibility was the watchword of a new group that papered pride demonstrations in New York that year. Queer Nation pleaded for a mission to change the way people talked about queerness. The flyer said that straight people lived free of fear and flaunted it to queer people. They dominated television, magazines, and street life. Queer people demanded free expression of their own sexuality—which it declared as privilege.

"Straight people will not do this voluntarily and so they must be forced into it," the Queer Nation manifesto read. "Straights must be frightened into it. Terrorized into it. Fear is the most powerful motivator. No one will give us what we deserve. Rights are not given they are taken, by force if necessary."

Queer Nation went beyond shock and horror at the *Hardwick* decision. "Since time began, the world has been inspired by the work of queer artists. In exchange, there has been suffering, there has been pain, there has been violence. Throughout history, society has struck a bargain with its queer citizens: they must pursue creative careers, if they do so discreetly. Through the arts queers are productive, lucrative, entertaining and even uplifting. These are the clear-cut and useful by-products of what is otherwise considered anti-social behavior. In cultured circles, queers may quietly coexist with an otherwise disapproving power elite."

"Being queer is not about a right to privacy," it challenged. "It is about the freedom to be public, to just be who we are," they declared. "Let's make every space a Lesbian and Gay space. Every street a part of our sexual geography. A city of yearning and then total satisfaction. A city and a country where we can be safe and free and more."[20]

The gay-rights movement had begun to pivot. Queer people outed themselves, outed those who would not make a public stand as queer, and fought back when queer-bashers bashed them. As in the civil-rights movement that preceded it, the time for contemplation had passed. The time for action had come.

Some tackled the new mode with zeal, but others were exhausted by the physical and emotional demands of keeping the queer community alive. The activist Randy Shilts had already been writing about AIDS for eight years when ABC's *Nightline* chose him as their "Person of the Week" during 1990's Pride Month. He had sounded alarms about the epidemic, then railed about how the government was letting "White House budget crunchers" decide how to research and treat the disease. He criticized the researchers, the blood banks that distributed infected blood, even the sex habits of queer people themselves. He had been critical in casting the epidemic into a recognizable story, that of tragedy, and in remaking the way people thought about the epidemic and queer people. It was overwhelming, he told *Nightline*: "I'm just about burned out."[21]

In his last few months in Miami Beach, Michael Hardwick greeted one of his long-ago friends from Atlanta to his studio. Woody Dykers came to South Beach for a few days, but none of it would be like the days when they had first met—when Hardwick, with boundless energy, real and infused, would stay up for days and go to every after-hour place, play cards in his dining room, attract a roomful of people who became his friends, let them have his house when he went to work, finish his shift and start it all over again.

When Woody saw him in Florida, Hardwick let him in through the iron-barred doors of his studio. It was a vast space with art in progress. The street was run-down, not much there in terms of businesses, but the beach was a couple of blocks away. Hardwick didn't have to go very far for coffee or food when he wanted either.

Woody saw a tiny kitchen in the back, a bathroom, and a ladder that went up to a mattress. There was no other bed, and for a couple of nights, Woody slept in the bay window at the front of the building. It might have felt cavelike and cool, the very embodiment of the idea of an artist who struggled. To a close friend, it felt profoundly sad.

Woody had known Hardwick wasn't doing well before he arrived in Miami but didn't understand how much Hardwick had physically declined until he saw him. He had just wanted to hang out with him in South Beach, to see him one more time. When Woody went out and danced to Deee-Lite's "Groove Is in the Heart," Hardwick stayed home. He didn't feel up to it. He rested and struggled to breathe.

The swing to the right had continued at the Supreme Court in 1990 when in July, eighty-four-year-old Justice William Brennan retired after suffering a stroke.[22] Brennan had so often sided with liberal causes along with Justice Thurgood Marshall, clerks had taken to referring to them in tandem. He had been on the deciding side in cases such as *New York Times v. Sullivan*, which in 1964 gave newspapers constitutional protection when sued for libel, and in *Shapiro v. Thompson*, which held in 1969 that the right to travel was protected by the Constitution as well.

Names circulated quickly on the replacement list, including Kenneth Starr and Clarence Thomas. Even a renomination for Robert Bork seemed possible when Republicans gave their stamp of approval for President George H. W. Bush's eventual nominee, David Souter. The future for the court's progressive wing seemed grim, particularly with the addition of "staunch conservative" Anthony Kennedy in 1987, who was appointed to the bench after Justice Powell retired.

Powell continued to make headlines, years after his tenure had ended. In an October 18, 1990, speech to the New York University Law School student body, the former justice made an astonishing mea culpa. In the Q&A session after his speech, Powell was asked whether any decision he made had given him doubt. *Bowers v. Hardwick*, he offered. "I think I probably made a mistake in that one." Upon rereading the decision and the dissent by Harry Blackmun, Powell said, "I thought the dissent had the better of the arguments."[23]

Powell confirmed to the *Washington Post* that he had made the remark. "That case was not a major case, and one of the reasons I voted the way I did was the case was a frivolous case" that had been developed "just to see what the court would do" on the topic of sodomy.[24]

Laurence Tribe believed Powell's admission decimated the moral authority that was supposed to have underpinned the decision. "The fact that a respected jurist who is indispensable to the majority conceded that on sober second thought he was probably wrong certainly will affect the way that future generations look at the decision," he said.

Powell shrugged it off. "So far as I'm concerned it's just a part of my past," he said, "and not very important." He said he hadn't thought more than a half-hour about the decision since switching his vote in 1986.[25]

Powell's indifference merited a scathing response from Sue Hyde of the National Gay and Lesbian Task Force's Privacy Project.[26] "I was at first glad to read in the October 26 edition of the *Washington Post* that you regret your vote in *Bowers v. Hardwick*," she wrote. "After all, Justice Powell, you created that majority. You cast the deciding vote to uphold the Georgia law criminalizing private, adult, consensual sex and you supported with your swing vote a decision which denies personhood and the fundamental right to be let alone to lesbian and gay people in the United States."

Hyde then tore into the former justice, writing that his misgivings about his vote betrayed no understanding of what the decision had meant for America's queer community. Far from being frivolous, Powell's vote had damaged them immeasurably. States continued to harass queer people for "crimes against nature," and to jail them.

A mother in Georgia had been denied custody of her seven-year-old son because, as a lesbian, she was considered an un-convicted felon. New Hampshire barred queer people from becoming foster parents because of *Hardwick*. Queer people could not be hired as law enforcement because of the assumption they were criminals. The military continued to discharge gay and lesbian people with the approval of the courts, which now had the *Bowers* decision to deny them a fundamental right to privacy.[27]

"Lesbian and gay people's lives are not frivolous and we are not frivolous people," Hyde wrote. "We are angry and resolute that the wrong you have done us should be set right as soon as possible." She suggested he should write to every state legislature where sodomy might be overturned to say that he had erred.

"And then, on behalf of Michael Hardwick, who was handcuffed, arrested, and spent many hours in jail awaiting release on bail, I ask this of you: please make sure that your colleagues on the U.S. Supreme Court—the sitting justices—know how you feel about your vote in *Bowers*," she concluded. "Your repudiation of your own vote in the case is the strongest argument for a review and a reversal by the court. Help to restore our faith in the ideals of justice and equal protection for all under the law."[28]

Hardwick had resigned himself to the fact that it would be his final work. Art had been the expression of his spirit, sometimes of his sexuality, but above all it had been his palliative therapy. He had bleached and burned and nicked his flesh to help others escape their everyday reality along with him. But art could no longer keep him alive. In his final installation for Squeeze, Hardwick and Alice painted huge poinsettias in neon and hung them from the ceiling.

On December 17, he gave his final interview to the *Miami Her-*

ald. He was stunned by Justice Powell's confession but said that the court case had inspired him to explore art as a means of expression. "It made me sure of myself," he said. "I'm not ashamed of who I am anymore." He had been determined to re-create himself after the 1986 decision, and now, he would create art for as long as he could.

"I'm not scared anymore," he said.[29]

Hardwick was out of money when Jack Kearney saw him for the last time. Kearney took him into his office, sat him down, and tried to convince him, *You're all right*, that he could give him something to help him get by.

Agitated, Hardwick couldn't stop moving. *You can't give me anything.* He barely looked at Kearney.

There's no way I'm going to get better.

Hardwick told Kearney he was going to head up and spend some time with his sister in Gainesville.

Susan and Mike came back to South Beach with their pickup truck and a trailer. Hardwick piled his few things into the trailer and into his Chevy truck, with Jumbo, too, and cleaned out the place in South Beach of his tools, books, and clothes. What remained of his artwork stayed behind. The caravan headed over the bridge into Miami, onto I-95 and the turnpike, before rolling out of the tropical Florida that he knew so well, back to Gainesville, where he had discovered himself.

He told Susan that most of his friends had been disowned by their families. When they became HIV positive, they had nowhere to turn but to their friends, who were all in the same position. It was a lonely way to die. At least it did not have to be that way for him.

Weeks later, a month later, Kearney hadn't heard from him. Someone told him that a new tenant had moved into Hardwick's studio on South Beach. Then, silence.

Landslide

Hardwick spent Christmas with his family. While Simone rocked on her new toy horse, Jasmine unwrapped teen-friendly clothes, and Robert tapped on a new word-processing computer, he tried to open a gift box, pulling at the ribbon with a skinny arm that struggled to summon the strength.

He called Jack Kearney a few weeks later. He told him that he had loved working with him at Squeeze. He told him that he was the best friend he'd ever had.[1]

The hallucinations grew deeper while he was living with Susan and Mike. He told them Kitty was pregnant. He struggled to stand on his own. When he got up from a nap on the back porch one afternoon he fell and bled. From then on, his family would divide up his care. He would spend a week with Kitty in her mobile home at the end of a dirt road in farm country, then a week with Susan and Mike nearby, then a week with Alice, who lived a half hour away in Gainesville. Alice had become a constant caregiver despite her own health issues, within the confines of the knotty relationships of both brother and sister and artist and artist.

By March 31, 1991, Easter Sunday, Hardwick could no longer care for himself. He laid on a chaise on the wooden deck behind Susan and

Mike Criss's home. Warmed by the sun and a white sweatshirt, he sipped from milkshakes to try to sustain himself. His hair had matted and curled into corkscrews. His beard had grown in because it was too difficult and dangerous to shave him. His face had hollowed out and his hands had grown even more sinewy. His nose stood out profoundly, with a bump in the ridge from where it had been broken long ago. His eyes had darkened. He struggled to move. Kitty told other family that he was dying from cancer.

On Easter, Susan brought her daughter Simone to the room where Michael rested, while Kitty sat next to Michael and held her granddaughter close to him.

"Simone, show Uncle Mikey your new shoes," Susan cooed as she recorded it on videotape. He reached out to Simone as she extended her foot, then beckoned her with the palm of his hand. "Go see him, Simone, can you give him a hug?"

Simone kicked her pink booties toward him as Kitty adjusted Simone's Easter bonnet. He stared at nothing while Kitty stroked his beard-dusted chin. She brought Simone close to him, then placed the bonnet on his head in jest. Hunched over on the leather couch, wrapped in a gray striped blanket, Hardwick became himself again for a moment, if the palest version.

"Hey . . . hey you're kicking the heck out of me," he said in a near whisper. "You're kicking the heck out of me . . ." he repeated, "you're kicking the heck out of me, yes you are," he told his niece as he played with her feet, "you're kicking the heck out of me," fussing with her feet and struggling with consciousness before he faded out.

When he first became ill, Susan had frantically sought for anything that could help him. She spent $600 a month to get him treatment and researched public assistance while his body tried to fend off complications. Once his immune system collapsed, nothing more would work.

Alice brought a group of friends to sing to Michael. It helped ease the grief, if only until the echo of the last chord fell silent. In the final weeks of his life, a port placed into his body dripped medicine to numb him. By Memorial Day, he had shrunk to sixty-five pounds and could no longer move from his bed. He curled into a fetal position and remained there.

You need to come over, Kitty told Susan on the phone. *Something's wrong with Jumbo.*

Susan raced over to her sister Alice's house to see what could be wrong. Jumbo was a big dog, a hundred pounds, perfectly healthy. He had lain down next to Hardwick—he was like his child, he loved him so much—and died.

Michael barely lived a few more days after that, until the evening of June 13, 1991. He did not speak, or eat, or move again. In his final moments he may have been visited by beautiful visions that rose and ebbed in a kaleidoscope, the hallucinations that often accompany death—in flight as Castaneda had promised, in peace as Baba had taught, robed in the wild vines that crept through Squeeze's rafters, at the summit of the giant statues that lorded over Club Nu. Hearing the heartbeat of the Avatar, the sweet whisper of lovers, the cries of an unfaithful one, the letters spoken to him in shock, the creak of his bedroom door. Then, adrift in the ocean, its salt stinging his reddened skin, the raft his family had built bore him gently toward home.

Epilogue

It had been nearly a year since Hardwick's nephew Robert and his friend Jorge had seen Michael in his Miami Beach studio. The young men had moved to Europe to study, then had flown to Africa for adventure. They backpacked into the Atlas Mountains on the Road of a Thousand Shebas, then traveled from Marrakesh down to Essaouira, where for four days, they drank mint tea and walked on the beach, blasted by wind as they watched kite surfers dance across the water.

On the night of June 13, 1991, Robert told Jorge about a grand plan he had quietly devised. He studied history; he knew now that he needed to interview his uncle, so that he could document all that had happened in his extraordinary life. The next morning, Robert stayed back at the hotel to plan.

Jorge wandered off to a peaceful stretch of the beach to read. As he hunted for a spot where the wind would be calm, where he could be alone, he saw someone lying in the sun—asleep, or so he thought. *How strange,* he thought, *the sand has started to cover his face.* Then he saw foam coming from the man's mouth.

He ran down the beach for help, but he knew the young Arab man was dead. He pantomimed for lifeguards to follow him. When the authorities finally arrived, he helped them carry the body to a path closest to the beach.

Shaken, Jorge ran back to the hotel, the sight of the man lodged in his brain, until he saw Robert sitting at a table outside of the hotel, motionless. While Jorge had been gone, Robert had called home to speak with his boyfriend about his idea to record Michael's life. He began excitedly but had to be stopped—

Oh my God, you haven't heard, Michael passed.

Robert ran to the beach. In a fugue, he fell down, landing next to a dead bird.

When he could, he rose to his knees and shook the sand from his clothes. He stumbled back to the hotel and braced himself in a chair at one of the tables outside of the Café de France. In his grief, he began to write a poem, pausing long enough to see Jorge as he crossed the worn cobblestones, coming toward him.

Jorge knew.

"Mein Onkel ist ein Stern," Robert told him quietly.

My uncle is a star.

After Hardwick's death on June 13, 1991, the *Gainesville Sun* noted only that he had come from Miami in December 1990, was an artist, and had died after a long illness. His family held a memorial service on June 18 for about thirty-five people. The strains of Yo-Yo Ma's classical cello, Hardwick's favorite, greeted guests. The physical therapist who had helped Susan with Jasmine's patterning exercises sang "Landslide" by Fleetwood Mac from the back of the room. Hardwick's niece Jasmine signed her eulogy, a reading from "The Sweetness of Peace."

"My brother Michael got involved in the world's purposes," Susan told those gathered. "If we all were committed to just one of our beliefs, strongly enough to stand up no matter what the consequences—and there were many for Michael—the world would be a better place," she said between halting pauses. After the service and cremation, Kitty and her son Patrick took Michael's ashes to Bonita Springs, on the west coast of Florida where Patrick lived, and cast them into the turquoise waters of the Gulf of Mexico.

It would be seventeen years before the decision in *Bowers v. Hardwick* was overturned. In 1998, a false report of someone brandishing a gun sent four police to a Houston apartment. There, officers encountered Tyron Garner and John Lawrence, who were said by at least two officers to be engaged in sex. An officer in charge at the scene insisted on filing sodomy charges, though two of the police officers had not seen any sexual activity, and the other two disputed whether they had seen oral or anal sex. After a plea of no contest, the men accepted Lambda Legal's help to argue in Texas courts that their convictions violated equal protection and privacy guarantees in the Constitution. When Texas denied their claims, they filed for a grant of certiorari in 2002 in what would become *Lawrence v. Texas*.

At the Supreme Court, Lawrence's case was argued by Paul Smith, an out gay lawyer and Yale Law School graduate who had once been a clerk for Justice Lewis F. Powell. Smith's case for Garner and Lawrence expressly argued that *Bowers v. Hardwick* should be overturned. On June 26, 2003, Laurence Tribe sat in court when Justice Anthony Kennedy pronounced, "*Bowers* was not correct when it was decided, and it is not correct today. *Bowers v. Hardwick* should be and now is overruled."[1] Hardwick had been vindicated, all those years later, twelve years after his death. Writing in dissent of the 6–3 decision were Justices Antonin Scalia, William Rehnquist, and Clarence Thomas.

There are so many more things I wish I could tell you about Michael Hardwick's life, but I don't know them. I have been unable to find the two women Hardwick said had drawn him to Atlanta, unable to reach others who knew him in Miami in the final years of his life, and unable to locate those who knew him during college and the years preceding his move to Atlanta.

So much died with him, despite the parts of his life that live on with his family, his friends, and in his art. The rest I ascribe to an irretrievable past of events gone unrecorded, mementos discarded, traumas long since buried. The past usually is unrecoverable, but it is especially difficult to document during Hardwick's time and in his community, where so many people died so quickly, and so young.

History is a kind of karmic recovery operation that inevitably raises more questions than it can answer. Historians try to resurrect people and re-create events to the best of our knowledge and ability—and while doing so we cast new shadows and uncover new stories for others to tell. The *point* of history is to provoke us into contemplation or into action, to learn what is presented to us as fact and then, often, to actively seek to disrupt that perception of truth. It is a radical pursuit of instability in the hope of achieving perfection, knowing it will always fail.

Historians litigate the past. We assemble evidence, write a narrative, argue a case, convict or free people from their sins, imaginary or real. Lawyers and judges hold a clear advantage against us: they litigate the future.

We all write the story every day that will preserve our lives, whether in trails of official documents or in social media posts. The legal system has a special privilege when it comes to its story. As some of the most astute legal minds ever to serve the public interest, lawyers and judges are keenly aware of what to omit from the record in the interests of their own story. Some Supreme Court justices may have destroyed materials that might have spoken to history better than those they chose to leave behind. Byron White was said to have shredded most of the documents of his work—paid for by U.S. taxpayers—after his retirement. This is power with no oversight. It fails us all.

To their credit, the more liberal Supreme Court justices were also more liberal with the documentation they left behind. Of the myriad thanks our nation owes Thurgood Marshall, a lesser one in the context of all that he did is for the early release of his archives, which were made available very soon after his death in 1993. Marshall's released files alarmed other justices with his simple act of transparency. In death, Marshall shed great light on many cases in which he had participated, including *Hardwick*. Even his former clerks were surprised. When memos on the *Hardwick* case were made public, Marshall's clerk and salty memo author Daniel Richman was among those whose moral clarity rang out from the page: "I certainly had zero idea that my memos would become public, ever," Richman told me when we spoke about his term with the court.[2]

Some of the conservative justices from the Hardwick term have walled off their archives until decades after their death. Warren Burger had his records sealed until ten years after the death of the last justice with whom he served; that keeps his records private until 2033, which will mark ten years after the death of Sandra Day O'Connor, whose archives have since been made available for research. As for Justice Rehnquist, the sole Supreme Court clerk to advocate against *Brown v. Board of Education*—leaving *Plessy v. Ferguson* as precedent—much of the contents of his archives will remain closed to all research until the death of the last justice with whom *he* served, either Justice

Anthony Kennedy or Justice Clarence Thomas. Rehnquist's archives from the 1998 impeachment of President Bill Clinton will remain closed until 2048.

The less these archives speak, the more remains obscured. These selective contributions to the historical record betray the fundamental pact these justices have with the American public. They sanction the release only of certain information and prevent the discovery of nuance that could enhance the interpretation of modern cases and issues. They leave the impression that they hold some higher allegiance to the Supreme Court itself instead of to the people they serve.

The people who want you to know and understand history will tell it to you. Those who don't will hide it, bury it, destroy it, or overturn it.

Hardwick died without knowing that his case would be overturned by *Lawrence v. Texas*, or that same-sex marriage would be declared constitutional in *Obergefell v. Hodges*, in 2015. Still, his life had a galvanizing effect on queer activists and their history. It also brought more allies to the cause, including Laurence Tribe, who told me that he wouldn't have been nearly as motivated to testify against Robert Bork and for Anthony Kennedy if it hadn't been for the *Bowers* decision. He had been warned several times that there were three things that he had done in his career that had kept him from a nomination to the Supreme Court of his own: his writings in favor of the legalization of drugs, his Bork testimony, and *Bowers v. Hardwick*.

"I couldn't be prouder of all three," he said.

When I spoke with him, Tribe had been tasked with writing about the direction in which the court had moved as its most recent appointees took their seats. The 2020 elections prevented further damage to democracy while it could still be triaged. Since then, former president Trump's appointees to the Supreme Court have ushered in an era of deconstruction, one in which the Supreme Court has played an outsized role in reversing many of the established rights of liberty that had been identified in the past half century. On June 24, 2022, the Supreme Court invalidated the right to make reproductive choices in *Dobbs v. Jackson Women's Health Organization*, which overturned *Roe v. Wade* and destabilized the entire body of jurisprudence that exists in the penumbra of the Fourteenth Amendment's due process clause.

In his concurrence with the majority opinion, Supreme Court Justice Clarence Thomas staked out the terrain of decisions that may yet come. "As I have previously explained," Thomas wrote, "'substantive due process' is an oxymoron that 'lack[s] any basis in the Constitution.'" Thomas added that "in future cases, we should reconsider all of this Court's substantive due process precedents, including *Griswold*, *Lawrence*, and *Obergefell*." Contraception, consensual adult sexual behavior, and same-sex marriage—all, in Justice Thomas's view, should be reconsidered and, by logical extension, overturned. In a galling turn of the phrase that demoted the idea of liberty to political wordplay, Thomas wrote that *Roe* had been "wrong the day it was decided."

The sea change in the jurisprudence of liberty troubles Tribe. Civil rights have more often and more thoroughly been protected by Congress, he says. It is the Supreme Court that has most often been the agent of chaos in American society.

"As an institution," he instructs, "it is equally capable of undermining progress toward justice and human rights as it is advancing that progress."

The court has failed to protect discrete and insular minorities as well as voting rights, he says. "Somehow, I had convinced myself that that was then, and now, after the Warren court, things would get better and better," he rues. "Well, there was no basis to assume that, and in fact, a lot of basis not to."

Tribe says he hasn't given up yet fully on the idea that the moral arc of the universe bends toward justice. But right now, "the court has a clear five-justice, hard-right, ideologically driven majority," he says. "I think there are five Robert Borks on the court right now."[3]

On a range of issues, but most obviously in *Dobbs*, today's Supreme Court has moved swiftly to reverse a half century of decisions that defined critical elements of modern American culture. In doing so, it has flouted public opinion. While the purpose of the court is not to mirror that opinion—which would have been disastrous during the civil-rights era—it should be a protector of the progress toward greater personal liberty that has shepherded our democracy into new political eras.

Instead, empowered with a decisive conservative majority, the current court has whittled away at carefully reasoned precepts of personal liberty and carefully constructed consensus decisions. In doing so it threatens to reduce the very idea of constitutional principles to caricature—a grab bag of conflicting positions and murky language to be exploited, and to be used to discriminate at will. The court's rightward turn, far out of step with public opinion on personal autonomy, threatens to destroy faith in the institution itself.

How can it uphold its purpose and the Constitution while it privileges the concepts of liberty that best mirror the political will of our time? A recent proposal would add justices to the Supreme Court every other year under every president, no matter their party. The nine most recently named would serve as the core court for appellate issues. The plan would, in effect, enact term limits of eighteen years for sitting justices, though it would not provide for compulsory hearings or votes on nominations within a reasonable period. The plan could cure the irregular and antediluvian way in which court vacancies are filled.

If enacted, it could bring the court into more close coordination not with public opinion but with a more common understanding of the political era in which it serves. It would acknowledge the Supreme Court as an institution that is political by its very nature. Each justice accedes to the court through a political process. Each brings their personal beliefs to the bench. Custom now leads many justices to retire when political advantage makes it possible to "retain" a seat. While they may not be directly or wholly influenced in every case by those factors, it is naïve to mistake their resulting concurrences and dissents as devoid of any influence from those powerful political forces. Claims that the court operates under some superhuman mantle of impartiality are facetious, at best.

Reform of the court has vexed all presidents who have tried. Any possible solution brings with it electoral peril. The very least that could be done—instituting an independently monitored code of conduct—seems out of reach. Thus far, we have failed to hold the court accountable for glaring ethical lapses. In doing so, we have failed to answer the challenges facing our democracy with the discipline and verve the moment demands.

To do so, we must first accept the truth about our democracy. The Supreme Court has been groomed—and not by queer people. It was groomed by those who operated under the veneer of originalism, a convenient label to mask retrogression. Nominees to the Supreme Court deceived senators as they falsely affirmed or suggested that they would hold to judicial precedents established over the past generations, then overturned those precedents when the opportunity came. Conservatives immersed themselves in a fifty-year effort to install the court of their choice and emerged the victors. It will take an equally powerful and sustained effort—one that makes an effective appeal for universal voting rights and access, for court term limits, for the end of gerrymandering, and for personal autonomy—to reverse that victory.

We must believe this to be possible. But we may also be at the beginning of an era in which the six-justice conservative majority finds itself with the cases and votes to overturn those critical decisions in *Griswold*, *Obergefell*, and *Lawrence*. If that happens, the symptoms of rot will deepen, perhaps slowly, perhaps quickly and painfully. We will relive a past in which rampant disease was ignored. When lives shattered by artificially imposed morality were discounted. When rights called into question were abrogated or denied. We will all be Michael Hardwick.

President Joseph R. Biden offered a more positive message for our future than I can muster. "I have never been more optimistic for the future of America," he wrote to me in August of 2023, in response to my questions about the future of the Supreme Court. "Our Nation has always turned crisis into opportunity, and I believe we are better positioned than any country in the world to lead in the 21st century and deliver real results for the American people."

He correctly identifies the best motivation to reform our judicial system: crisis. As of this writing, various state officials have met Justice Thomas's challenge and asserted that, given the necessary Supreme Court ruling, they will resume the enforcement of antiquated sodomy laws still on the books.[4]

Are we on the cusp of a return to *Hardwick*-era sexual surveillance? Sue Hyde offers a guarded answer. "It's not as if people are not doing things," she said. "But what I do not see is that, even though there is a broad recognition of the threat to any right, or any notion of equality that is attached to the right to privacy . . . what I don't see is that there is a concerted coalition effort to organize people."

"It needs to be a fight to the death," she continued, with all implied hyperbole, "and we need to win."

Our democracy should further the rights of all citizens each time we reexamine the law and its ideals. To ensure that pragmatic approach to the law we can—and must—address the shortcomings of the Supreme Court's ethical standards and its composition. If we do not, we are destined for decline. We will trade our Constitution of aspiration for the more primitive frame of selective originalism.

The choice is ours, all of ours. Either we will live as equals, or we will live under tyranny.

Acknowledgments

This book would not have been possible were it not for the cooperation of Michael Hardwick's remaining family, or those who have already passed away.

Today, not far from the college where Hardwick discovered himself, tunnels of water oaks and the occasional brace of mailboxes line a road that leads from Gainesville, Florida, into the country, where Hardwick's sister Susan and her husband Mike live with Jasmine and tend to a beautiful garden with lilies, goats, friendly dogs, and a grandchild.

For a long time, Kitty Hardwick lived nearby, where she volunteered for gay hotlines and instructed parents how to get over their shock and love their child when they came out. "I'm just happy I chose to be close to my children and accept them, no matter what," she said in 1986. "Parents who can't deal with it lose so much. It's been hard and painful, but I'm proud of my son."[1] Both of her sons would die before her: Michael in 1991, Patrick from an undetected heart condition in 1994.

Alice Dale Hardwick Hehr moved onto the land where Kitty lived and built herself an off-the-grid home from lumber and plastic sheeting, lined with gravel and furnished with a bed and a little statue of the Buddha. She worked in an adjacent space she had built into a studio and produced compelling artwork: she wound rope into a female bust, unraveling it from the bottom, rendering it unstable. Alice began to experience persistent infections and ignored pleas from the family to see a doctor. She didn't want to know. In 2004, she died from cancer. Before she died, she choreographed her funeral and produced the program for the memorial service. It shows her body, suspended in space, arms extended in a Christlike pose, soaring into the blackness of the universe.

The family did not understand then that the vicious squabbles that frequently erupted between Alice and Kitty had any medical cause. They realized only late in her progression that Kitty suffered from dementia. She died in 2008.

The Hardwick-Weston-Browning-Chriss clan now extends over several states. Robert Hardwick Weston lives in upstate New York with his partner Roberto. Both are creators, artists, and teachers who work in a studio framed by hills studded with hydrangea and light-pink yarrow, patrolled by a thickly muscled hound named Archer. Simone lives near her parents and sister.

At Thanksgiving, the family says a prayer and repeats the names of those they have lost. Jasmine always speaks for Mike.

Dwight Sawyer, the man arrested with Michael Hardwick, saw his sodomy charge dismissed, and lived for years in Atlanta with his partner Joey, until they split up. Sawyer went on to work for FEMA in Washington, D.C., where he died on February 4, 1996, from complications from AIDS.

"There's only a handful of us left that remember this time period," Miss Puss told me on a phone call that had us both in stitches and near tears for almost three hours. "I often wonder how different my life would be," she said, "if my brothers were still here."

"It still makes me want to cry just thinking about it," said Abby

Rubenfeld, when asked about the status of queer people in the wake of the Supreme Court's same-sex ruling. "Especially having worked on and lived through the *Hardwick* case and reading that opinion where the U.S. Supreme Court was so dismissive, so disrespectful, so dehumanizing, and having lived through all that . . . When *Lawrence* was decided, *that* made me cry. At the time, I talked to every person that had worked on *Hardwick*—of course a lot of the men in particular had died from the AIDS epidemic—but any of the people that I talked to who had worked on *Hardwick*, they all had the same reaction: we were all beside ourselves crying, so grateful that we had been vindicated and there was finally language in the books to overcome this hateful, horrible language in the *Hardwick* opinion." Rubenfeld practices law in Nashville, Tennessee.

Kathy Wilde stayed in contact with Hardwick and recalled him as "great fun." At the end of his life, he became embittered about the case, but not about their friendship. "We talked about doing hikes together, but we never wound up getting to do that," she says. "In the final days he got very discouraged and felt like his life had been wasted. We'd lost the case, and what was there to show for the energy and time? So it's quite sad he didn't live to see the vindication in the *Lawrence* case."[2] She now directs litigation for Disability Rights Oregon.

Evan Wolfson championed the cause of same-sex marriage after his work on *Bowers v. Hardwick*. In 2002, he looked back on the decision with hope that soon, queer people would be able to join in legal union and would be given the equal protection of the law. "I often think of Michael Hardwick's courage," he said, "of Larry Tribe's and other nongay allies' support, and of our own rising empowerment. And I still proudly wear that pink triangle lapel pin, summoning others to fight injustice and to join us in shaping America's civil rights history."[3] He founded and leads Freedom to Marry, an organization credited with laying the framework for the eventual *Obergefell* decision that granted same-sex marriage rights in the United States. He now takes that fight to other countries around the world.

Michael Hobbs retired from his law practice. He writes that, at the time of the Supreme Court arguments, he had argued that consensual sodomy did not fall within the prevailing moral values of the country at that time. "Obviously, those prevailing values could and did, in my view, evolve," he reports from retirement. "I don't see any chance that the overall ruling in *Bowers v. Hardwick* could be revived by the application of that standard today."[4]

Michael Bowers practices law in Athens, Georgia. In 1997, during a campaign for governor of Georgia, Bowers's long-running affair with Anne Davis became public.[5] Bowers admitted the affair and resigned his commission with the Air National Guard, then suspended his campaign for governor. He had resigned as attorney general earlier that year when he launched his gubernatorial run. By 2015, Bowers would make news when he sided with queer activists and wrote legal opinions that decried pending "religious freedom" bills in Georgia, which he deemed were "nothing but an excuse to discriminate." Still a Republican, Bowers said that his opinions on same-sex marriage had changed over the years, and that if it were sanctioned by law, he would support it. "Regardless of what my personal beliefs are," he said, "I don't want to see anybody discriminated against. And I especially don't want to see the law violated or the law contorted and that's why I undertook this assignment."[6] He would not, however, change the way he approached *Hardwick*: "At the time I thought I was doing right, and as I look back I still think I did what I had to do given the law."[7]

Keith R. Torick lives in the greater Atlanta area, according to his social media pages. In 1986 he told the *Washington Post* that he regretted the arrest and that he thought the law had been poorly written. "I didn't do it to get my name in the law books," he said. "I don't want my name associated with it."[8]

Acknowledgments

Jack Kearney remained a fatherly presence among clubgoers in Fort Lauderdale, where he stayed in touch with former Squeeze crew members and close to his daughter and granddaughter. "I kind of cried when [Hardwick] died," he told me, saying he "was very happy to be his friend." Michael was a beautiful person, and the friendship they had, Jack said, he'd never had with anyone else. He kept one piece of art that Michael created: the neon hand that hung over the bar at Squeeze, which can be seen in the 1992 Jim Belushi movie *Traces of Red*, at about the twenty-eight-minute mark. The artwork reminded him of Michael's hands, Jack said—gnarled and busy, but open. Kearney died in May of 2024.

Many people played obvious roles Hardwick's life, but others will never be acknowledged, simply because they only connected with him in remote or casual ways. I thank the people who expressed kindness to Hardwick during his time in the Seed, to the people who sheltered him when he was exploring his identity, to the teachers who introduced him to the world of nature, to the people who fed him when he had almost no money to support himself, and to the many people in the Miami and Fort Lauderdale nightclub scene who were amazed by his work and kept coming back for more, a simple act of affirmation that sustained him when little else could.

And while agents and editors rarely get top billing, Beth Marshea and Amy Cherry deserve to, because they have given my writing its home in your hands.

Among Hardwick's many friends from Atlanta, I spoke with and depended heavily on the memories of those closest to him and his friend Dwight Sawyer: Jim Bass, Arthur Cantrell, Woody Dykers, Joey Potter, Gil Robison, "Miss Puss," Kirk Slusser, and Anna Ware.

Hardwick's legal team of warriors contributed greatly to my

knowledge of the case: Jay Kohorn, Abby Rubenfeld, Laurence Tribe, Kathy Wilde, and Evan Wolfson. I'm grateful for the help of Judge Amy Totenberg, and that of Anne Goldstein, who provided the only known copy of Hardwick's handwritten statement about his sodomy arrest, from her archives. Thanks also to Kathy McGillicuddy, who provided access to Laurence Tribe's archives.

Among those associated with the Supreme Court justices, its 1986 decision, and its fallout, I must thank Nancy Blackmun, William Eskridge, Pamela Karlan, Daniel Richman, Robin Shahar, and Cliff Sloan.

From the Miami–Fort Lauderdale eras of Hardwick's life, I thank Doug Crosse, Danny Garcia, Caprice Harrold, Marcia Herold, Jack Kearney, Kyle Plyler, Kim Stark, Lori Tanner, Danny Tenaglia, and David Vance. My special thanks to Brad Lamm for helping revive some of the social network that Hardwick created, and for bringing me many steps closer to Hardwick through his vivid memories.

ACT UP veterans were crucial in recalling the impact of Atlanta and Washington, D.C., acts of civil disobedience. Those who gave invaluable help in this process include Matt Liam Ebert, Garance Franke-Ruta, Michael Frisch, Michelangelo Signorile, Ellen Spiro, and John Voelcker.

Other activists who helped me describe pivotal moments from the 1987 March on Washington and the 1990 ACT UP Atlanta actions include Chris Cash, Karen Chance, Holly Crenshaw, Michelle Crone, Jeff Graham, Hillel Gray, Sue Hyde, Nancy Langer, Cathy Woolard, and Andrew Wood.

Mike's friends from his childhood, Gene and Patty, made sure I knew about his wit as well as his truancy.

This book would have been much more difficult to write without the excellent reporting of Tracie Cone, Art Harris, Peter Irons, Jill Young Miller, Cliff O'Neill, and Robrt Pela. Joyce Murdoch and Deborah Price's standout volume of queer Supreme Court history proved an invaluable guide to information out of my reach.

Archives provided a mountain of information on the Supreme Court case as well as Hardwick's world. The archivists who helped me sift through history include Morna Gerrard, Leah Lefkowitz, Serena McCracken, Pam McGorry, Isaac Fellman, James Duran at the Vanderbilt Television News Archive, and the staffs at the Stonewall National Museum and Archives, the Library of Congress, the State Library of Florida, the New York Public Library, Cornell University, the University of Southern California, William and Mary University, and Princeton University.

Many thanks to my fellow historians, Joseph Perry and John McMillian, and to H. Robert Baker, who helped me grapple with the fundamentals of constitutional history.

Deborah Briggs and the family of Hyam Plutzick welcomed me to the Betsy Hotel in Miami Beach, where I wrote the first passages about Hardwick's life in Florida. Place matters.

So does family. Hardwick's cousin Debbie Dundas provided me with family home movies and her own memories. Family friend Jorge Alberto Perez contributed much about Hardwick's artwork and his Miami scene.

None of this would have happened without my husband's love and enduring patience, as well as his endless connections to Atlanta history. While writing, we realized that Michael's lover Cliff Hovan had worked for my husband years ago. In that moment, I realized Michael's story had never been out of reach. How could it be? It never was very far from our own.

Sources

Interviews

Jim Bass, June 13, 2021.
Susan Browning-Chriss, Simone Chriss, and Robert Hardwick Weston: June 16, 2021; October 23, 2021.
Joey Potter, June 18, 2021.
Evan Wolfson: June 16, 2021; August 16, 2022.
Jill Young Miller, by email, June 24, 2021.
Jack Kearney: July 5, 2021; November 24, 2021; May 5, 2022.
Jim Bass, by email, July 6, 2021.
Louis Levenson, August 9, 2021.
Robert Hardwick Weston: August 15, 2021; July 13, 2023.
David Vance, by email, September 7, 2021.
Marcia Herold, September 13, 2021.
Doug Crosse, by email, September 22, 2021; April 16, 2022.
Paul Orofino, by email, October 16, 2021.
Peter Irons, by email, October 23, 2021.
Daniel Richman, October 26, 2021.
Robin Shahar: October 26, 2021; November 19, 2021.
Andrew Schultz, by email, October 26, 2021.
William Eskridge, October 27, 2021.
Robrt Pela, November 10, 2021.
Jack Pelham, November 12, 2021.
Jeff Graham, November 22, 2021.
Matt Liam Ebert, December 7, 2021.

Michael Frisch, December 16, 2021.
Hillel Gray, December 24, 2021.
On behalf of Mike Clutter, by email, February 13, 2022.
Chris Cash, February 18, 2022.
Susan Kay Gilbert, by email, March 3, 2022.
Joyce Murdoch, March 17, 2022.
Arthur Cantrell, March 18, 2022.
Anna Ware, March 18, 2022.
Nancy Blackmun, by email, March 27, 2022.
Woody Dykers: April 11, 2022; April 29, 2022; May 22, 2022.
Michelangelo Signorile, by email, April 11, 2022.
Holly Crenshaw, April 15, 2022.
Jay Kohorn, April 18, 2022.
Debbie Dundas, April 25, 2022.
Lori Tanner, April 29, 2022.
Cliff O'Neill, May 4, 2022.
Caprice Herrold, by email, May 11, 2022.
Robin Sexner Cole, by email, May 11, 2022.
Gil Robison, May 20, 2022.
Kirk Slusser, June 8, 2022.
Sue Hyde, July 21, 2022.
Brad Lamm: August 5, 2022; July 18, 2023.
John Foutz, August 7, 2022.
Cathy Woolard, August 12, 2022.
Jorge Perez, August 14, 2022.
Abby Rubenfeld, August 15, 2022.
Pamela Karlan, August 19, 2022.
Sander Gilman, August 19, 2022.
Gene, September 2, 2022.
Michael Chriss, September 17, 2022.
Susan Browning-Chriss, September 17, 2022.
Jasmine Browning, September 18, 2022.
Jessica Hehr, September 21, 2022.
Nancy Langer, September 30, 2022.
Kathy Wilde, October 14, 2022.
Karen Chance, October 17, 2022.
Claudia Senesac, October 19, 2022.
Michelle Crone, December 17, 2022.

Cliff Frierson, January 22, 2023.
Nick Danna, January 27, 2023.
Ted Binkley, February 16, 2023.
Kim Stark, April 13, 2023.
Patty, April 13, 2023.
Laurence Tribe, April 16, 2023.
"Miss Puss," May 13, 2023.
Michael Hobbs, July 5, 2023.
Danny Garcia, July 14, 2023.
Cliff Sloan, July 25, 2023.

Books and Academic Journals

Bronski, Michael. *A Queer History of the United States*. Beacon Press, 2011.

Brooks, Peter. *Seduced by Story*. New York Review Books, 2022.

Carpenter, Dale. *Flagrant Conduct: The Story of Lawrence v. Texas*. W. W. Norton, 2013.

Eskridge, William. *Dishonorable Passions: Sodomy Laws in America 1861–2003* (Viking, 2008).

Goldstein, Anne B. "History, Homosexuality, and Political Values: Searching for the Hidden Determinants of *Bowers v. Hardwick*." *Yale Law Journal* 97, no. 6 (May 1988): 1073–1103.

Hartog, Hendrik. "The Constitution of Aspiration and 'The Rights That Belong to Us All.'" *Journal of American History* 74, no. 3 (1987): 1013–1034.

Irons, Peter. *The Courage of Their Convictions: Sixteen Americans Who Fought Their Way to the Supreme Court* (Free Press, 1988).

Klarman, Michael J. "How *Brown* Changed Race Relations: The Backlash Thesis." *Journal of American History* 81, no. 1 (1994): 81–118.

Murdoch, Joyce, and Deb Price. *Courting Justice: Gay Men and Lesbians v. the Supreme Court*. Basic Books, 2002.

Page, Benjamin I., Robert Y. Shapiro, and Glenn R. Dempsey. "What Moves Public Opinion?" *American Political Science Review* 81, no. 1 (1987): 23–43.

Prager, Joshua. *The Family Roe*. W. W. Norton, 2021.

Severs, George J. "Reticence and the Queer Past." *Oral History* 48, no. 1 (2020): 45–56.

Shilts, Randy. *And the Band Played On: Politics, People and the AIDS Epidemic, 20th Anniversary Edition*. St. Martin's Press, 2007.

Tribe, Laurence H. *The Invisible Constitution*. Oxford University Press, 2018.

Yang, Alan S. "Trends: Attitudes Toward Homosexuality." *Public Opinion Quarterly* 61, no. 3 (1997): 477–507.

Notes

Preface

1. Robrt L. Pela, "It Happened One Night: Will the Public Let Michael Hardwick Forget One Infamous Sex Act and Move On?" *Advocate*, January 16, 1990, 50.

Prologue

1. *Cruise* vol. 7, no. 26, June 25–July 1, 1982, 2 (Atlanta Lesbian and Gay History Thing papers and publications, ahc.MSS773, Kenan Research Center at the Atlanta History Center).
2. *Cruise* vol. 7, no. 26, June 25–July 1, 1982, 2.
3. Jim Bass interview.
4. Hank Ezell, "Fireworks Fan Loves Seeing It All Go Up in Smoke," *Atlanta Constitution*, July 4, 1982.
5. Jesse Dorris, "Patrick Cowley Is One of Disco's Most Important Producers. These Are His Must-Hear Deep Cuts," *Pitchfork*, January 17, 2018.
6. John D'Emilio and Estelle B. Freedman, *Intimate Matters: A History of Sexuality in America* (University of Chicago Press, 2013), 277.
7. Some sources cite landscape design as his path of study, along with Sanskrit, while others name botany. Santa Fe College does not maintain course catalogs from the era, but administrators confirm Hardwick studied there.
8. Art Harris, "'A Good Cop, but Badge-Heavy,'" *San Francisco Chronicle*, September 7, 1986.

9 Multiple versions of this story exist in Peter Irons's *The Courage of Their Convictions*, in newspapers, and in the public record.

Adrift

1 Daniel J. Weeks et al., *The Papers of Thomas A. Edison: New Beginnings, January 1885–December 1887* (Johns Hopkins University Press, 2015).
2 "Pin-A-Pola Factory to Be Built, Owners Pleased with Prospect," *Miami News*, August 21, 1915.
3 Classified ad, *Miami News*, October 14, 1924.
4 "Boston Services Unite Couple," *Miami Herald*, September 12, 1944.
5 Art Harris, "The Unintended Battle of Michael Hardwick," *Washington Post*, August 21, 1986.
6 No alleged instances of physical cruelty by either Kitty or Rick have been documented; the phrase had become commonly cited as a reason for divorce, most often as emotional cruelty.

Devils and Gods

1 Gene interview.
2 Patty interview.
3 Gene interview.
4 Ibid.
5 Florida Statute F.S. 800.02.
6 Peter Irons, *The Courage of Their Convictions* (Free Press, 1988), 392.
7 Dennis Wiedman and J. Bryan Page, "Drug Use on the Street and on the Beach: Cubans and Anglos in Miami, Florida," *Urban Anthropology* 11, no. 2 (1982): 213–235.
8 House of Representatives, *Drugs in Our Schools: Hearings Before the Select Committee on Crime, Ninety-Second Congress, Second Session, Miami, Florida* (U.S. Government Printing Office, 1972). The information from this section is drawn from this record.
9 Susan Browning-Chriss recalls only that he was arrested, not for which specific charge or on which date.
10 Yvette Cardozo, "Art Barker: The Seed Consumes Him," *Fort Lauderdale News*, May 21, 1972.
11 House of Representatives, *Drugs in Our Schools*.
12 Cardozo, "Art Barker: The Seed Consumes Him."
13 Anomaly Documentaries, *Inside "The Seed," Florida's Youth Cult*. YouTube, https://www.youtube.com/watch?v=M0XY2AI3ABI.

14 Frank Eidge, "Ex-Comedian Adopts Drugs Users for the Seed," *Playground Daily News*, August 20, 1972.
15 Steffi Cooper, "U.S. Aid Triples Rehab Fund for the Seed," *Fort Lauderdale News*, January 26, 1972.
16 Judith Miller, "The Seed: Reforming Drug Abusers with Love," *Science* 182, no. 4107 (1973): 40–42.
17 Mike Morgan, "Sammy, the Seed, and Love," *Fort Lauderdale News*, April 9, 1972.
18 Yvette Cardozo, "A Seed That Grew and Grew," *Fort Lauderdale News*, May 21, 1972.
19 Ibid.
20 It's unclear whether this could be Michael Hardwick.
21 Cardozo, "A Seed That Grew and Grew."
22 Ibid.
23 Maia Szalavitz, "The Cult That Spawned the Tough-Love Teen Industry," *Mother Jones*, September/October 2007.
24 Miller, "The Seed: Reforming Drug Abusers with Love," 41.
25 Ibid.
26 Cardozo, "A Seed That Grew and Grew."
27 "The Seed Receives Mental Health Grant," *Fort Lauderdale News*, January 22, 1972.
28 Combined, the Barkers' salaries would equal nearly $150,000 in late-2023 dollars.
29 "Editorial: Seed Is Put in Perspective," *Miami Herald*, October 14, 1972. At the time, homosexuality was still classified as a mental disorder.
30 Cardozo, "Art Barker: The Seed Consumes Him," 34.
31 Michael Reece, "Domestic Santa Fe," *Nouveau*, undated (assumed to be 1988–1989), 23. From the Michael Hardwick portfolio, courtesy of Robert Hardwick Weston.
32 Pete Townsend, "In Love with Meher Baba," *Rolling Stone*, November 26, 1970.
33 James Ivory, "Jai Baba!" *New Yorker*, June 13, 1969.
34 Ibid.
35 Ibid.
36 Thomas Robbins, "Eastern Mysticism and the Resocialization of Drug Users: The Meher Baba Cult," *Journal for the Scientific Study of Religion* 8, no. 2 (1969): 308–317.
37 Townsend, "In Love with Meher Baba."

38 Dick Wich, "People in the News," *Elmira Star-Gazette*, February 2, 1969.
39 Jessica Hehr interview.
40 Ann Forbes, "Me in the Arms of God!" *When He Takes Over*, ed. Bal Natu (Meher Baba Books, 1988), 21–26.
41 Reece, "Domestic Santa Fe," 23.

Atlanta

1 Streaming Science, "Conservation Conversation," September 18, 2019.
2 Art Harris, "The Unintended Battle of Michael Hardwick," *Washington Post*, August 21, 1986.
3 Peter Irons, *The Courage of Their Convictions* (Free Press, 1988), 392–393.
4 Harris, "Unintended Battle."
5 Irons, *Courage*, 393.
6 Marlin Beach House flat files, Stonewall National Museum and Archives, Fort Lauderdale, Florida.
7 Stephanie Mansfield, "New Rites of Lauderdale," *Washington Post*, April 20, 1977.
8 "'Boys' Made Fort Lauderdale a Star," *Miami Herald*, December 21, 1980.
9 Ibid.
10 John Dolen, "Landmark Marlin," *Fort Lauderdale Magazine*, November 7, 2019.
11 Ibid.
12 William N. Eskridge, *Gaylaw: Challenging the Apartheid of the Closet* (Harvard University Press, 2009), Introduction.
13 *One, Incorporated, v. Olesen*, 355 U.S. 371 (1958).
14 Dan Rather, "Bryant on Television," Dan Rather, Journalist, https://danratherjournalist.org/interviewer/whos-who.
15 "Anita Bryant Confronted in 1977 (Who's Who) Interview," YouTube, https://www.youtube.com/watch?v=fABwascm12s.
16 Ibid.
17 Jesse Monteagudo, "Memories Of Pride," Southfloridagaynews.com, March 12, 2012, https://southfloridagaynews.com/Jesse-Monteagudo/memories-of-pride.html (accessed February 12, 2023).
18 Bea Moss, "The Grove Goes Up . . . and Up," *Miami Herald*, February 12, 1978.
19 Ibid.
20 "Scouting Coconut Grove," *New York Times*, March 27, 1977.
21 "'Hotel Scarface' Recounts Glamorous, Infamous Epicenter of Miami's Cocaine Days," *PBS NewsHour*, December 27, 2017.
22 Dr. Joseph Trainer, "Marriage Doctor," *Miami News*, January 31, 1978.

23 Irons, *Courage*, 393.
24 Paul Orofino interview.
25 Michael Reece, "Domestic Santa Fe," *Nouveau*, undated (assumed to be 1988–1989), 23.
26 Irons, *Courage*, 393.
27 "Townsend Passion Play Closes Season After Attack," *Knoxville News-Sentinel*, August 23, 1980.
28 Michael's sister believes he began reading the Castaneda series not long after the first volumes were published in the late 1960s and early 1970s.
29 Castaneda portrayed his books as nonfiction, but in the decades since their publication, it has become generally accepted that they are works of pure fiction—and plagiarism, in part, due to some dozens of pages of quotes that appeared to have been lifted from classic texts.
30 Joshua Rothman, "The Crazy History of 'Star Wars,'" *New Yorker*, December 17, 2014.
31 Carlos Castaneda, *Journey to Ixtlan: The Lessons of Don Juan* (Simon & Schuster, 1972).
32 Mike Chriss interview.
33 Irons, *Courage*, 393.
34 "Retired Firefighter Hardwick Dies," *Miami News*, February 18, 1981.
35 Harris, "Unintended Battle."

Crime of Passion

1 Richard L. Eldredge, "Backstreet: An Oral History of Atlanta's Most Fabled 24-Hour Nightclub," *Atlanta Magazine* (blog), October 9, 2020.
2 Cliff Frierson interview.
3 Barbara Gervais Street, "The Gaying of Atlanta," *Atlanta Constitution*, December 12, 1982.
4 Ibid.
5 Ibid.
6 Larry Bush, "Atlanta's Mayor Andy Young," *Advocate*, December 9, 1982, 21–24.
7 Ibid.
8 Ibid.
9 Ibid.
10 Ibid.
11 WGST News (Atlanta), 1981–2008—excerpts, "Atlanta's Gays: A Life of Their Own," Peabody Awards Collection, 81003 NWR 1 of 1, Walter J.

Brown Media Archives & Peabody Awards Collection, University of Georgia, Athens.

12 Lawrence K. Altman, "New Homosexual Disorder Worries Health Officials," *New York Times*, May 11, 1982.
13 Ibid. In 1992 the agency would change its name to the Centers for Disease Control and Prevention.
14 Arthur Cantrell interview.
15 Ibid.
16 Gil Robison, "Teenage Gay Bashers Busted in Piedmont Park," *Metropolitan Gazette*, June 17–23, 1982 (Atlanta History Center).
17 "L/G/T Proclamation Goes into Effect Without Mayor's Signature," *Metropolitan Gazette*, June 17–23, 1982 (Atlanta History Center).
18 "Club Exile Raided by Atlanta Police, Four Arrested," *Metropolitan Gazette*, July 1–7, 1982 (Atlanta History Center).
19 "Anita Bryant, Gays' Minister Visit Discotheque in Atlanta," *Oklahoman*, June 29, 1982.
20 Gil Robison, "Anita Bryant Spotted Boogying at Limelight," *Metropolitan Gazette*, July 1–7, 1982 (Atlanta History Center).
21 "Anita Bryant, Gays' Minister Visit Discotheque."
22 "Thousands March on Georgia State Capitol," *Metropolitan Gazette*, July 1–7, 1982 (Atlanta History Center).
23 Louis Levenson interview. In a late interview with the *Advocate* eighteen months before his death, Hardwick would allege the following: "This guy had ten ongoing cases of homosexual harassment to his credit. Four of the [people he arrested] had been physically abused afterward by strangers."
24 Kirk Slusser interview.
25 Peter Irons, *The Courage of Their Convictions* (Free Press, 1988), 394.
26 Ibid.
27 Ibid.
28 Michael Hardwick statement prepared for ACLU attorneys.
29 Ibid.
30 Irons, *Courage*, 394.
31 Ibid., 395.
32 Hardwick did not mention this attack in his statement to his ACLU attorneys. However, still frames of his mug shots—available through footage that aired in 1986 on NBC News—show Hardwick with a noticeable left black eye and small cuts on his face. Kirk Slusser confirms that he witnessed

Michael's condition on the day of the assault. Further confirmation comes from Dwight Sawyer: "I do know that the Sunday before the arrest, Michael was beaten by a group of guys. [. . .] I do know at the time that speculation was that these were police officers, off-duty, or whatever. And you have to keep in mind that Michael's house was on Ponce Place, is only two blocks away from what was then, the station house." See Ralph Ginn, "Hardwick's Counterpart Discusses Arrest and Case," NBC News, October 24, 1986.

33 Leada Gore, "'Last Lynching in America' Shocked Mobile in 1981, Bankrupted the KKK," AL.com, April 26, 2018.
34 Joey Potter interview.
35 In this account shared by Irons, Hardwick suggests that he came home alone with Dwight Sawyer. Sawyer contradicts this and says they came home with a group. Some in the social group attribute this to heavy drinking and drug use among the people who regularly went to Hardwick's house to party.
36 Ginn, "Hardwick's Counterpart," 6–7.
37 It is unclear whether Torick ever received or saw the note from the clerk about the warrant or if he had the authority to invalidate it. According to the arrest report, he detained the two men at 12:10 p.m. Hardwick in various accounts timed the arrest from between 8:30 and 10:30 a.m.
38 Kirk Slusser interview.
39 Hardwick later said that he had left the door cracked. See Irons, *Courage*, 395, and Richard Laermer, "Michael Hardwick: The Man Behind the Georgia Sodomy Case," *Advocate*, September 2, 1986, 38–41, 110.
40 Irons, *Courage*, 395.
41 Ibid.
42 Ibid.
43 Lowe, "Long Uphill Climb," 4.
44 Hardwick ACLU statement.
45 Kirk Slusser interview.
46 Ginn, "Hardwick's Counterpart," 6–7.
47 Joey Potter interview.
48 Greg McDonald, "GA Suits Have Warned Against Jail Fires," *Atlanta Constitution*, November 9, 1982.
49 Ginn, "Hardwick's Counterpart," 6–7.
50 Hardwick ACLU statement.
51 Robrt L. Pela, "It Happened One Night," *Advocate*, January 16, 1990, 51.

52. Irons, *Courage*, 396.
53. Laermer, "Michael Hardwick."
54. Ibid.
55. Ginn, "Hardwick's Counterpart," 6–7.
56. Ibid.
57. Ibid.
58. Joey Potter, Facebook post, https://www.facebook.com/groups/2973108472722616/permalink/3394597043907088.
59. Jim Bass interview.

Private Matters

1. Ralph Ginn, "Hardwick's Counterpart Discusses Arrest and Case," NBC News, October 24, 1986, 6–7.
2. As Dwight recounts in his interview, "I will decline to state his name."
3. Ginn, "Hardwick's Counterpart," 6–7.
4. Leigh Ann Wheeler, *How Sex Became a Civil Liberty* (Oxford University Press, 2012), 40.
5. GA Code § 16-6-2 (2020).
6. Peter Irons, *The Courage of Their Convictions* (Free Press, 1988), 397.
7. Bill Banks, "John Sweet, Activist and Lawyer, Dies at 77," *Atlanta Journal-Constitution*, June 11, 2020.
8. Richard Laermer, "Michael Hardwick," *Advocate*, September 2, 1986.
9. Irons, *Courage*, 396.
10. Laermer, "Michael Hardwick."
11. Marilyn Goldstein, "Michael Hardwick Went Public with His Private Life," *Newsday*, August 4, 1986.
12. Laermer, "Michael Hardwick."
13. Art Harris, "The Unintended Battle of Michael Hardwick," *Washington Post*, August 21, 1986.
14. Ginn, "Hardwick's Counterpart," 6–7.
15. Hardwick would later recall this moment to the *Advocate* in 1986 as follows: "The judge kind of chuckled and asked my attorneys how I pled, and they said 'Guilty' with no argument. We didn't want them to get suspicious as to what we were up to."
16. In the record, "Selser"—and as noted, Slusser was a guest at the home. Hardwick had another roommate.
17. Torick requested a lab report, which indicated about three grams of marijuana.

18 Harris, "Unintended Battle."
19 Irons, *Courage*, 382.
20 Harris, "Unintended Battle."
21 Irons, *Courage*, 383.
22 Ibid.
23 *Bowers v. Hardwick*; American Civil Liberties Union Records: Subgroup 2, Legal Case Files Series, MC001-02-04, Public Policy Papers, Department of Special Collections, Princeton University Library.
24 Krista Reese, "The Lights Went Out in Georgia," *George*, May 1998, 70.
25 Ginn, "Hardwick's Counterpart," 6–7.
26 Email from Kathy Wilde, August 8, 2023.
27 Kathy Wilde interview.
28 William Eskridge, *Dishonorable Passions* (Viking, 2008), 1.
29 Ibid.
30 Ibid., 185.
31 The core of Brandeis's dissent would frame the later 1967 Katz decision, which reasoned the government had to produce a warrant to wiretap the phones of citizens.
32 National Constitution Center, "Interpretation: The Fourteenth Amendment Due Process Clause," https://constitutioncenter.org/the-constitution/articles/amendment-xiv/clauses/701.
33 *Loving v. Virginia*, 388 U.S. 1 (1967).
34 *Eisenstadt v. Baird*, 405 U.S. 438 (1972).
35 *Roe v. Wade*, 410 U.S. 113 (1973).
36 In 2022, the Supreme Court held in a 5–4 decision in *Dobbs v. Jackson Women's Health Organization* that no such right to abortion existed in or was implied by the Constitution's due process clause, and *Roe* was overturned.
37 Box III.78, folder 33–34, *Hardwick v. Bowers*, 1986–1996, American Civil Liberties Union of Georgia Records, Richard B. Russell Library for Political Research and Studies, University of Georgia Libraries, Athens, Georgia.
38 Ibid.
39 Ibid.
40 "Mayor Young Signs Lesbian/Gay Proclamation," *Cruise*, June 17–23, 1983, https://www.houstonlgbthistory.org/cruise.html.
41 Maria Helena Dolan, "2000 March for Lesbian/Gay Day in Atlanta," *Cruise*, June 17–23, 1983, https://www.houstonlgbthistory.org/cruise.html.

42 Dyana Bagby, "Celebrating 44 Years of Atlanta Pride and Who We Are," *Georgia Voice*, October 10, 2014.

43 "Shirley Franklin Speaks at Atlanta Gay Center," *Cruise*, June 17–23, 1983, https://www.houstonlgbthistory.org/cruise.html.

44 "Michael Hardwick Interviewed," *Cruise*, July 8–14, 1983, https://www.houstonlgbthistory.org/cruise.html.

45 Ibid.

46 The 1983–1984 Atlanta city directory shows a Michael D. Hardwick at 811 Ponce de Leon Place and another on Peachtree Road. It cannot be confirmed if the latter listing is also valid for Hardwick, though friends recall that another friend lived in the same building.

47 "Michael Hardwick Interviewed."

48 Dick Williams, "Are Homosexual Rights Really Their Wrongs?" *Atlanta Journal*, July 3, 1983.

49 Ibid.

50 Heather Murray, "Fearing a Fear of Germs," Historians.org, October 2, 2020.

51 Frank M. Johnson Papers, 1865–1999 (bulk 1955–1995), box 364, folder 8, Library of Congress.

52 Lambda amicus briefs, August 22, 1983. ACLU of Georgia archives, University of Georgia.

53 Ibid.

54 Ibid.

55 Eskridge, *Dishonorable Passions*, 251.

The Boys of Summer

1 Harold v. Shumacher, "A Cook's Tour of a Neighborhood That's Changed Its Course," *Atlanta Journal*, April 3, 1982.

2 Peter Irons, *The Courage of Their Convictions* (Free Press, 1988), 399.

3 Art Harris, "The Unintended Battle of Michael Hardwick," *Washington Post*, August 21, 1986. None of his old friends could identify the person, or if they even existed.

4 While both Montagnier and Gallo and their teams had isolated the virus independently, it later was discovered that some of Gallo's samples used in his research were obtained from Montagnier's cultures. The teams at the Pasteur and the NIH would both be credited with the discovery of the HIV virus later, but only after presidents Reagan and Mitterrand brokered an end to an increasingly tense legal battle over patent rights for

HIV testing. See Dr. Howard Markel, "How the Discovery of HIV Led to a Transatlantic Research War," March 24, 2020, PBS.org.
5 "AIDS," #89596, *ABC Evening News for Monday, April 23, 1984* (Vanderbilt TV News Archive).
6 See Michel Foucault, *The History of Sexuality, Volume 1* (Vintage, 1990), 149.
7 Ibid., 151.
8 "AIDS," #87850, *ABC Evening News for Friday, November 23, 1984* (Vanderbilt TV News Archive).
9 Frank Page, "AIDS on the Increase," *Gay Center News*, December 6, 1984 (Georgia State University Archives, Special Collections).
10 Ibid.
11 Frankie Goes to Hollywood, "Frankie Goes To Hollywood - Relax (Official Video)," YouTube, uploaded April 3, 2018, https://www.youtube.com/watch?v=Yem_iEHiyJ0.

Justified

1 "International Civil Rights: Walk of Fame: Elbert Tuttle," National Park Service, https://www.nps.gov/features/malu/feat0002/wof/elbert_tuttle.htm.
2 Robert D. McFadden, "Frank M. Johnson Jr., Judge Whose Rulings Helped Desegregate the South, Dies at 80," *New York Times*, July 24, 1999.
3 Richard Kavanaugh, "Sodomy Statute Challenged in Georgia," *Around the Clock: The Gay Weekly*, January 25, 1985.
4 Longstaff would remain in the country. See Mike Anglin, "Richard Longstaff," *Dallas Way*, December 8, 2017.
5 "SUPREME COURT / HOMOSEXUAL RIGHTS," #542593, *NBC Evening News for Tuesday, March 26, 1985* (Vanderbilt TV News Archive).
6 Richard Cohen, "Keep It Quiet," *Washington Post*, October 2, 1984.
7 "SUPREME COURT," #87186, *ABC Evening News for Monday, October 1, 1984* (Vanderbilt TV News Archive).
8 Brian Hamacher, "'Dadeland Mall Massacre': Thursday Marks 40th Anniversary of Infamous 'Cocaine Cowboys' Shootout," *NBC 6 South Florida* (blog), July 11, 2019.
9 Ibid.
10 Ibid.
11 Associated Press, "Conference on AIDS Begins in Atlanta," *New York Times*, April 16, 1985.
12 Phyllis Kravitch letter to Frank Johnson, April 1, 1985. Frank M. John-

son Papers, 1865–1999 (bulk 1955–1995), box 364, folder 8, Library of Congress.

13 Joyce Murdoch and Deb Price, *Courting Justice* (Basic Books, 2002), 281.

14 U.S. Court of Appeals for the Eleventh Circuit, 760 F.2d 1202 (Eleventh Cir. 1985), May 21, 1985.

15 Associated Press, "Court Says Sex Statute Violates Constitutional Rights," *Macon Telegraph and News*, May 22, 1985.

16 Ann Woolner, "Sodomy Law Violates Privacy, Court Rules," *Atlanta Constitution*, May 22, 1985.

17 Ibid.

18 Ibid.

19 Krista Reese, "The Lights Went Out in Georgia," *George*, May 1998, 72.

20 Stephen Breyer, Pamela S. Karlan, Richard S. Arnold, Karen Nelson Moore, and Norval Morris, "In Memoriam: Harry A. Blackmun," *Harvard Law Review* 113, no. 1 (1999): 1–25.

21 Breyer et al., "In Memoriam," 2.

22 Nancy Blackmun email, March 27, 2022.

23 A Kennedy appointee to the federal circuit, Marshall took the Supreme Court seat of Thomas Campbell Clark, who had succeeded Frank Murphy. Murphy died in 1949, and though he was engaged to a woman, many believed him to have been in a long-term relationship with Edward G. Kemp. See Murdoch and Price, *Courting Justice*, 19.

24 *Stanley v. Georgia*, 394 U.S. 557 (1969).

25 "Thurgood Marshall," *Oyez*, https://www.oyez.org/justices/thurgood_marshall.

26 Associated Press, "Justice Brennan Calls Criticism of Court Disguised Arrogance," *Los Angeles Times*, October 13, 1985.

27 "John Paul Stevens," *Oyez*, https://www.oyez.org/justices/john_paul_stevens.

28 "Harry A. Blackmun," *Oyez*, https://www.oyez.org/justices/harry_a_blackmun.

29 "Byron R. White," *Oyez*, https://www.oyez.org/justices/byron_r_white.

30 "Sandra Day O'Connor," *Oyez*, https://www.oyez.org/justices/sandra_day_oconnor.

31 Byron R. White Papers, 1961–1992, box II:35, folder 6, Library of Congress.

32 The archives of Justice John Paul Stevens contain a memo from Rehnquist to O'Connor, written in 1993, that still held that *Plessy* only prohibited dis-

crimination, and that it did not require integration. See Richard L. Hasen, and Dahlia Lithwick, "There's Unsettling New Evidence About William Rehnquist's Views on Segregation," *Slate*, June 1, 2023.

33 Associated Press, "FBI Releases Rehnquist Drug Problem Records," NBC News, January 4, 2007.

34 Joyce Murdoch and Deb Price were able to capture an incalculably valuable snapshot of the machinations behind the *Hardwick* case at the court in their book *Courting Justice*. While I have cited a handful of their most incisive reporting here, I have left their sterling account as an admirer—and have combed through other sources to find fresh details. Go read their book.

35 "Lewis F. Powell, Jr.," *Oyez*, https://www.oyez.org/justices/lewis_f_powell_jr.

36 September 28, 1985, memo from William Stuntz to Lewis F. Powell, *Bowers v. Hardwick*, Supreme Court Case Files Collection, box 129, Powell Papers, Lewis F. Powell Jr. Archives, Washington & Lee University School of Law, Virginia.

37 Ibid.

38 William J. Brennan Papers, 1945–1998 (bulk 1956–1990), box I:711, folder 7, Library of Congress.

39 Daniel Richman interview.

40 Kathy Wilde interview.

41 Christina Pazzanese, "As He Prepares to Retire, Laurence Tribe Retraces His Path from Teen Immigrant Math Whiz to Leading Constitutional Law Scholar and Admired Professor," *Harvard Gazette*, June 24, 2020.

42 Ibid.

43 Ibid.

44 Ibid.

45 Laurence Tribe interview.

46 William Domnarski, "Q&A with Laurence Tribe of Harvard Law School," *Daily Journal*, August 12, 2021.

47 William Eskridge, *Dishonorable Passions* (Viking, 2008), 238.

48 Ibid., 5.

49 Letter from Robert Remar to Burt Neuborne, July 31, 1985. American Civil Liberties Union, American Civil Liberties Union Records: Subgroup 2, Legal Case Files Series, 1947–1995, *Bowers v. Hardwick*, 1985, box 1251, Special Collections, Princeton University Library.

50 Abby Rubenfeld interview.
51 Letter from Laurence Tribe to Kathy Wilde, November 13, 1985. Laurence Tribe Archives.
52 Ibid.
53 Minutes of the November 16, 1985, meeting, Ad Hoc Task Force to Challenge Sodomy Laws, Donald F. Baker Collection (The Dallas Way) in The Portal to Texas History, University of North Texas Libraries, https://texashistory.unt.edu/explore/collections/DFBAKER.
54 Laurence Tribe interview.
55 Ad hoc task force second day meeting, 13. The spellings of "wiff" and "sturring" have been corrected from the original in my use of the text.
56 Ibid., 14.
57 Bowers brief to Supreme Court, December 19, 1985.
58 Kim Green, "2015 Nashvillians of the Year: How Abby Rubenfeld and Bill Harbison Helped to Change History," *Nashville Scene*, November 25, 2015.
59 Abby Rubenfeld interview.
60 Memo from Pamela Karlan to Harry Blackmun. Harry A. Blackmun Papers, 1913–2001 (bulk 1959–1994), box 451, folder 7, 14, Library of Congress.
61 Ibid., folder 7, 13.
62 Murdoch and Price, *Courting Justice*, 287.
63 Bowers reply brief, March 21, 1986.
64 William J. Brennan Papers, 1945–1998 (bulk 1956–1990), box I:711, folder 7, Library of Congress.
65 Ibid.
66 Karlan memo to Blackmun, 26, 21.
67 Powell Papers, *Bowers v. Hardwick*, Supreme Court Case Files Collection, box 129.
68 Memo from Daniel Richman to Thurgood Marshall. Thurgood Marshall Papers, 1949–1991 (bulk 1961–1991), box 376, folder 2, 3, Library of Congress.
69 *Courting Justice*'s authors believe this would have been dictated the Saturday prior, as was Powell's custom.
70 Powell Papers, *Bowers v. Hardwick*, Supreme Court Case Files Collection, box 129.

Theater

1 Buren Batson, "*Bowers vs. Hardwick*: Equal Justice Under Law," *Gay Center News*, April 11, 1986.

2. Kathy Wilde interview.
3. Evan Wolfson interview.
4. Peter Irons, *The Courage of Their Convictions* (Free Press, 1988), 399.
5. William Domnarski, "Q&A with Laurence Tribe of Harvard Law School," *Daily Journal*, August 12, 2021.
6. Ibid.
7. All quoted material comes from the official transcript of the case: *Bowers v. Hardwick*, 478 U.S. 186 (1986).
8. Ibid.
9. Batson, *"Bowers vs. Hardwick."*
10. Ibid.
11. Ibid.
12. Irons, *Courage*, 399.
13. Evan Wolfson interview.
14. Batson, *"Bowers vs. Hardwick."*
15. Laurence Tribe interview.
16. Sexual Orientation Law 2006: Kathleen Sullivan, YouTube, https://www.youtube.com/watch?v=i0vK5yXftSM. "Chief Justice Burger, who had a habit of . . . having his head slip down to his chest into apparent slumber during the argument, popped up and said, 'What about brother-sister incest?'"
17. Irons, *Courage*, 399.
18. Batson, *"Bowers vs. Hardwick."*
19. Ibid.
20. Laurence Tribe interview.
21. Batson, *"Bowers vs. Hardwick."*
22. Letter from Gene Guerrero to Burt Neuborne and Ira Glasser, April 2, 1986. ACLU of Georgia archives, University of Georgia.
23. Abby Rubenfeld interview.
24. Evan Wolfson interview.

Reversal

1. Pam Karlan said, during our interview, that 1986 represented the peak of abortion rights in America, while it arguably marked the nadir of the gay rights movement.
2. Bill Moyers, "Mr. Justice Blackmun," *In Search of the Constitution*, April 16, 1987 (transcript available at BillMoyers.com).
3. "The Justice Harry A. Blackmun Oral History Project," Harry A. Blackmun Papers, Library of Congress.

4   William Eskridge, *Dishonorable Passions* (Viking, 2008), 244–245.
5   Lyle Denniston, "Justice Byron White: A Retrospective," Constitution-Center.org, October 16, 2021.
6   "You Say 'Huana, I Say 'Juana: Has High Court's Spelling Gone to Pot?" *National Law Journal*, April 14, 1986.
7   Denniston, "Justice Byron White."
8   Adam Lipton, "Exhibit A for a Major Shift: Justices' Gay Clerks," *New York Times*, June 8, 2013.
9   Many sources come up with similar or paraphrased versions of this.
10 Lipton, "Exhibit A."
11 Stephen Breyer, Pamela S. Karlan, Richard S. Arnold, Karen Nelson Moore, and Norval Morris, "In Memoriam: Harry A. Blackmun," *Harvard Law Review* 113, no. 1 (1999): 1.
12 Memo from Michael Mosman, April 1, 1986. Powell Papers, Lewis F. Powell Jr. Archives, Washington & Lee University School of Law, Virginia.
13 *Courting Justice* offers that Mosman had written to Powell on April 2 that he, Bill Stuntz, and Ann Coughlin all believed that Powell should reverse and write an opinion declaring punishment for sodomy unconstitutional; Coughlin said to the authors that she never advocated reversal. See Joyce Murdoch and Deb Price, *Courting Justice* (Basic Books, 2002), 306.
14 Much of the record of these votes comes through the papers of Thurgood Marshall which—in a shock to many who served along with him on the Supreme Court, or clerked for him, had agreed in 1991 to release his papers through the Library of Congress shortly after his death, which came in 1993. See Neil A. Lewis, "Rare Glimpses of Judicial Chess and Poker," *New York Times*, May 25, 1993.
15 Moyers, "Mr. Justice Blackmun."
16 Murdoch and Price, *Courting Justice*, 309.
17 Kathy Wilde interview. She adds that she didn't find out about the decision not to approach Powell's clerks until after the decision: "I was really furious."
18 Letter from Warren Burger to Lewis Powell, April 3, 1986. Powell Papers, Lewis F. Powell Jr. Archives, Washington & Lee University School of Law, Virginia.
19 Ibid.
20 Ibid.
21 Murdoch and Price, *Courting Justice*, 313.
22 Byron R. White Papers, 1961–1992, box II:50, folder 3, Library of Congress.

23 Lewis, "Rare Glimpses."
24 Ibid.
25 Breyer et al., "In Memoriam," 2.
26 Moyers, "Mr. Justice Blackmun."
27 Pamela Karlan interview.
28 "The Justice Harry A. Blackmun Oral History Project."
29 Ibid.
30 Moyers, "Mr. Justice Blackmun." In this interview, Blackmun clearly, if elliptically, refers to Powell's vote shift in the *Hardwick* case.
31 Moyers, "Mr. Justice Blackmun."
32 William F. Buckley Jr., "Crucial Steps in Combating the Aids Epidemic; Identify All the Carriers," *New York Times*, March 18, 1986.
33 *Pride and Progress*, Episode No. 16 [2], "The Right Stuff," Episode No. 192, April 16, 1986 (Gay Cable Network Archives; MSS 231; 231.0682; Fales Library and Special Collections, New York University Libraries).
34 Marc Slavin, "ACLU Puts National Resources into Gay Rights," *Bay Area Reporter*, June 26, 1986.
35 George Mendenhall, "'The Future Is Ours, Says Lambda's Stoddard," *Bay Area Reporter*, May 29, 1986.
36 The long history of attribution of this opinion to Pamela Karlan was initiated in part by remarks Blackmun made in 1995 during an oral history interview: "Professor Karlan, of course, was my clerk that year that worked on this case and did a lot of very effective writing, and I owe a lot to her and her ability in getting that dissent out. She felt very strongly about it, and I think is correct in her approach to it. I think the dissent is correct, and I've stated publicly more than once that it will be the law someday, and then people say, 'What makes you think so?' Well, I don't need to go into reasons for that." For more, see "The Justice Harry A. Blackmun Oral History Project." In our interview, Karlan told me that early drafts circulated among all of Blackmun's clerks, with his thoughts and cited cases. "The basic structure of the opinion was pretty clear before I sat down to do any drafting," she said. "My job was to turn that into something that looked more like a Supreme Court opinion and less like a philosophical, you know, a philosophical position."
37 Moyers, "Mr. Justice Blackmun."
38 Dissent remarks read from the bench by Harry Blackmun. Harry A. Blackmun Papers, box 451, folder 9, Library of Congress.
39 "The Justice Harry A. Blackmun Oral History Project."

40 Message from Thurgood Marshall to Harry Blackmun. Harry A. Blackmun Papers, box 451, folder 7.

Backlash

1 Peter Irons, *The Courage of Their Convictions* (Free Press, 1988), 400.
2 David Lowe, "Michael Hardwick's Long Uphill Climb," *San Francisco Sentinel*, August 15, 1986.
3 Richard Laermer, "Michael Hardwick," *Advocate*, September 2, 1986, 110.
4 Kim Green, "2015 Nashvillians of the Year: How Abby Rubenfeld and Bill Harbison Helped to Change History," *Nashville Scene*, November 25, 2015.
5 Kathy Wilde interview.
6 Ibid.: "I was caught up in the, in the maelstrom of press at that point. And I'm sure that Michael had known from other sources. It seems like I should have called him, but it wasn't something that occurred to me cause he had been so out of the picture for so long."
7 Ibid.
8 "SUPREME COURT / SODOMY," #310601, *CBS Evening News for Monday, June 30, 1986* (Vanderbilt TV News Archive).
9 Evan Wolfson, "Bowers v. Hardwick," *Advocate*, November 12, 2002, 94.
10 Kirk Slusser interview.
11 Ralph Ginn, "Hardwick's Counterpart Discusses Arrest and Case," NBC News, October 24, 1986, 6–7.
12 "SUPREME COURT / SODOMY," #103388, *ABC Evening News for Monday, June 30, 1986* (Vanderbilt TV News Archive).
13 William Eskridge, *Dishonorable Passions* (Viking, 2008), 252.
14 Lowe, "Long Uphill Climb."
15 Larry Rohter, "Friend and Foe See Homosexual Defeat," *New York Times*, July 1, 1986.
16 Cal Thomas, "Opinion: Gay Wrongs," *Plano Daily Star-Courier*, July 13, 1986.
17 "A Government in the Bedroom," *Newsweek*, July 14, 1986.
18 John Rechy, "A High Court Decision and a Sense of Betrayal," *Los Angeles Times*, July 6, 1986.
19 John Wetzl, "Top Court's Decision Bashes Gays," *San Francisco Sentinel*, July 4, 1986. The number is reported as a hundred, a few hundred, and up to 2,000 as given by the *Bay Area Reporter*.
20 Marc Sandalow, "S.F. Gays, Lesbians Vow to Fight / Sodomy Ruling Stirs Protest," *San Francisco Chronicle*, July 1, 1986.

21 Mary C. Dunlap, "Gay Men and Lesbians Down by Law in the 1990's USA: The Continuing Toll of *Bowers v. Hardwick*," *Golden Gate University Law Review* 24 (1994).
22 William G. Blair, "City's Homosexuals Protest High Court Sodomy Ruling," *New York Times*, July 3, 1986.
23 Ibid.
24 Sarah Schulman, *Let the Record Show: A Political History of Act Up New York 1987–1993* (Farrar, Straus and Giroux, 2021), 100.
25 Ibid.
26 Peter Freiberg, "Supreme Court Decision Sparks Protests," *Advocate*, August 5, 1986, 12.
27 Ibid.
28 Alan Lewis, "300 Rally Against Supreme Court Sodomy Ruling," *Gay Center News*, July 18, 1986 (Georgia State University Archives, Special Collections).
29 Joan Hanauer, "The Four-Day Party for the Statue of Liberty's 100th," UPI, July 7, 1986.
30 Alan Finder, "Police Halt Rights Marchers at Wall St.," *New York Times*, July 5, 1986.
31 Freiberg, "Supreme Court Decision."
32 Hanauer, "Four-Day Party."
33 Freiberg, "Supreme Court Decision."
34 Nancy Langer interview.
35 Samuel Maull, "Rally Protests Court's Sodomy Ruling," *Herald Statesman*, July 5, 1986.
36 *Pride and Progress*, Episode No. 29 [2] "The Right Stuff," July 15, 1986 (Gay Cable Network Archives; MSS 231; 231.0695; Fales Library and Special Collections, New York University Libraries).
37 Freiberg, "Supreme Court Decision."
38 Maull, "Rally Protests."
39 Freiberg, "Supreme Court Decision."
40 Fred Bruning, "Challenger's Outrage Led to Case," *Newsday*, July 2, 1986.
41 Tina Montalvo, "Miami Native Who Lost Sodomy Suit Calls High Court Ruling Frightening," *Miami Herald*, July 2, 1986.
42 Frank M. Johnson Papers, 1865–1999 (bulk 1955–1995), box 364, folder 78, Library of Congress
43 Montalvo, "Miami Native."
44 "A Government in the Bedroom," 38. In the *Newsweek* poll, only 34 percent

said that the states should be able to bar consenting private homosexual behavior; no accounting for the remaining 9 percent. The survey noted that when not delimited to homosexual sex, those polled wanted to keep the government out of their bedrooms, 74–18 percent. However, when asked, fewer respondents said homosexuality was an accepted alternative lifestyle—down to 32 from 34 percent in June 1982. Some 25 percent were avoiding homosexuals because of AIDS, up from 13 percent—and 44 percent were avoiding places where homosexuals "may be present," versus 28 percent in June 1982.

45 Lowe, "Long Uphill Climb."
46 *Phil Donahue Show*, July 1982, an in-depth interview with Michael Hardwick and Kathy Wilde; from the personal collection of Kathy Wilde.
47 Hardwick would tell the *Sentinel* that Donahue had planned to pair him with Jerry Falwell, but he had refused to appear. When Donahue promised the show to him alone, he agreed. "I didn't trust Donahue at first," he told the *Sentinel*. "I thought he was up to something." See Lowe, "Long Uphill Climb."
48 Irons relates this story in *Courage*, but Kathy Wilde has no recollection of it. Kathy Wilde says she never was informed by CNN that Falwell would be a part of the interview.
49 Nat Henthoff, "The Dred Scott Parallel," *Washington Post*, July 11, 1986.
50 Robert Lindsey, "Homosexuals, Upset by Ruling, Plan Drive to Abolish Anti-Sodomy Laws," *New York Times*, July 5, 1986.
51 Ibid.
52 Al Kamen, "Powell Changed Vote in Sodomy Case," *Washington Post*, July 13, 1986.
53 Letter from Laurence Tribe to Kathy Wilde. Laurence Tribe Archives.
54 "Boisterous Gay Protest Greets Supreme Court Justice," *Santa Cruz Sentinel*, July 18, 1986.
55 Herbert Michelson, "Gays Taunt Justice O'Connor," *Sacramento Bee*, July 17, 1986.
56 Ibid.
57 Ibid.
58 Letter from Abby Rubenfeld, "Agenda, July 18–19 meeting," July 17, 1986. National Gay Task Force Archives, Cornell University.
59 "For Life & Love: We're Not Going Back!" *Etcetera*, July 25–31, 1986 (Special Collections and Archives, Georgia State University Library).

At Liberty

1. David Lowe, "Michael Hardwick's Long Uphill Climb," *San Francisco Sentinel*, August 15, 1986.
2. Art Harris, "The Unintended Battle of Michael Hardwick," *Washington Post*, August 21, 1986.
3. Harris, "Unintended Battle."
4. Peter Irons, *The Courage of Their Convictions* (Free Press, 1988), 402.
5. Harris, "Unintended Battle."
6. Irons, *Courage*, 402.
7. Harris, "Unintended Battle."
8. Lowe, "Long Uphill Climb," 4.
9. Richard Laermer, "Michael Hardwick," *Advocate*, September 2, 1986, 110.
10. Marilyn Goldstein, "Michael Hardwick Went Public with His Private Life," *Newsday*, August 4, 1986.
11. Torick told the paper he "never had a complaint from a gay."
12. When contacted, the management of the bar—one of whom had owned the bar since its inception—said the bar did not have security during that time.
13. Harris, "Unintended Battle."
14. Ruth Marcus, "Powell Sees No Major Court Shift," *Washington Post*, August 13, 1986.
15. Renee D. Turner, "Man Continuing Bid to Challenge State Sodomy Law," *Atlanta Constitution*, September 8, 1986.
16. Letter from Laurence Tribe to Kathy Wilde, September 24, 1986. Laurence Tribe Archives.
17. "VIOLENCE AGAINST GAYS," #306983, *CBS Evening News for Tuesday, October 21, 1986* (Vanderbilt TV News Archive).
18. *Pride and Progress*, Episode No. 1 [2], "The Right Stuff," December 31, 1986 (Gay Cable Network Archives; MSS 231; 231.0719; Fales Library and Special Collections, New York University Libraries).
19. Evan Wolfson interview.
20. Thomas Paine, *Rights of Man* Part Two (1792).
21. *Pride and Progress*, Episode No. 42 [2], "The Right Stuff," October 13, 1986 (Gay Cable Network Archives; MSS 231; 231.0707; Fales Library and Special Collections, New York University Libraries).
22. Michel Martin and Emma Bowman, "In Newly Found Audio, A Forgotten Civil Rights Leader Says Coming Out 'Was an Absolute Necessity,'" NPR, January 6, 2019.
23. Ibid.

24 Henry Louis Gates, "Who Designed the March on Washington?" *The Root*, https://www.pbs.org/wnet/african-americans-many-rivers-to-cross/history/100-amazing-facts/who-designed-the-march-on-washington.

25 Ibid.

26 "Gays Protest Court's Sodomy Ruling," *San Francisco Chronicle*, October 9, 1986.

27 George Mendenhall, "Scalia Nixed Gay Privacy Rights; Reagan Court Nominee Doesn't Believe in Constitutional Right to Privacy," *Bay Area Reporter*, June 26, 1986.

28 Letter from Abby Rubenfeld, October 7, 1986. Laurence Tribe Archives.

29 Evan Wolfson interview.

30 Ibid.

31 Charles Seabrook, "Hotel Lobby Offers Variety of Opinions About AIDS," *Atlanta Constitution*, February 25, 1987.

32 Petrelis said the TV exposure from this moment led to the conversation with Larry Kramer that led to the formation of ACT UP. See Michael Petrelis, "Let's Talk HIV: 'United in Anger'—The ACT UP Doc," *Edge Media Network*, December 17, 2011.

33 Philip M. Boffey, "Homosexuals Applaud Rejection of Mandatory Tests for AIDS," *New York Times*, February 26, 1987.

34 Tom Austin, "Club Nu," *Miami New Times*, July 18, 1990.

35 Club Nu closed in July of 1990.

36 Danny Garcia interview.

37 Letter from Mary Grace Neville to Michael Hardwick, Hardwick archive, Robert Hardwick Weston.

38 Bill Moyers, *For the People*, June 11, 1987, transcript available at https://billmoyers.com/content/for-the-people.

39 Thurgood Marshall, "The Constitution's Bicentennial: Commemorating the Wrong Document?" *Vanderbilt Law Review* 1337 (1987): 40.

40 Ibid.

41 Ibid.

42 Fred Bruning, "For Blacks, a Bittersweet Bicentennial," *Newsday*, May 31, 1987.

43 Irons, *Courage*, 402.

44 Ibid.

45 Lien filed against Michael Hardwick, Miami–Dade court records.

46 "SUPREME COURT / POWELL REPLACEMENT," #556932, *NBC Evening News for Sunday, June 28, 1987* (Vanderbilt TV News Archive).

47 *Dronenburg* was denied rehearing by a panel of judges including Ruth Bader Ginsburg, who wrote that she denied it because the *Doe v. Commonwealth* 1976 Supreme Court case was controlling in the matter.
48 Gerald M. Boyd, "Bork Picked for High Court," *New York Times*, July 2, 1987.
49 Ibid.
50 "A Supreme Act of Civil Disobedience," *Etcetera*, vol. 3, no. 36 (Special Collections, Georgia State Library and Archives).
51 Laurence Tribe interview.
52 Christina Pazzanese, "As He Prepares to Retire, Laurence Tribe Retraces His Path from Teen Immigrant Math Whiz to Leading Constitutional Law Scholar and Admired Professor," *Harvard Gazette*, June 24, 2020.
53 "Bork Nomination Day 7, Part 1," C-SPAN, October 17, 1987.
54 Linda Greenhouse, "Washington Talk: The Bork Hearings; For Biden: Epoch of Belief, Epoch of Incredulity," *New York Times*, October 8, 1987.

March

1 *Pride and Progress*, Episode No. 43 [2], "The Right Stuff," October 21, 1987 (Gay Cable Network Archives; MSS 231; 231.0761; Fales Library and Special Collections, New York University Libraries).
2 Joan E. Biren, *For Love and for Life: The 1987 March on Washington*, 1990 (Joan E. Biren Queer Film Museum Collection, Archives Center, National Museum of American History).
3 Ibid.
4 *Pride and Progress*, Episode No. 43.
5 Biren, *For Love and for Life*.
6 Michael Hardwick is commemorated in two different panels, one bearing his name and another, stitched by attendees at a legal conference in 1996, bears his name and the symbol of the scales of justice.
7 Biren, *For Love and for Life*.
8 "Person of the Week (Cleve Jones)," #105955, *ABC Evening News for Friday, October 16, 1987* (Vanderbilt TV News Archive).
9 Biren, *For Love and for Life*.
10 On January 13, 1988, the Supreme Court held 5–3 that no infringement of the students' First Amendment rights had occurred, since the course was an extension of a learning environment, implicitly subject to editing by teachers and other faculty.
11 Michelle Crone interview.

12 In a memo from Justice Blackmun's archives, Wong described the security concern and directed court officers and employees on special procedures that, it was hoped, would thwart a direct confrontation. Harry A. Blackmun Papers, Library of Congress.
13 Ibid.
14 Biren, *For Love and for Life*.
15 "WASHINGTON, DC/GAY RIGHTS PROTEST," #105883, *ABC Evening News/World News Tonight*, October 13, 1987 (Vanderbilt TV News Archive).
16 His affinity group—part of a fifth wave, gathered at Site F, included T. J. Richard Anthony, San Francisco; Holly Crenshaw and Karen Chance, Atlanta; Mark Randolph Stevens, Indianapolis; Laney Day, Los Angeles; and Michael Quirk, San Francisco. Support included Stebbo Hill and Chris Cash, Atlanta; Phyllis Rowe, Indianapolis; Hillel Gray, D.C.; and Dennis Dullea, Los Angeles. One more name is illegible: "H al al / C. Cattineza," perhaps from San Francisco.
17 Biren, *For Love and for Life*.
18 Conversation with Maria Helena Dolan, 2022.

Bliss

1 Craig Pittman, "Miami Vice: How an Icon of 80s Cool Transformed a City and the Landscape of Television," *CrimeReads* (blog), July 17, 2019.
2 Natalie O'Neill, "Gays Leave Unfriendly South Beach for Fort Lauderdale," *Miami New Times*, January 14, 2010.
3 Ibid.
4 Peter Irons, via email.
5 Lori Tanner interview.
6 Ibid.
7 Caprice Herrold interview.
8 Lori Tanner interview.
9 Ibid.
10 Joan E. Biren, *For Love and for Life: The 1987 March on Washington*, 1990 (Joan E. Biren Queer Film Museum Collection, Archives Center, National Museum of American History).
11 Adam Liptak, "Surprising Friend of Gay Rights in a High Place," *New York Times*, September 2, 2013.
12 Testimony from Laurence Tribe, *Hearings Before the Committee on the Judiciary, United States Senate, One Hundredth Congress, First Session on the Nomi-*

nation of Anthony M. Kennedy to Be Associate Justice of the Supreme Court of the United States, 90-878 (U.S. Government Printing Office, 1989).

13 "The War Conference," *Houston LGBT History* (blog), https://www.houstonlgbthistory.org/warconference.html.

14 Ibid.

15 Ibid.

16 Heather Dewar, "Stars-Studded Fundraisers Put on Ritz to Fight AIDS," *Miami News*, March 14, 1988.

17 Michael Lasandra, "Star-Studded AIDS Benefit Loses Financial Luster," *Miami News*, March 9, 1988.

18 Jane Woolridge, "It's Difficult to Raise Money for AIDS," *Miami Herald*, March 10, 1988.

19 Ibid.

20 Ibid.

21 "Gay Rights Activists Protest at Supreme Court," UPI, June 30, 1988, https://www.upi.com/Archives/1988/06/30/Gay-rights-activists-protest-at-Supreme-Court/2116583646400.

22 "Two Supreme Court Protesters Singled Out," *Southern Voice*, July 21, 1988.

23 Hal Straus, "Convention to Be Rich, Varied Stage," *Atlanta Constitution*, July 17, 1988.

24 Ibid.

25 Bill Montgomery, "Protestors of Practically All Persuasions to Sound Off at Democratic Convention," *Atlanta Journal-Constitution*, July 10, 1988.

26 "Klan and Skinheads Meet with Wall of Anger, Not Allowed to March," *Southern Voice*, July 21, 1988.

27 Ibid.

28 Ibid.

29 Robert Byrd, "Police Thwart Gay 'Kiss-In;' Shouting Match Disrupts Anti-Abortion Rally," Associated Press, July 18, 1988, https://apnews.com/article/e48c8e73b824baf470cfca28a083965c.

30 Gerry Yandel and Kathy Trecheck, "From Chants to Kisses, Streets of Downtown a Pageant of Protests," *Atlanta Constitution*, July 19, 1988.

31 Lou Chibbaro Jr., "Convention Protests Focus on Discrimination, Sodomy Laws," *Washington Blade*, July 22, 1988.

32 Jim Galloway, "Young on Tightrope Between Police, Gay Protestors in 'Apology,'" *Atlanta Constitution*, July 21, 1988.

33 "Preliminary Speeches; Platform Speeches," C-SPAN, July 19, 1988.
34 Gann died in 1990, at the age of thirty-six.
35 Jill Young Miller, "The Metamorphosis of Michael," *Sun Sentinel*, September 10, 1989.
36 Cyn Zarco, "Fifth Street Shenanigans," *Miami News*, October 14, 1988.
37 Cyn Zarco, "Restaurateur Gets Surprise Birthday Party," *Miami News*, November 11, 1988.
38 Unattributed clipping from Michael Hardwick archives.
39 "Leonard Horowitz, Industrial Designer, 43," *New York Times*, May 10, 1989.
40 Meher Baba, "The Reincarnating Individual," in DISCOURSES 7th ed (Avatar Meher Baba Perpetual Public Charitable Trust, 1987), 337–338.
41 Tom Zucco, "South Beach to Die For," *Tampa Bay Times*, October 8, 1995.
42 Sandra Schulman, "Squeeze's Seventh: There Is Always an Alternative," *Sun-Sentinel*, February 29, 1996.
43 Ibid.
44 Doug Crosse email.
45 Miller, "Metamorphosis of Michael."
46 Ibid.
47 Ibid.
48 Ibid.
49 Ibid.

Silence

1 Robrt L. Pela, "It Happened One Night," *Advocate*, January 16, 1990.
2 Ibid.
3 Ibid.
4 Ibid.
5 Ibid.
6 "Ann Northrop," ACT UP Oral History Project, https://actuporalhistory.org/numerical-interviews/027-ann-northrop.
7 Joshua Barone, "Yo-Yo Ma Is Finding His Way Back to Nature Through Music," *New York Times*, December 15, 2022.
8 *Nouveau* magazine, from the Michael Hardwick archive, publication date unknown, 22.
9 Darren J. Hughes, "Blending with an Other: An Analysis of Trance Channeling in the United States," *Ethos* 19, no. 2 (June 1991): 161–184.

Notes to pages 265–274

10 Michael Reece, "Domestic Santa Fe," *Nouveau*, undated (assumed to be 1988–1989), 23
11 Jill Young Miller, "The Metamorphosis of Michael," *Sun Sentinel*, September 10, 1989
12 Ibid.
13 Elyse J. Singer and April D. Thames, "Neurobehavioral Manifestations of HIV/AIDS: Diagnosis and Treatment," *Neurologic Clinics* 34, no. 1 (February 2016): 33–53.
14 Janny Scott and Lynn Simross, "AIDS: The Therapies : From Acupuncture to Licorice to Visualization," *Los Angeles Times*, August 16, 1987.
15 Hughes, "Blending with an Other."
16 "'Gay America Loves You,' Billboard, Looking South Down the Downtown Connector, Atlanta, Georgia, June 20, 1990," Digital Library of Georgia, https://dlg.usg.edu/record/gsu_ajc_4755?canvas=0&x=955&y=1402&w=3448.
17 Radicalarchives, "Neighbors Network: 'Hatred in Georgia' and Other Publications (1989–1994)," January 16, 2013, https://radicalarchives.org/2013/01/16/neighbors-network-publications.
18 Pat Pheifer, "Activist Keith Gann Dies of AIDS at 36," *Minneapolis Star Tribune*, May 10, 1990.
19 "GAY PRIDE," #575824, *NBC Evening News for Sunday, June 24, 1990* (Vanderbilt TV News Archives).
20 "The Queer Nation Manifesto," *History Is a Weapon* (blog), https://www.historyisaweapon.com/defcon1/queernation.html.
21 "PERSON OF THE WEEK (RANDY SHILTS)," #129294, *ABC Evening News for Friday, June 22, 1990* (Vanderbilt TV News Archive).
22 Al Kamen, "Liberal Justice Brennan Quits Supreme Court, Giving Bush Chance to Buttress Conservatives," *Washington Post*, July 21, 1990.
23 Maer Roshan, "Ex-High Court Justice Flip-Flops on Sodomy Case," *Outweek*, November 14, 1990, 16.
24 Ruth Marcus, "Powell Regrets Backing Sodomy Law," *Washington Post*. October 26, 1990.
25 Ibid.
26 Letter from Sue Hyde to Lewis F. Powell. National Gay Task Force Archives, folder 100-65, Cornell University.
27 Ibid.
28 Ibid.
29 Tracie Cone, "Landmark by Design," *Miami Herald*, December 17, 1990.

Landslide

1 Interview with Jack Kearney.

Epilogue

1 *Lawrence v. Texas*, 539 U.S. 558 (2003).
2 Daniel Richman interview.
3 K. K. Ottensen, "Current Supreme Court Is Damaging to the Country, Law Scholar Warns," *Washington Post Magazine*, August 16, 2022.
4 Texas Attorney General Ken Paxton said in 2022 that should the Supreme Court vitiate the privacy ruling in 2003's *Lawrence v. Texas*, he would be "willing and able" to prosecute Texans for sodomy. See Trudy Ring, "Texas AG Ken Paxton 'Willing and Able' to Defend Sodomy Law," *Advocate*, June 30, 2022.

Acknowledgments

1 Art Harris, "The Unintended Battle of Michael Hardwick," *Washington Post*, August 21, 1986.
2 Patrick Saunders, "The Reboot of Mike Bowers," *Georgia Voice*, March 4, 2015.
3 Evan Wolfson, "Gods & Monsters: *Bowers v. Hardwick*," *Advocate*, November 12, 2002, 94.
4 Interview with Michael Hobbs by email.
5 Kevin Sack, "Georgia Candidate for Governor Admits Adultery and Resigns Commission in Guard," *New York Times*, June 6, 1997.
6 Saunders, "Reboot." Bowers's support for same-sex marriage would become the law of the land on June 30, 2015, when the Supreme Court decided in its favor in *Obergefell*.
7 Saunders, "Reboot."
8 Art Harris, "'A Good Cop, but Badge-Heavy,'" *San Francisco Chronicle*, September 7, 1986.

Index

A&B Bonding, 69
ABC (ABC News), 100, 173, 214, 270
abortion, xiii, 34, 93, 153
ACLU. *See* American Civil Liberties Union
ACLU of Georgia, 76, 86, 123, 124, 141
ACLU of Louisiana, 123
acquired immunodeficiency syndrome. *See* HIV/AIDS
ACT UP, 217, 238, 253–57, 259–61, 268
Ad Hoc Task Force to Challenge Sodomy Laws, 120, 123, 124, 127, 138, 188
Advocate, xv, 191, 251, 261–62
AID Atlanta (group), 89
AIDS (AIDS epidemic). *See* HIV/AIDS
AIDS Awareness Day, 88
AIDS Quilt, 212–14, 217, 237
Alamillo, Joseph Melville ("Joe," stepfather), 15
Albany, Ga., 105
Allen, Ivan, 52
Allen, Peter, 234
All Souls Church (Washington, D.C.), 208
American Bar Association (ABA), 194, 231
American Civil Liberties Union (ACLU), 51, 71–74, 76, 77, 86, 123, 124, 141, 150, 161–62, 185, 202; *See also* Tribe, Laurence; Wilde, Kathleen "Kathy"
American Constitutional Law (Tribe), 122
American Medical Association, 106

American Psychological Association (APA), 127–28, 157–58
American Public Health Association, 127
anal sex, 33, 37, 81–83, 111, 148, 183, 255
Angelo (DJ at Backstreet), 49
antifungals, 241
antivirals, 241
Arizona Supreme Court, 116
Arkansas, 41
Arlington National Cemetery, 214
Arrington, Marvin, 88
Art Deco style architecture, 226, 252
Asner, Ed, 234
Asphalt Jungle, The (film), 32
Atlanta Business and Professional Guild, 194–95
Atlanta City Council, 58, 72, 88
Atlanta Constitution, 51
Atlanta–Fulton County Stadium, xix
Atlanta Gay Center, 51, 101
Atlanta Journal-Constitution, 91, 95, 195
Atlanta Municipal Court, 62, 63, 71, 74
Atlanta nightlife codes, xvii, xxiii–xxiv
Atlanta Police Department, 51, 58, 61, 94, 141, 193, 237–38; *See also* Torick, Keith R.
Ault, Steve, 231
Aunt Fanny's Cabin (Atlanta restaurant), 235
Austin Cary Forest, 27
azidothymidine (AZT), 160, 173, 196, 241, 267

331

Baba, Meher, 22–25, 41, 230, 241–42, 264, 265, 277
Backstreet (Atlanta nightclub), 45, 49–51, 54–56, 62, 96
Bacuranao, Cuba, 4
Bahamas, 5
Baker, Donald, 79, 123
Baker v. Carr, 34
Baker v. Wade, 79, 90, 118, 123–25, 178, 207
Barbara Gervais Street (Atlanta), 51
barbiturates, 16
Barker, Arthur Robert, 16–21
Barker, Shelly, 16–18, 20
Barrett, Richard, 236
Bass, Jim, 50
Batson, Buren, 76, 141–43, 149–50
Battery Park (New York City), 180–81
Beatles, the, 22
Bells Are Ringing (film), 44
Bentsen, Lloyd, 239
Bethesda, Md., 110
Biden, Joseph R., and administration, 207–9, 288
Billboard Project, 267
Bill of Rights, 85, 205
Birmingham, Ala., 66
birth control, 33–34, 71, 85, 134, 285
Black, Hugo, 117, 164
Black civil rights, 52, 65–66, 85, 105, 112–13, 117, 154, 197, 257–58
Blackmun, Harry, 107, 113–15, 119, 125, 130, 140, 142, 148, 153–56, 159, 160, 164–67, 185, 204, 272
Blackstone, William, *Commentaries of the Laws of England*, 82–83
Blalock, Harvey, 5, 6
Blanche (co-employee), 39, 264
Blondell, Joan, 30
blood transfusions, 186
Board of Education of Oklahoma City v. National Gay Task Force, 107, 124, 125
Boat House (Fort Lauderdale restaurant), 242
Bolton, Arthur, 77
Bork, Robert, 207–9, 231, 271, 284, 286
Boston, Mass., 49
Boutilier, Clive, 106
Bowers, Michael, 77–78, 94, 112, 117, 126, 173
Bowers v. Hardwick, 271–73
  and ACLU, 124–25
  and Ad Hoc Task Force to Challenge Sodomy Laws, 120, 123, 124
  amicus briefs in, 127–28
  anti-queer backlash following, 195, 272–73
  decision, xi, 162–67, 171–72
  denial of rehearing, 195
  and *Dronenburg v. Zech*, 117
  and equal protection, 198–99
  and gay-rights movement, 186–89, 199–200, 218, 230, 234, 269
  grant of certiorari, 118–20, 123
  and "Homo 101" briefs, 126, 155
  and *Lawrence v. Texas*, xiii
  memos circulated during, 129–35, 283
  oral arguments, 129
  overturning of, 281
  Lewis Powell as deciding vote in, 125–26, 207
  Powell's regret about, 270–71
  privacy issues, 125, 129, 197, 231, 288
  proceedings, 137–51
  reactions to decision, 172–81
  state's argument in, 126–27
"Boys of Summer, The" (song), 102
Bradley, Dan, 206
Brandeis, Louis, 84, 164
Brennan, William, 114, 119–20, 125, 125, 130, 140, 143–44, 156, 164, 271
Briggs, John, 180
Browning, Jasmine (daughter of sister Susan), 28–29, 40, 44, 50, 245–46, 275, 280
Browning-Chriss, Simone (daughter of sister Susan), 263–64, 275, 276
Browning-Chriss, Susan Hardwick (sister), 3–9, 24, 25, 27–29, 40, 43, 44, 245, 246, 263–64, 274–77, 280–81
Brown v. Board of Education, 112, 114, 116, 117, 137, 283
Bryan, William Jennings, 232
Bryant, Anita, 34–35, 37–39, 59, 216, 253
Buchanan, Rick, 178
Buchmeyer, Jerry, 79
Buckley, William F., Jr., 160–61
Bulldogs (Atlanta nightclub), 54–55, 194
Burey, Vivian, 114
Burger, Warren, 114, 115, 118, 120, 125, 139, 144, 145, 149, 154, 156–59, 163, 177, 179, 180, 194, 198, 200, 283

Index

Bush, George H. W., 239, 271

Cades Cove, Tenn., 41, 43
California, 161, 180, 197
"Call to Action, A," 231–32
Camus, Albert, 266
  The Plague, 265
Canada, 106
Capitman, Barbara, 241
Capitol Building, 213
Capitol Police, 217
Carey v. Population Services, 93, 111, 141
Carlson, Steven, 180
Carney, Art, 16
Cars, the, 36
Carswell, G. Harrold, 113
Carter, Jimmy, and administration, 52, 86, 206
Car Wash bar, xviii, xxii
Castaneda, Carlos, 265–66, 277
  The Teachings of Don Juan: A Yaqui Way of Knowledge, 41–42
Castro district (San Francisco), 33
CBS (CBS Evening News), 34, 195
Center City neighborhood (Philadelphia), 202
Centers for Disease Control (CDC), 53–54, 53–54, 101, 110, 200, 254, 259–61
Central Intelligence Agency (CIA), 116
Central Park (New York City), 179
Chabner, Bruce A., 53
Chance, Karen, 220–21
Charlie's Bunion, 43–44
Chattahoochee River, 64, 102
Chavez, Cesar, 215
Cheek, Bob, 63
Cherokee people, 43
Chicago, Ill., 115
China, 121
Chinnis, C. Cabell, 155–57
Christianity, 41
Chrysler, xx
Cincinnati, Ohio, 72, 178
City University of New York, 206
civil rights movement, 105, 197, 235; *See also* Black civil rights; gay rights (gay-rights movement)
Clark, Dorothy, 113
Clay, Dana, 234

Clingman's Dome, 41
Clinton, Bill, and administration, 235, 284
Club Baths (Atlanta), 62
Club Baths (Miami), 39, 110
Club Cheers (Miami), 227–30, 240
Club Exile (Atlanta), 58
Club Nu (Miami), 201–2, 227, 244, 277
CNN, 173–74, 237
Coca-Cola, 187
cocaine, 12, 15, 16, 36, 100, 109, 131, 228
Coconut Grove, Fla., 12, 30, 35–37, 39, 199, 232
Commentaries of the Laws of England (Blackstone), 82–83
Committee on Drug Abuse, 18
Communist Party, 197
Compound S, 160
Comstock Act (1873), 71
Congressional Cemetery, 211–12
Connecticut, 84
conservatives (conservative movement), 38–39, 86, 92, 107, 114, 116, 118, 160–61, 174–75, 206, 215–16, 231, 236, 240, 287–88
constitutional rights. *See* U.S. Constitution; *individual rights, e.g.*: privacy, right to
Contemplation of Justice (statue), 219
contraception, 33–34, 71, 85, 134, 285
Coots, Jerry G., 63
Coral Gables, Fla., 30, 109, 242
Cove (Atlanta nightclub), xvii–xxiii, 49, 55–57, 61, 64, 66, 68–70, 75, 96, 102
Cowley, Patrick, xxi
Cowley, Sylvester, xxi
Cox, Archibald, 208
Crawley, Paul, 81–82
Crazy Ray'z (Atlanta bar), 88
Chriss, Mike, 40, 43, 245–46, 274–76
Chriss, Susan (sister). *See* Browning-Chriss, Susan Hardwick (sister)
Crone, Michelle, 216
Crown & Anchor bar (Provincetown, Mass.), 49
cruel and unusual punishment, 150, 156
Cruise, xvii, 89
Cuba, 4, 5
Cuban Missile Crisis, 7
Cubans (Cuban Americans), 109, 226
Curran, James W., 110

Index

Dade County, Fla., 10, 20, 34, 35, 38, 206
Dade County Sheriff's Department of Morals, 12
"Dadeland Massacre," 109
D'Alema, Guy, 59
Dallas, Tex., 178
Dallas Gay Alliance, 79
Daughters of Bilitis, 32
David (childhood friend), 12
Davis, Anne, 78
Davis, Robert, 56, 57
Davis, Sammy, Jr., 18, 19
D.C. Metropolitan Police, 217–18
Dear, Noach, 186
de Bolt, George, 268
deconstruction, 285, 286
Deering, John, 36
DeKalb County Police, 259
Delaplaine, Andrew, 240
DeLaria, Lea, 257
Dellinger, Walter, 209
Democratic National Convention (Atlanta, 1988), 235–40
desegregation, xii, 34, 114
Devo, 50
didanosine (ddI), 241, 267
Dobbs v. Jackson Women's Health Organization, 285, 286
Doe v. Commonwealth's Attorney of Richmond, 34, 38, 72, 83, 87, 94, 105–6, 110, 111, 119, 126, 132
Dolan, Maria Helena, 87–88
Domingo, Placido, 179
Donahue, Phil, 182–86
Donald, Michael, 65–66
Douglas, William O., 115, 141
"Do You Wanna Funk" (song), xxi
drag performers (drag bars), 39, 51, 109
Dred Scott v. Sanford, 112–13, 137, 175
Dronenburg v. Zech, 117–19, 207
drug trade, 36, 109
due process clause, 77, 79, 84, 85, 118, 134, 141, 163, 285
Dukakis, Michael, 235, 238, 239
Duke University, 160, 209
Dunlap, Mary C., 176
Dykers, Woody, 56, 65, 270–71
Dykes on Bikes, 268

Earle, Brent Nicholson, 211
Eaves, Reginald, 53
Edison, Thomas Alva, 4
Eighth Amendment, 156, 158, 164
Eisenhower, Dwight D., and administration, 113, 115
Eisenstadt v. Baird, 33, 85, 112, 131, 148
elections of 2020, 284–85
Ellis Island, 179
English common law, 82–83, 163
equal protection (equal protection clause), 79, 128, 207
Escher, M. C., 229, 244, 247

Falwell, Jerry, 92, 173–74, 184
Fancher, R. D., 259
Federal AIDS Task Force, 110
Federal Bureau of Investigation (FBI), 60, 197, 207
Feminist Majority Foundation, 215
Fierstein, Harvey, 196
Fifth Amendment, 76, 80, 85
First Amendment, 32, 76, 85, 142, 216
Fleetwood Mac, 36, 40, 44, 280
Florida, 13, 137–38, 206–7
Flushing, N.Y., 206
Foley Square (New York City), 180
Fontainebleau Hotel (Miami), 234
Food and Drug Administration (FDA), 101
Forbes, Ann, 25, 264
Fortas, Abe, 113
Fort Lauderdale, Fla., 16, 17, 19, 30–32, 39–40, 242–43
Fort Myers, Fla., 4
Foucault, Michel, 230, 266
  History of Sexuality, 97, 98
Fourteenth Amendment, 76, 77, 79, 80, 85, 112, 141, 158, 163, 285; *See also* due process clause
Fourth Amendment, 80, 85, 160, 165–66
Foutz, John, 54–55
Francis, Connie, 31
Frankie Goes to Hollywood, 101–2
Fraser, James Earle, 137
Frozen, Ira, 237
Fulani, Lenora, 237
Fulton County, Ga., 52, 76

Gabor, Zsa Zsa, 234
Gainesville, Fla., 27, 40–41, 246, 263–64, 274
Gainesville Sun, 280

Gallo, Anthony, 96
Gallus (Atlanta nightclub), 95–96, 100–102
Gann, Keith, 238–39, 268
Garner, Tyron, 281
Gatien, Peter, 57
Gatlinburg, Tenn., 40–45
Gay Cable Network, 161
"gay cancer," xxi
Gay Men's Chorus, 60
Gay Men's Health Crisis, 179
Gay Pride, 35, 58–61, 87, 91, 253, 258, 267–69
Gay Pride Day, 38, 58, 88
Gay Pride march (Atlanta, 1982), 58
Gay Pride Month, 270
Gay Pride Parade (New York City), 268
Gay Pride Week, 52, 60, 268
gay-related immune deficiency (GRID), 53
gay rights (gay-rights movement)
  and ACLU, 72–73, 120, 123–24, 162
  in Atlanta, 51–53
  civil rights movements compared with, 269
  conservative backlash to, 38–39, 87–88
  and efforts to repeal sodomy laws, 80–81, 88, 198, 235, 253–54
  Michael Hardwick and, xii–xv, 78–79, 88, 89, 91, 126–28, 195–98, 204, 221, 232, 253, 281–84, 288
  and *Hardwick* decision, 178–80, 182, 186–89
  and HIV/AIDS, 200–201, 211–15, 217–19, 230, 232–35, 237–39, 253, 259–60
  and March on Washington, 189, 199–201
  in national media, 268, 270
  roots of, 32–35
  and Supreme Court justices, 118, 153, 163–64
  and U.S. Constitution, 107, 198–99
  and "War Conference," 230–32
Gene (childhood friend), 11, 12
Georgetown University, 114
George Washington University Hospital, 116
Georgia Bureau of Investigation, 60
Georgia Constitution, 80
Georgians Opposed to Archaic Laws (GOAL), 90

Georgia sodomy laws; *See also Bowers v. Hardwick*
  ACLU and efforts to repeal, 71–73, 76, 117–18, 161–62
  and AIDS epidemic, 86
  arrest and charging of Michael Hardwick under, xi–xii, 66–70, 76
  gay-rights movement and efforts to repeal, 80–81, 88, 198, 235, 253–54
  Michael Hardwick's view of, 89, 90, 192–93, 197
  penalties under, 156
  previous arrests under, 52, 58–59, 76–77
  U.S. Constitution and, 76, 77, 79–80, 86–87, 106, 111, 130–31, 134, 135, 149, 150, 156
Georgia State Capitol, 60
Georgia State University, xxiv
Ginsburg, Douglas, 231
Gleason, Jackie, 16
Go-Go's, 64
Goldberg, Whoopi, 215
Goldstein, Marilyn, 191–93
Gorin's Homemade Ice Cream, 235
Grace House (Minnesota hospice facility), 268
Grady Hospital (Atlanta), 98–99
Graff, Leonard, 234
"Great March, The," 200
Green, Bob, 34
Greenwich Village, 179
Griswold v. Connecticut, 33, 85, 86, 112, 115, 130, 141, 148, 285, 288
Growth Concept Environmental Design, 39

Hagin, Chris, 238
Haitians, 109
Hall, Robert H., 86, 87, 92
Hallandale Beach, Fla., 39
Hamilton, George, 30
Hardwick, Alice (sister). *See* Herr, Alice Dale Hardwick
Hardwick, Billy Dale "Rick" (father), 3–5, 8–11, 27–28, 45
Hardwick, Kathleen "Kitty" Blalock Alamillo (mother), 3–10, 15, 16, 19, 29, 64–65, 73, 74, 275–77, 281
Hardwick, Mary Lou (stepmother), 27–28

Hardwick, Michael David; *See also Bowers v. Hardwick*
  and ACLU, 71–74, 76, 77
  Advocate interview, 251–53, 261–62
  AIDS diagnosis, 247
  arrest of, at March on Washington protest, 219–21
  arrest of, for sodomy, xi–xii, 66–69
  arrest of, for speeding, 16
  as artist, 201–2, 225–29, 240–41, 243–44, 246, 248–49, 249, 251–53, 263, 267–68, 273
  as Backstreet bartender, 45, 49, 50, 54–56
  at Club Cheers, 227–29, 240
  and coworker Blanche, 39
  at CUNY ceremony, 206
  and dog Jumbo, 201, 277
  Phil Donahue interview, 183–85
  drug use, 12, 15, 16
  and Woody Dykers, 270–71
  and emergence of AIDS epidemic, 98–99
  family background and childhood, 3–12
  final decline and death, 275–77
  final interview, 273–74
  firing of, from Peachtree Plaza Hotel, 90–91
  first court date, 70, 71
  first signs of illness, 230, 247
  funeral service, 280–81
  as Gallus bartender, 95–96, 100
  in Gatlinburg, 40–45
  gay-bashing assaults on, 57–58, 64–65
  and gay rights movement, xii–xv, 78–79, 88, 89, 91, 126–28, 195–98, 204, 232, 253, 281–84, 288
  and Georgia sodomy laws, 80–81, 87, 90, 127, 255
  and Michael E. Hobbs, 143
  and Cliff Hovan, 37, 40–41, 43
  and Jack Kearney, 243–44, 247, 249, 274, 274, 275
  and Brad Lamm, 229–30
  love of outdoors, 43–44
  and "Marlboro Man," 44–45
  and Miami, 109
  move to Atlanta, 45
  Bill Moyers interview, 202–4
  and Ernie Mule, 54–57
  Newsday profile of, 191–93
  Officer Torick on, 193–94
  physical appearance of, 27
  reaction to Supreme Court ruling, 171–72, 174–76, 181–82
  relations with family, 27–29
  and Dwight Sawyer, 65–69, 71, 72, 74, 78, 173, 194
  sexual identity of, 29
  spiritual life, 22, 25, 27, 28, 41–42, 264–67
  at Squeeze, 242–44
  at Supreme Court, 135, 137–39, 146, 147, 149–51, 159, 182
  at "the Seed," 16, 19, 21, 27
  ticketing of, for public drinking, xxii–xxiv, 61–63
  and Laurence Tribe, 146
  and Jorge Vasquez, 37, 192
  view on Georgia sodomy laws, 89, 90, 192–93
  and Kathy Wilde, 81–82, 108–9, 151, 195
  and Evan Wolfson, 138, 147, 150–51, 196, 199
Hardwick, Patrick "Pat" (brother), 3, 5, 7–9, 28, 281
Hardwick, Robert (son of sister Susan). *See* Weston, Robert Hardwick
Hardwick, Susan (sister). *See* Browning-Chriss, Susan Hardwick
Hardwick's Sassy Sodomites (activist group), 218
Haren, Christian, 44–45
Haring, Keith, 267–68
Harlan, John Marshall, II, 85, 86, 116, 122, 129, 134, 147, 147, 164
Harris, Art, 191–94
Harrold, Jan, 228
Hart, Dolores, 30
Harvard Law School, 113, 117, 121–23, 125
Harvard University, 121
Harvey Milk Plaza (San Francisco), 175–76
Hauser, Tim, 232–33
Hay, Colin, 56
Haynsworth, Clement, 113
Hays, Henry, 65–66
Hazelwood School District, et al., v. Cathy Kuhlmeier, et al., 216

Heckler, Margaret, 96
Hehr, Gerald, 8, 24
Helms, Jesse, 231
Henley, Don, 102
Hernandez, Juan Carlos, 109
Herndon, H. Judd, 72, 74, 75, 81, 123
heroin, 15, 16, 18, 29
Herr, Alice Dale Hardwick (sister), xxi, 3, 5–9, 22, 24–25, 28, 29, 229, 243–46, 248–49, 266–67, 273, 275, 277
Higginbotham, A. Leon, Jr., 205–6
Hilton Hotel (San Francisco), 187–88
history (historiography), 282
History of Sexuality (Foucault), 97, 98
HIV/AIDS (HIV/AIDS epidemic)
   American Psychological Association on, 127–28
   and *Bowers v. Hardwick*, 132, 162, 173, 184, 186
   and conservatives, 86, 92, 160–61, 174–75, 231, 236
   emergence of, 53–54
   and gay-rights movement, 200–201, 211–15, 217–19, 230, 232–35, 237–39, 253, 259–60
   and government power, 97–98, 230
   Michael Hardwick on, 192–93, 203
   in national media, 100, 214, 270
   notable victims of, 267–68
   rapid growth of, in mid-1980s, 100–101, 110
   and Reagan administration, 88, 214, 215, 238–39
   scientific advances regarding, 96–97, 160, 195–96
   and sodomy laws, 86, 127–28, 235
   in South Florida, 110, 206, 241
Hobbs, Michael E., 105, 139–43, 149
Holiday, Billie, xxi, 29
Holmes, Oliver Wendell, 165
"Homo 101" briefs, 126, 155
Homosexual, The (documentary), 12
homosexuality
   Florida's criminalization and stigmatization of, 12–15
   growing public awareness of, 37–38
   as pathology, xxi, 157–58
   Lewis Powell's views on, 125, 129, 131, 133–35, 155–57
Hoover, J. Edgar, 197

Horowitz, Leonard, 241
Houston, Tex., 281
Hovan, Bill, 30, 37, 40–41
Hovan, Cliff, 37, 40–41, 43
Howar, Barbara, 34–35
Howard University, 114
HTLV-III virus, 96
Hudson, Rock, 221, 233
Huelsenkamp, Alice (great aunt), 5
Huelsenkamp, Bertha (great aunt), 5
Huelsenkamp, Catherine Zair Filer (great grandmother), 4, 5
Huelsenkamp, Clemens J. "C.J." (great grandfather), 4–5
Huelsenkamp, Kathleen ("Nanny," grandmother), 4–6, 10
Huelsenkamp, William (great uncle), 5
Hughes, Langston, 114
Human Rights Campaign, 196
Humm, Andy, 231
Hunter, Joyce, 231
Hunter, Nan, 123, 202
Hyde, Sue, 257, 272–73, 288–89

Iacocca, Lee, xx
Illinois, 33, 83
"I'm Coming Out" (song), 50
Immaculate Conception Church (Washington, D.C.), 258–59
Immigration and Nationality Act (1952), 106
Inman, Richard, 14–15
In Search of the Constitution (public television series), 202–4
Institut Pasteur, 96
interracial marriage, 85
intimacy, 86, 128, 130, 141, 145–48
Iroquois Onondaga Nation, 206
IRS Building (Washington, D.C.), 212

Jackson, Jesse, 215, 235, 238
Jackson, Robert, 116, 166
Jackson Memorial Hospital (Miami), 206–7
Jacobs, Raymond, 179
Jeanne-Claude and Christo, 225
Jennings, Peter, 214
"Jetson birds" (artwork by Planet Beach), 227
Jim (bartender friend), xxii–xxiii

Jim Crow, 114, 197
Johnson, Frank, 105, 110, 111, 130
Johnson, Holly, 101
Johnson, Howard R., 74
Jolie, France, 50, 56
Jones, Cleve, 195, 212–14, 217
Jones, Grace, 50
Joplin, Janis, 24
judicial activism, xiii
judicial restraint, 132, 207
Jumbo (dog), 201, 241, 243, 245, 263, 274, 277

Kansas City, Mo., 5
Kaposi's sarcoma, 53
Karlan, Pamela, 130
karma, 252, 264
Katz v. United States, 122, 164
Kearney, Jack, 243–45, 247–49, 274, 275
Keith's Cruise Bar (Hallandale Beach, Fla.), 39
Kellogg, Jim, 123
Kennedy, Anthony, 230–31, 281, 284, 284
Kennedy, John F., and administration, 115
Kennedy, John F., Jr., 239
Kentucky, 178
Key West, Fla., 31
Kight, Morris, 237
King, Evelyn "Champagne," 50
King, Martin Luther, Jr., 105, 132, 197
Knowles, James, 65–66
Koch, Ed, 254
Kohorn, Jay, 123–24, 188
Koukoutchos, Brian, 125, 138
Kowalski, Sharon, 212, 220
Kravitch, Phyllis, 105–6, 110, 119
Ku Klux Klan, xx, 65–66, 88, 236, 237

Lambda Legal Defense and Education Fund, 92–94, 120, 123, 127, 128, 138, 162, 177–78, 281
Lamm, Brad, 229–30
Langer, Nancy, 123, 176–81
La Paloma (Miami nightclub), 30
LaRouche, Lyndon, 161
Larry King Live, 173–74
Laurel Falls, Tenn., 41
Lavender Hill Mob, 200–201
LAV virus, 96

Lawrence, John, 281
Lawrence v. Texas, xiii, 281, 284, 285, 288
Lee, Robert E., xx
Lenox Mall (Atlanta), xix
"Lesbian/Gay Male/Transperson Pride Day" (Atlanta), 58, 88
lesbians (lesbian activism), 28, 51, 56, 58, 88, 175, 207, 215, 218–19, 259, 273
Levenson, Louis, 73, 77
Levi, Jeff, 187
Lewis, John, 72, 195
libel laws, 271
Limelight (Atlanta nightclub), 57, 59
Lincoln University, 114
Lizard Lounge (Fort Lauderdale bar), 248
Lolita (Nabokov), 32
Longstaff, Richard, 106
Los Angeles, Calif., 33
Louisiana, 123
Loving v. Virginia, 85, 147
Lowe, Michael, 238
Lucas, George, 42
Lyons, Oren, 206

Ma, Yo-Yo, 264, 280
Mahesh, Maharishi, 22, 25
Malley v. Briggs, 154
Manhattan Transfer, 232–33
Mapplethorpe, Robert, 267
Marbury v. Madison, 137
March On (Los Angeles activist group), 237
March on Washington (1979), 60, 188, 189
March on Washington (1987). *See* National March on Washington
March on Washington Committee, 208
March on Washington for Jobs and Freedom (1963), 132, 197
Maricopa County, Ariz., 116
marijuana (marijuana laws), 15, 22, 36, 67, 68, 70, 74–76, 108, 154–55, 231
Marilyn Manson and the Spooky Kids, 242
Marlin Beach Hotel (Fort Lauderdale), 30–32, 35, 37, 40
Marshall, John, 137
Marshall, Thurgood, 114, 115, 119, 120, 122, 125, 132–33, 138, 140, 143–44, 156, 164, 167, 204–6, 207, 271, 283
Matlovich, Leonard, 212

Index

Mattachine Society, 14, 32
Maui, Hawaii, 204
Mayo Clinic, 113
McAuliffe, Hinson, 52
McCraw, Russ, 59
McCutchan, Mark, 64
McDonogh, Michael, 234
McGreivy, Susan, 88
medical privacy, 161, 206–7
Meese, Ed, 114
Men at Work, 56
meningitis, 186
Meredith, James, 105
Merhige, Robert, 83
Metropolitan Community Church (Washington, D.C.), 212
Miami, Fla., 5, 7, 12, 13, 29–30, 35, 38, 40, 109, 199; *See also* Coconut Grove, Fla.
Miami Beach, Fla., 13, 15, 16, 30, 109–10, 199, 201–2, 225–30, 240, 246; *See also* South Beach, Fla.
Miami Design Preservation League, 241
Miami Herald, 38, 181–82, 273–74
Miami International Airport, 11
Miami Vice (television show), 226
Michael Hardwick and the Sodomites (group), 219, 220
Milk, Harvey, 188, 211–12
Mimieux, Yvette, 30
Minneapolis, Minn., 195
Minnelli, Vincente, 44
Miranda v. Arizona, 194
Missouri, 118
Mobile, Ala., 65, 66, 69, 72, 74
Monroe Manor complex (Atlanta), 49
Montagnier, Luc, 96
Montgomery, Ala., 59, 105
Moore, Chris, 57
Moore, Tommy, 227, 227
Moore v. City of East Cleveland, 134, 141, 147
Moral Majority Report, 92
Morgan, Tracy, 259–60
morphine, 16
Morris, Winston, 58
Morrison, Helane, 119
Mosman, Michael, 131–33, 155–56
Moyers, Bill, 202–4, 206
MTV, 101, 192
Mule, Ernie, 54–57
Murphy, Frank, 138
Mutiny Hotel (Miami), 36, 109

NAACP, 114
Nabokov, Vladimir, *Lolita*, 32
Nalley, Jim, xvii
Napper, George, 51, 236
National Cancer Institute (NCI), 53, 53–54, 160
National Committee for Sexual Civil Liberties, 120
National Farm Workers Association, 215
National Gallery of Art, 215
National Gay and Lesbian Rights Project, 202
National Gay and Lesbian Task Force, 81, 107, 148, 187, 234, 272
National Institute of Mental Health, 20
National Institutes of Health, 110
National Lesbian & Gay Rights Project, 88
National Mall (Washington, D.C.), 197, 211, 212–13
National March on Washington (1987), 189, 199–201, 208, 211–21, 230, 231
National Movement, 236–37
National Museum of American History, 215
National Organization for Women (NOW), 128, 178, 215
Nazi Germany, 200
NBC Nightly News, 268
Nevada, 118
New Age philosophies, 25, 41–42
"New Frontier Octatarian" (artwork by Michael Hardwick), 227
New Hampshire, 273
New Jersey, 114
Newsday, 191–93, 206
Newsweek, 162, 175, 182, 239
New York City, 24, 33, 44, 100–101, 123, 175–81, 186, 188–89, 194, 196, 199, 201, 202, 254, 268, 268–69
New York State, 177
New York Times, 160, 173
New York Times v. Sullivan, 271
New York University Law School, 271–72
Nightline, 270

1984 (Orwell), 97–98
Ninth Amendment, 80, 85
Nixon, Richard, and administration, 15–16, 18, 113, 115–17, 208
Nor, Buddy, 177
Norman, Pat, 175
North Carolina, 43
Northrop, Ann, 254
Northwestern Law School, 115
nuclear weapons, 216

Obergefell v. Hodges, 284, 285, 288
obscenity, 32–33, 71
O'Connor, John, 254
O'Connor, Sandra Day, 107, 116, 117, 125, 146, 156, 187–88, 283
Official Code of Georgia, 80
Ohio, 178
O'Keefe, Georgia, 247
Oklahoma, 107
Olmstead v. United States, 84
Olympic Games (Atlanta, 1996), 235
Omni Coliseum (Atlanta), 236, 238
One Inc. v. Oleson, 32–33
Operation Sail 1986, 179
oral sex, 37–38, 67, 75, 82, 127, 183–85, 194
originalism, 114, 287, 289
Orwell, George, 114
    1984, 97–98
Oscar Wilde Bookshop (New York City), 173

Pacino, Al, 109
Padula, Margaret, 207
Padula v. Webster, 207
Paine, Thomas, *Rights of Man*, 196
painkillers, 16
Palladium (New York City), 201
Panama City, Fla., 37
Panesso, Jimenez, 109
Paris, France, 31, 96, 98, 212
Parkman, Steve, 202
Parks, Rosa, 105, 239
Parrish, Maxfield, 247
Pasteur Institute, 110
Patty (childhood friend), 12
Payton v. New York, 130
PBS, 202–4
Peaches Back Door (Atlanta nightclub), 49

Peachtree Manor Hotel (Atlanta), 58
Peachtree Plaza Hotel (Atlanta), 61, 90–91
Peacock Inn (Miami), 36
Pegasus (Gatlinburg health-food store), 42, 44
Pela, Robrt, xv, 251–53, 262, 263
Pelosi, Nancy, 214–15
People magazine, 34
Perez, Jorge Alberto, 246, 279–80
Perlman, Itzhak, 179
Perry, Troy, 212
Pershing missiles, 216
Petrelis, Michael, 254
Philadelphia, Penn., 200, 202
Piedmont Park (Atlanta), xvii, 58, 88, 102, 268
Pin-a-Pola, 4–5
pink triangle symbol, 173, 200, 211, 214
Pitcock, Charles and Mary Alice, 5
Plague, The (Camus), 265
Planet Beach, 227
Plessy, Homer, xii
Plessy v. Ferguson, xii, 113, 116, 137, 283
pneumocystis carinii, 53
pneumonia, 186
Poe v. Ullman, 84–85, 86, 134, 146–47
Ponce de Leon Place (Atlanta), x–xi, xxiv, 56, 62, 66, 68, 78
Postmortem (magazine), 242
Potter, Joey, 65, 66, 69, 78
Powell, Lewis F.
    appointment of, 117
    background of, 116–17
    and *Baker v. Texas*, 123
    and *Board of Education of Oklahoma City v. National Gay Task Force* decision, 107
    concurring opinion of, 163–64
    on direction of the Court, 194
    equivocation of, in *Bowers* case, 187
    and granting of certiorari to *Bowers v. Hardwick*, 119
    and Michael Hobbs, 140, 141
    as key vote in *Bowers v. Hardwick*, 125–26, 155–59, 187, 207
    and *Lawrence v. Texas*, 281
    regret later expressed by, 271–72, 274
    resignation of, 207
    and Laurence Tribe, 145–47, 150
    views on homosexuality, 125, 129, 131, 133–35, 155–57

Index

Power of Silence, The (Castaneda), 265
Prentiss, Paula, 30
Presley, Elvis, 32
Pride Week. *See* Gay Pride Week
Princeton University, 127
privacy, right to, xiii–xiv, 33–34, 76, 77, 79, 80, 83–86, 93, 96–98, 111, 114, 115, 125, 126, 130–32, 154, 165–66, 183, 206–7, 209
Privacy Project (National Gay and Lesbian Task Force), 272
pro-life movement, 255–56
Proposition 6 (California), 180
"Protect America's Children" campaign, 38
Provincetown, Mass., 31, 49
Public Health Trust of Dade County, 206
public school teachers, 107
Punch Bowl (Boston bar), 49
Puss, Miss, 56, 57, 65, 78, 98–99

Queer and Present Danger, 218
Queer Nation, 268–69

Rainbow Falls (Tennessee), 43
Ramblin' Raft Race (Atlanta), 64
Raphael, Sally Jesse, 182
Rauschenberg, Robert, 232
Reagan, Ronald, and administration, xx, 88, 98, 107–8, 179, 180, 214, 215, 231, 238, 262
Rechy, John, 175
Rehnquist, William, 116, 118–20, 125, 146, 147, 156, 196, 281, 283–84
"Relax" (song), 101–2
reproductive privacy, 33–34
reproductive rights, 285
Richard B. Russell Building (Atlanta), 178
Richards, Ann, 235
Richman, Daniel, 132–33, 283
Richmond, Va., 117
Richter, Roz, 173
Riggins, John, 188
Rights of Man (Paine), 196
right to privacy, xii
Rivera, Geraldo, 182
Robinson v. California, 154
Roe v. Wade, xiii, 33–34, 85–86, 112, 113, 116, 118, 130, 148, 153, 156, 164, 183, 207, 285

Romulus, N.Y., 216
Roosevelt, Franklin, and administration, 117
Ross, Diana, 50
Roswell, Ga., 94, 194
Rubenfeld, Abby, 120, 123, 127, 128, 138, 150–51, 172, 188–89, 194–95, 198–99
Rumours (Fleetwood Mac), 40
Russell, Lloyd "Papa," xviii, xxi, xxiv, 55, 69, 70
Rustin, Bayard, 132, 196–98
Rutledge, Wiley, 115

Safe Sex Sluts, 218
St. Patrick's Cathedral (New York City), 254, 261
St. Paul, Minn., 38, 113, 238
Salvation Army, 233
"sanctity of the home," 131, 134, 165–66
San Francisco, Calif., 33, 100–101, 121, 134, 175–76, 187–88, 194, 195, 213, 268
San Francisco Sentinel, 191
Santa Fe Community College, 27
Saturday Night Massacre, 208
"Save Our Children" movement, 34
Sawyer, Dwight, 65–69, 71, 72, 74, 76, 78, 81, 94, 173, 194
Scalia, Antonin, 198, 281
Scarface (film), 109
Schechner, William, 268
Scott, Dred, xii, 126
"Seed, the," 16–21, 27
Seeger, Peter, 72
Selma, Ala., 195
Senate, 209, 231
Senate Judiciary Committee, 207, 209
Seneca Women's Peace encampment, 216
"separate but equal," xii
sex education, 13, 254
"Sexual Privacy and the Constitution" (panel discussion), 202
sex workers, 76–77, 91
Shapiro v. Thompson, 271
Shaw, E. Clay, Jr., 31–32
Sheppard, Ben, 20
Sheridan Square (New York City), 176–77, 179
Shilts, Randy, 270
Siegel, Aron, xx

Silencing the Internal Dialogue (artwork by Michael Hardwick), 240, 241
"Situation" (song), xxi
60 Minutes, 34
Slaton, Lewis, 76–77, 86–87
slavery, 206
Slusser, Kirk, 62–63, 65–68, 74, 75, 78, 173
Smeal, Eleanor, 178
Smith, Allison Sue, 176–77
Smith, Kevin, 237
Smith, Paul, 281
Smithsonian National Museum of Natural History, 215
Smoke Rise Mountain Community (Gatlinburg, Tenn.), 40–41
sodomy (term)
  historical definitions of, 37, 38
  mentioning/discussion of, in the media, 81–82, 183, 203
sodomy laws; *See also Doe v. Commonwealth's Attorney of Richmond*; Georgia sodomy laws
  and AIDS epidemic, 86, 127–28, 235
  American Psychological Association on, 127–28
  efforts to repeal, 33–34, 39, 80–81, 88, 178, 186–87, 187–88, 253–54, 256, 258; *See also* Ad Hoc Task Force to Challenge Sodomy Laws
  history of, xiii, 79, 82–86, 119, 154, 163, 178
Soft Cell, xxi
Sojourner, Sabrina, 257–58
Sorensen, John, 12, 13
Souter, David, 271
South Beach, Fla., 109, 240–41, 245, 270–71, 274
South Dakota, 41
Southern Baptists, 82
Southern Voice, 237
Southwest Miami Senior High School, 8
Soviet Union, xx
Spanish-American War, 4
Spiritualist movement, 266
Spiro, Ellen, 254
Sports Page bar (Atlanta), 64
Springfield, Dusty, 101
Squeeze (Fort Lauderdale nightclub), 242–45, 247–49, 252, 273, 275, 277
Stanford Law School, 116
Stanford University, 231
Stanley v. Georgia, 83, 114, 115, 130, 142, 145, 148, 156, 164
Stark, Kim, 240–42
Starr, Kenneth, 271
Star Wars (film series), 42
Statue of Liberty, xx, 179–81, 218
statute of limitations, 181, 191
Stein, Gertrude, 212
Stevens, John Paul, 115, 125, 125, 140–43, 153, 156, 159, 164
Stevenson, Don, 98–99
Stewart, Potter, 121–22
Stoddard, Tom, 162, 177–78
Stone Mountain, Ga., xix–xx
Stoner, J. B., 236
Stonewall riots, 33
"Stonewall Then, Atlanta Now," 59–60
Strasburg, Va., 41
Streisand, Barbra, 101
substantive due process, 84, 285
Sullivan, Kathleen, 123–25, 129
Sumrall, Clint, 71, 90
SUNY-Buffalo, 206
Superior Court of Fulton County, 76
Supreme Court; *See also individual cases, e.g.: Bowers v. Hardwick; individual justices, e.g.: Powell, Lewis F.*
  civil rights cases, xii, xiii
  obscenity cases, 32–33
  prior queer-related rulings, 106–7
  rightward turn of, 107, 286
  term limits proposed for, 286–88
Supreme Court Building, 112, 208, 216, 218
Supreme Court Plaza (Washington, D.C.), 198
Sweet, John, 72–74, 76, 77, 79
Sweet Gum Head (Atlanta drag bar), 51, 56
"Sweetness of Peace, The" (song), 280
Sydney, Australia, 31

"Tainted Love" (song), xxi
Tanner, Lori, 228
Taylor, Elizabeth, 232, 233
Teachings of Don Juan, The: A Yaqui Way of Knowledge (Castaneda), 41–42
tea dances, xix
Tenaglia, Danny, 227

Index

Tennessee, 29, 40, 43
Texas, 79, 85, 90, 118, 118, 119, 178, 207, 235
Third Amendment, 80
"Third Floor Bar" (Gallus nightclub, Atlanta), 95–96
Thom, Janice, 268
Thomas, Cal, 174–75
Thomas, Clarence, 271, 281, 284, 285, 288
Thomas Paine Park (New York City), 196
Thompson, Karen, 212
thrush, 53
Tiegs, Cheryl, 234
Toklas, Alice B., 212
Tokyo, Japan, 31
Tomb of the Unknown Soldier (Arlington National Cemetery), 214
Torick, Keith R., xi–xii, xviii–xxiv, 61–63, 66–68, 74–76, 89, 94, 193–94
Trainer, Joseph, 38
transgender people, 58, 91, 109
Tribe, Laurence, 93, 107, 120–26, 128, 129, 131, 133–34, 138–40, 143–50, 155, 172, 195, 198, 199, 208–9, 231, 272, 281, 284–86
  American Constitutional Law, 122
Trump, Donald, and administration, 285
Turchin, John, 201
Turchin, Robert, 201
Turchin, Tom, 201
Turtle Clan (Iroquois Onondaga Nation), 206
Tuttle, Elbert P., Sr., 105
Tyler, Robin, 215–17, 231

Uncle Charlie's (Coral Gables nightclub), 109, 171, 227
United Kingdom, 106
United Nations, 52
University of South Alabama, 65
U.S. Constitution (constitutional rights); *See also individual amendments*
  and birth control, 71
  and Court's rightward turn, 286
  due process clause, 77, 79, 84, 85, 118, 134, 141, 163, 285
  and gay rights, 106–7, 175, 176, 198–200, 202, 204

  and Georgia sodomy laws, 76, 77, 79–80, 86–87, 106, 111, 130–31, 134, 135, 149, 150, 156
  and intimacy, 128, 141, 148
  and obscenity, 83
  and presidential powers, 208
  and protection from libel, 271
  and right to privacy, xii, xiii, 83, 84, 93, 111, 114, 126, 128–31, 165–66, 202, 209, 281
  and right to travel, 271
  "silences" of, 121, 187, 205–6
  200th anniversary of, 200, 204–5
U.S. Court of Appeals for the District of Columbia, 115
U.S. Court of Appeals for the Eleventh Circuit, 94, 105, 108, 110–12, 128, 156, 162
U.S. Court of Appeals for the Tenth Circuit, 107
U.S. Department of Health and Human Services, 96
U.S. Department of Justice, 115, 208
U.S. Park Police, 211
U.S. Postal Service, 32
USS *Iowa*, 179
Utley, Garrick, 268

"Vacation" (song), 64
Vaid, Urvashi, 234
Vara, Carmine, 49
Vara, Henry, 49
Vara, Vicki, 49
"Vaseline Valley," 49
Vazquez, Jorge, 37, 39, 192
Venice, Fla., 109
Vietnam War, 12, 18, 183
Virginia, 83, 85, 87, 105, 116–17, 155, 231
Vizcaya mansion (Miami), 36

Wahl, John, 188
Waldo, Fla., 28
"War Conference, The," 230–32
Warner, Arthur, 120
Warner, John, 233
War on Drugs, 15–16, 23
Warren, Earl, 85, 112, 114, 115, 144, 194, 205, 285–86
Washington, D.C., 60, 178, 194, 200, 211, 234

Washington and Lee University, 116–17
Washington Post, 187, 191, 272
Watergate scandal, 208
Watson, Thomas E., 256
"Way We Were, The" (song), 101
Weaver, George, 140
Webb City, Mo., 27–28, 45
Weston, Robert Hardwick (son of sister Susan), 24, 40, 44, 246–47, 275, 279–80
WFOR-TV, 174
Where the Boys Are (film), 30
"Whip It" (song), 50
White, Byron, 115, 118–20, 125, 148, 154–56, 159, 160, 162–63, 166, 172, 173, 283
White, Douglas, 177
White Album (the Beatles), 22
white supremacists, 236–37; *See also* Ku Klux Klan
Whittaker, Charles, 115
"Who Can It Be Now?" (song), 56
Who's Who (television program), 34

Wichita, Kans., 38
Wilde, Kathleen "Kathy," 77, 79–82, 87, 92, 94, 105–6, 108–9, 111, 117–18, 120–21, 123, 124, 151, 157, 172, 176, 178, 181–83, 185, 194–95
Williams, Dick, 91–92, 195
Willis, Alexander, 234
Windmill Towne shopping center (Gatlinburg, Tenn.), 42
Winfrey, Oprah, 182
Winnie (Miss Puss's mother), 98–99
Wolfson, Evan, 128, 138, 147, 150–51, 161–62, 173, 196, 199
Wong, Alfred, 116, 218
WTVJ (TV station), 12
WXIA (TV station), 81–82

Yale Law School, 115, 130, 132, 281
Yaz, xxi
"You Make Me Feel (Mighty Real)" (song), xxi
Young, Andrew, 52–53, 58, 88, 236, 238
Young, Neil, 36